IMAGES
of America

CLINTON COUNTY

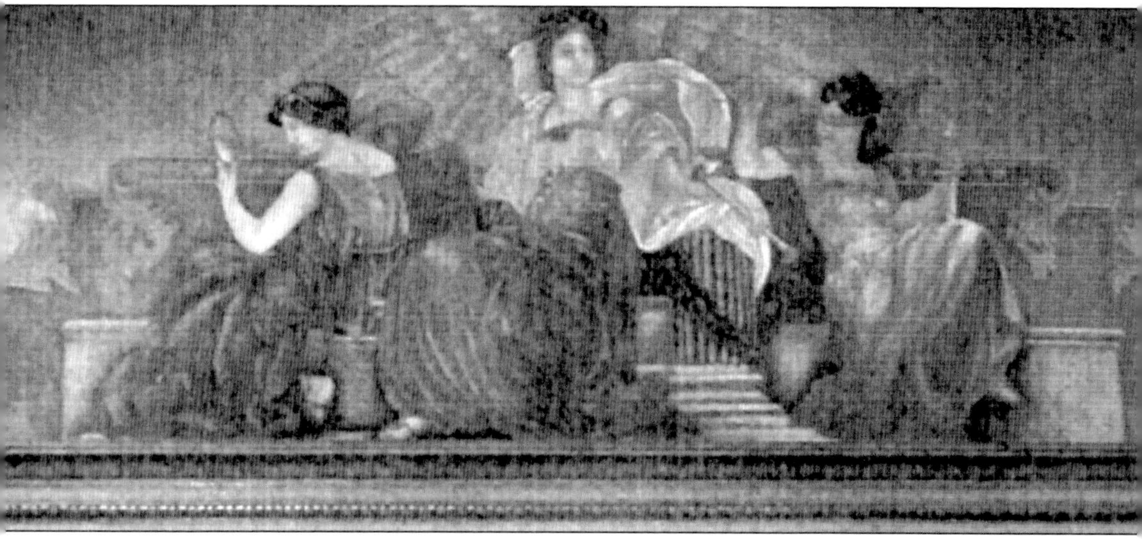

In 1901, W.G. Andrews, a local fresco artist, painted the magnificent mural of *Three Sisters of Justice* in the South District Courtroom of the Clinton County Courthouse. The mural decorates the wall between the oak paneling behind the judge's bench and the ceiling. With over 100 years of age, the mural is still an awesome sight when one visits that hall of justice in the recently renovated courthouse. (Photograph from the Clinton County Historical Society archives.)

IMAGES
of America

CLINTON COUNTY

Clinton County Historical Society

ARCADIA
PUBLISHING

ISBN 978-0-7385-3224-0

Published by Arcadia Publishing
Charleston, South Carolina

Printed in the United States of America

Library of Congress Catalog Card Number: 2003114306

For all general information contact Arcadia Publishing at:
Telephone 843-853-2070
Fax 843-853-0044
E-mail sales@arcadiapublishing.com
For customer service and orders:
Toll-Free 1-888-313-2665

Visit us on the Internet at www.arcadiapublishing.com

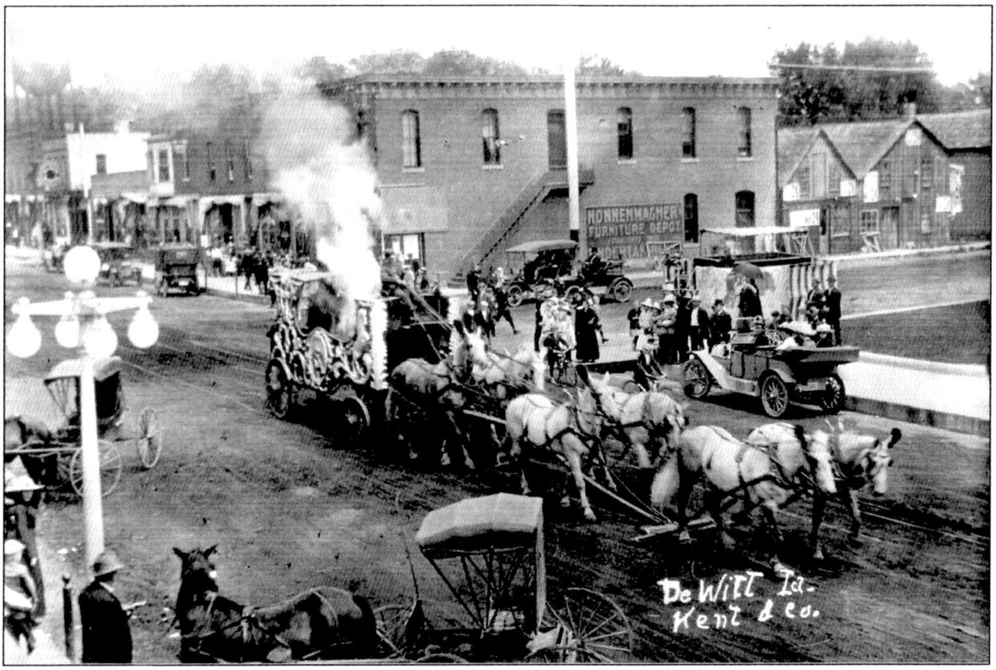

Kent & Co. captured this six-horse-drawn circus wagon going down the main street in DeWitt in 1908. One can almost hear the music and feel the excitement in the air. (Photograph from the Clinton County Historical Society archives.)

Contents

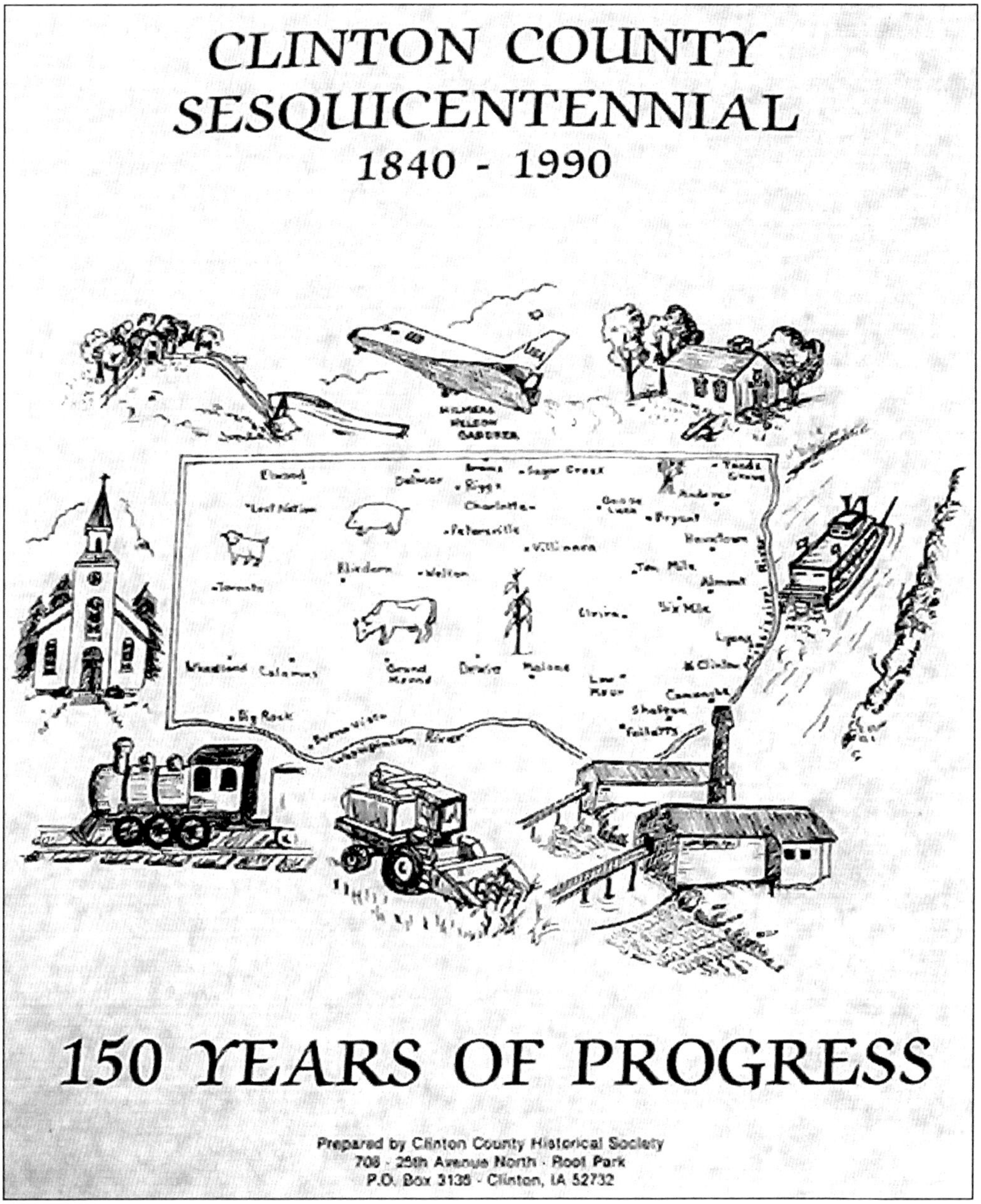
CLINTON COUNTY
SESQUICENTENNIAL
1840 - 1990
150 YEARS OF PROGRESS
Prepared by Clinton County Historical Society
708 - 25th Avenue North - Root Park
P.O. Box 3135 - Clinton, IA 52732

INTRODUCTION

Because of its location across the Mississippi River, Clinton County, Iowa, was once considered to be the "far west." It was also considered a land of opportunity for early immigrants. Covering a total of 880 square miles, the county is located midway between the north and south borders of the state of Iowa, with the Mississippi River as its eastern border and the Wapsipinicon River as its southern border.

On January 11, 1840, Clinton County was organized by the Territorial Legislature and the first three commissioners, Elijah Buell, George Griswald, and Robert C. Bourne, were elected in August of that year. Township lines were drawn, redrawn, and changed as the years went on and the population of the county increased. The county seat was originally located in Camanche, then moved to DeWitt, and relocated to Clinton, where it remains today. By 1860, the county population had grown to 17,000, and is now approximately 50,000.

Farming remains the largest industry in the county and all crops of the temperate climate do well in the fertile soil. Manufacturing industries have mainly settled along the Mississippi River while the interior of the county retains its rural heritage.

The rivers, bordering the county, played an important part in the development of the county and remain a vital resource today. Originally, the Mississippi River was the county's only connection to the outside world, until the railroads crossed the Mississippi River in the 1850s. The railroads opened the interior of the county and allowed the farming community easier access to worldwide markets for their produce. The towns and villages grew up around the railroad depots and stations. Interior roads followed the paths of the Indians who were roaming the land before it was opened up for settlement.

Today, Clinton County is a wonderful place to live and raise families. The land those first settlers saw has been enhanced over the years until it sparkles with promise and beauty. The Clinton County Historical Society thanks all who have freely given their time and photographs which have allowed us the opportunity to complete this project and share these many memories.

One

Early History

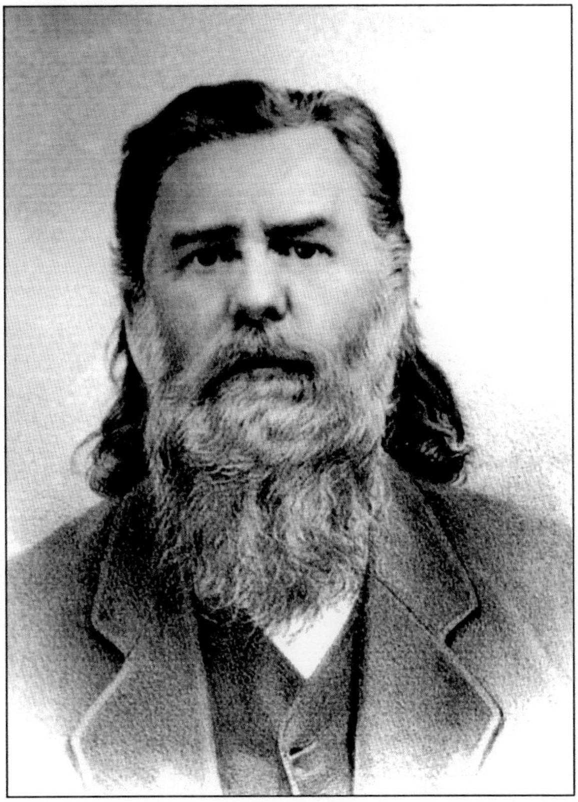

James D. Bourne was the first postmaster in Clinton County. The first post office was at the American Fur Company on the Wapsipinicon River at the settlement named Monroe across from McCausland in Scott County. During the times the river couldn't easily be crossed, dogs were used to ferry the mail by swimming from one shore to the other side. In 1839, Mr. Bourne was appointed to the new office of Sheriff of Clinton County. He usually dressed in buckskins and a slouched straw hat and his "native" appearance often surprised those meeting him for the first time. (Photograph from the Clinton County Historical Society archives.)

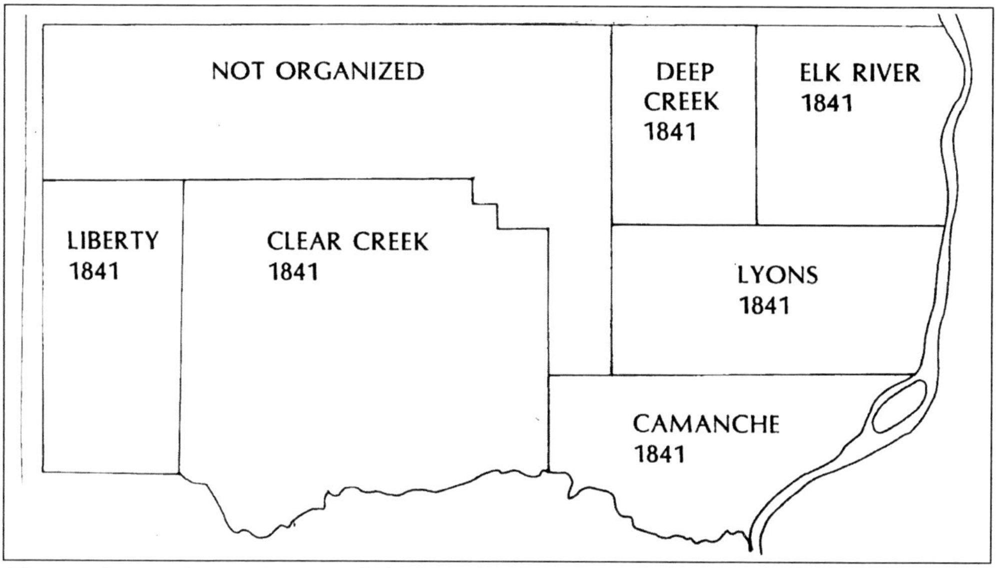

Clinton County, having been settled in 1835 at Lyons by Elijah Buell, was already organized into six townships by 1841. Clear Creek was later divided into Welton and Berlin townships. By 1852, the county had grown to 13 townships and would grow rapidly within the next 20 years. (Photograph from the Clinton County Historical Society archives.)

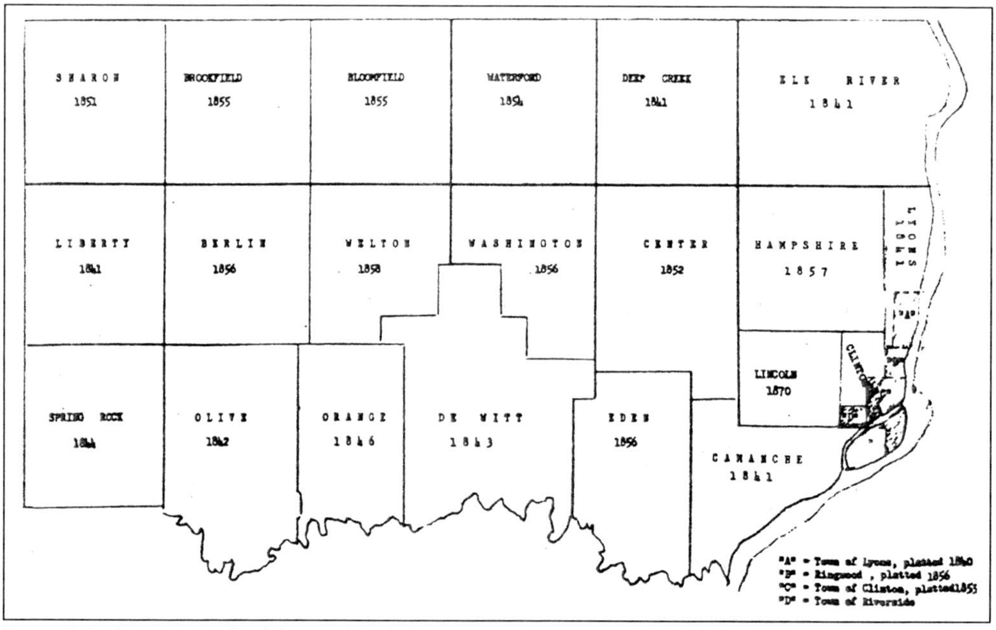

By 1876, the county had been divided into 21 townships. Today, the county is down to 18 townships as the townships surrounding the city of Clinton have been absorbed into the city. In 1919, Berlin Township was re-named Grant Township as the people of the county wanted no connection with anything German. (Photograph from the Clinton County Historical Society archives.)

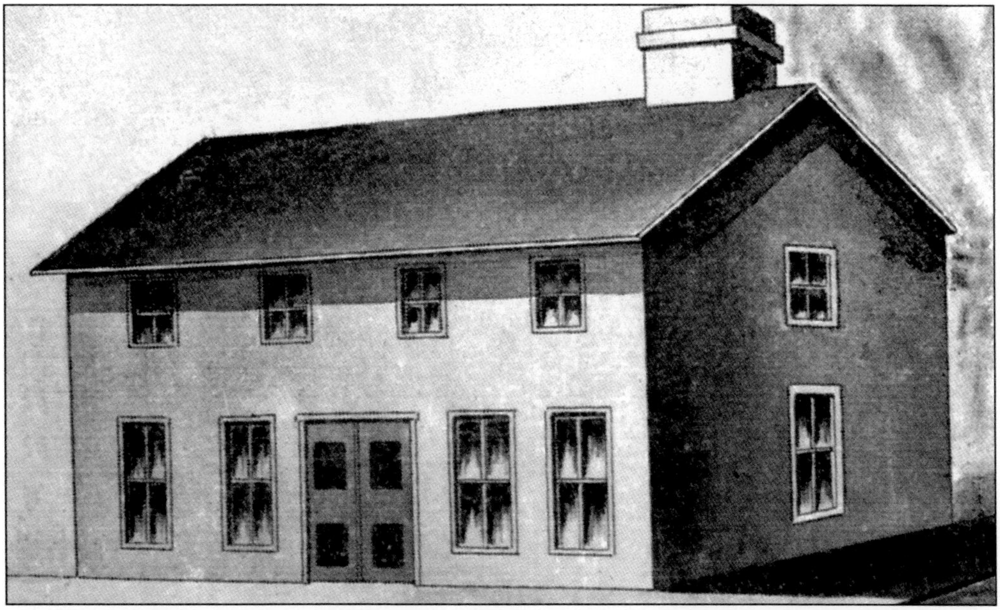

On July 4, 1838, the Iowa territory was organized. On January 11, 1840, the Territorial Legislature passed an act to organize the county of Clinton and made Camanche the county seat. This artist's sketch of a proposed courthouse was advertised in 1843. Most authors list Camanche as the location for this 1843 courthouse, however, by that time, the county seat had been moved to Vandenberg, later re-named DeWitt. (Photograph from the Clinton County Historical Society archives.)

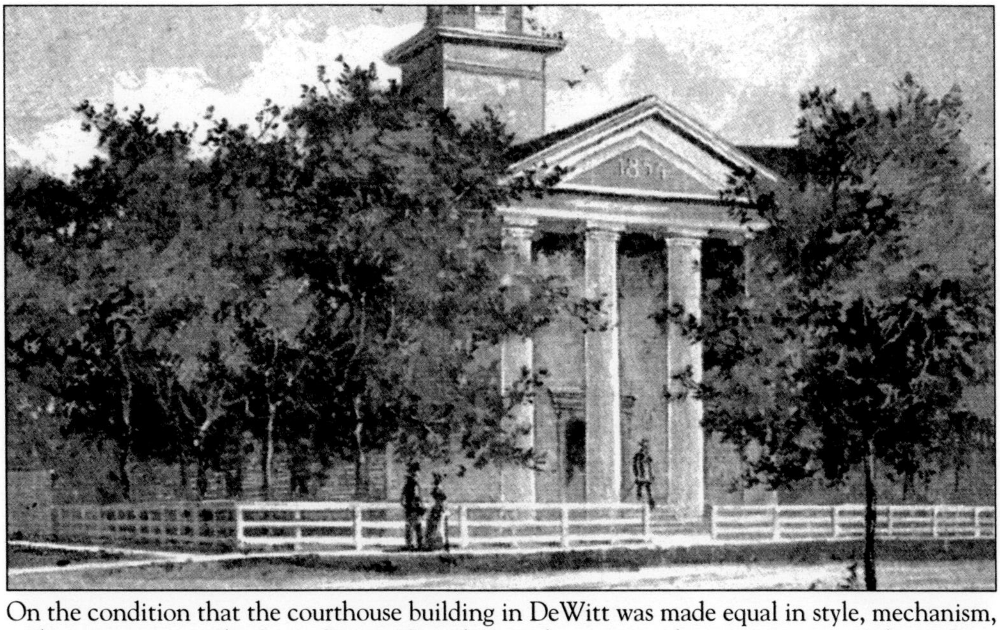

On the condition that the courthouse building in DeWitt was made equal in style, mechanism, and construction as the Scott County Courthouse, the contract for construction was let on June 23, 1853. It was built, at a price of $5,900, on the east side of the public square and ready for occupancy in 1854. A jail was built in 1855 at a price of $1,668. (Photograph from the Clinton County Historical Society archives.)

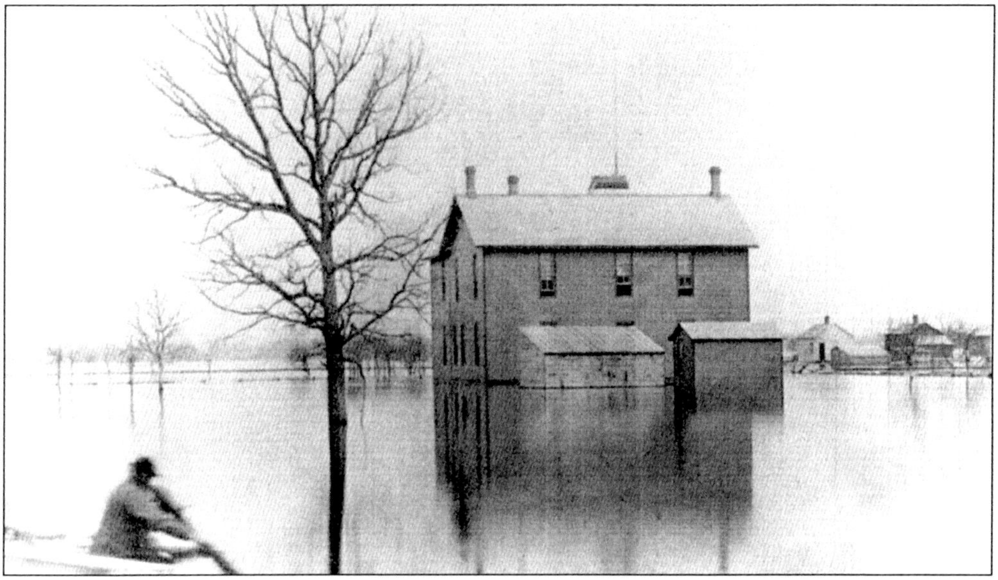

With Clinton and Lyons the largest cities in the county, the people of both cities were clamoring for Clinton to become the county seat. After months of meetings, a county election was held on the second Tuesday of October, 1869, to determine if the county seat would relocate to "Block 8" in Clinton. The vote tallied a 511 majority in favor of the relocation and sealed the move from DeWitt to Clinton. Plans were immediately made and a temporary building was quickly erected. On November 21, 1869, the new courthouse was occupied by the first session of the district court in Clinton. Preceding the vote, pictures of a pool of high water, labeled "Block 8," with fishermen sitting on its shores were circulated against the move. That prediction of high water came true as shown in this 1888 photograph of the temporary courthouse. (Photograph from the Clinton County Historical Society archives.)

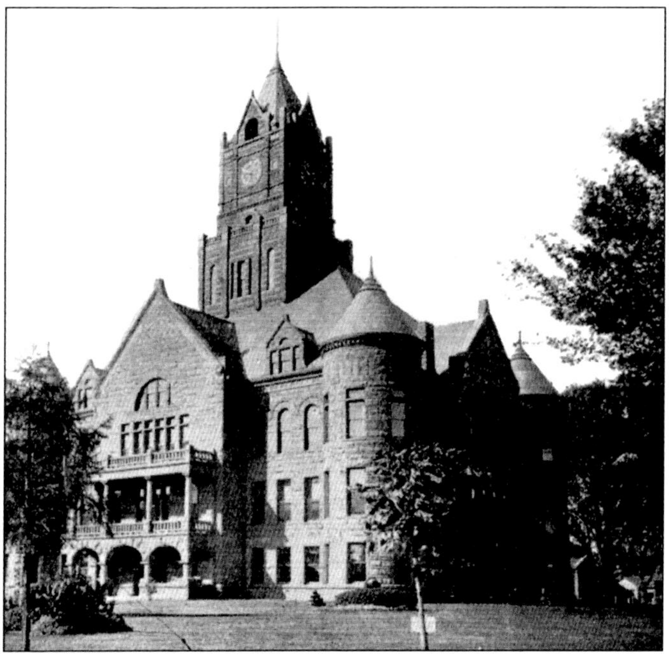

On March 15, 1892, a county election was held to determine if a new courthouse, not to exceed $100,000, would be built on "Block 8." A majority of 539 voters favored the new building. By August 1897, after two more elections to secure tax-levied construction funds, a magnificent courthouse was completed at a total cost of $168,000. One hundred years later, the completely refurbished courthouse was re-dedicated to the people of Clinton County in September of 2003. (Photograph from the Clinton County Historical Society archives.)

Two

CAMANCHE AND EDEN TOWNSHIPS

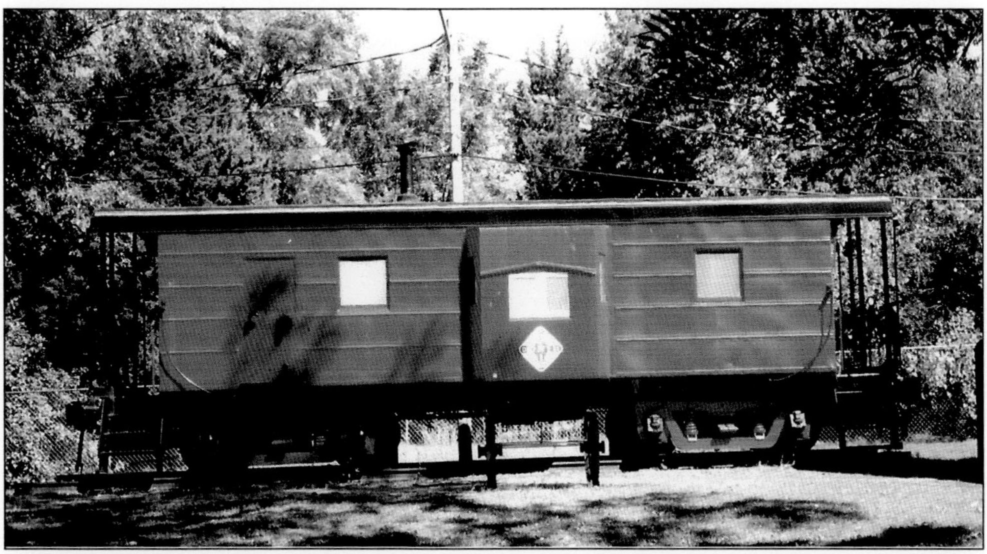

By 1979, this Dri-line caboose which had been donated to the city of Camanche by the Milwaukee & CNW Railroads to be used as a museum. It was celebrated with a grand opening on August 22, 1982. The caboose was moved to its present location on the Camanche Library grounds in 1986 at a cost of $1,500. A group of Camanche volunteers joined Dri-line section men to lay the track where it stands. The caboose museum can be seen by appointment through the Camanche Historical Society. (Photograph from the Clinton County Historical Society archives.)

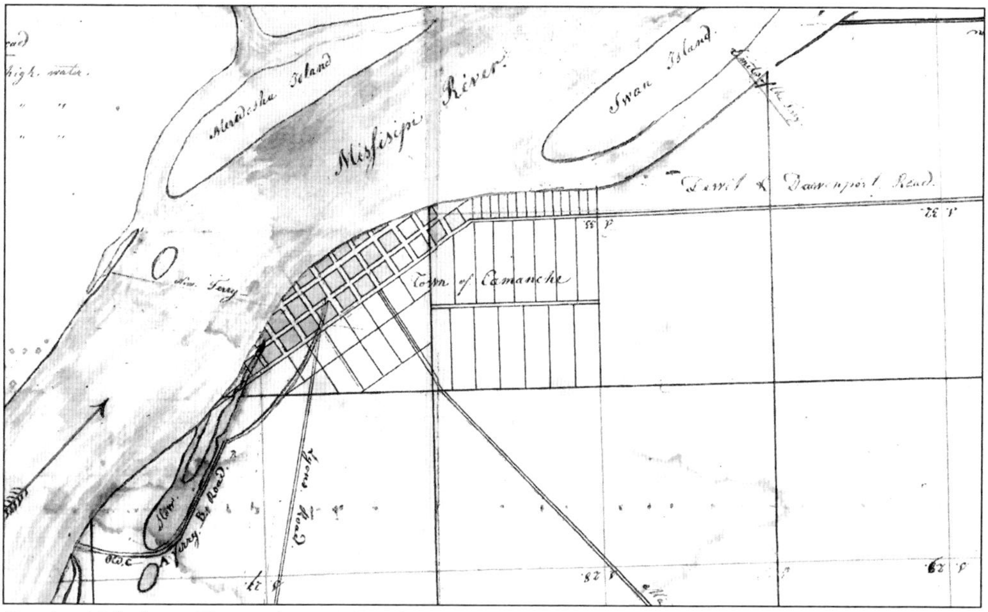

On the 11th day of December, 1850, Thomas C. Dyer, J.P., stated that Auguste Brion personally appeared before him, as a justice of the peace, and swore that this plat was a true one as set forth. Auguste Brion had produced a plat of the town and vicinity of Camanche as of December 1, 1845, using a grapevine as a surveyor's tool. (Map donated to the Clinton County Historical Society in memory of E.R. Seymour by Phil and Ruth Fedderson.)

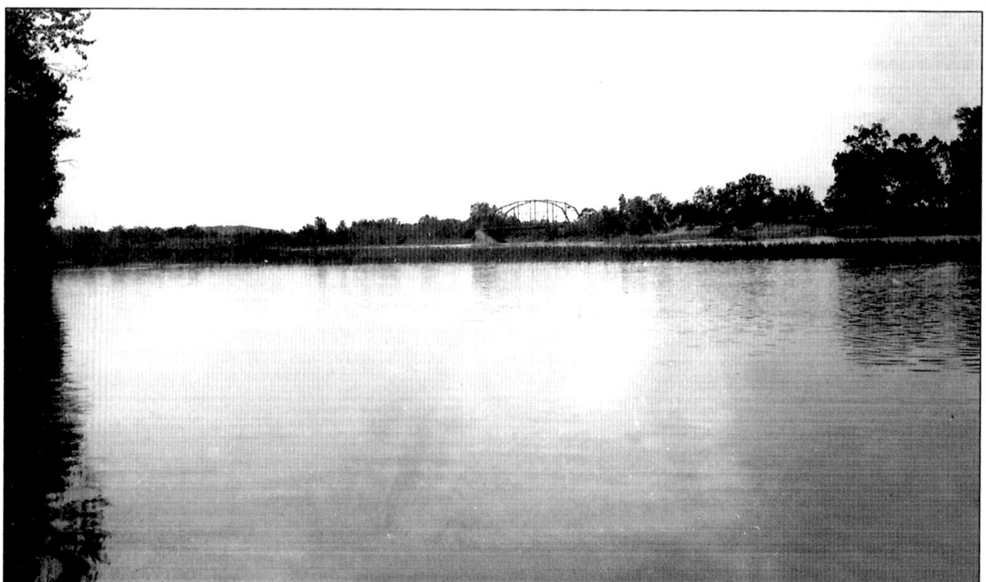

In the mid-20th century, the Docia Bridge in Illinois could be seen rising majestically in the horizon when viewed from about three miles south of Camanche, looking across the Mississippi River. (Photograph courtesy of Bill and Lucille Wharff.)

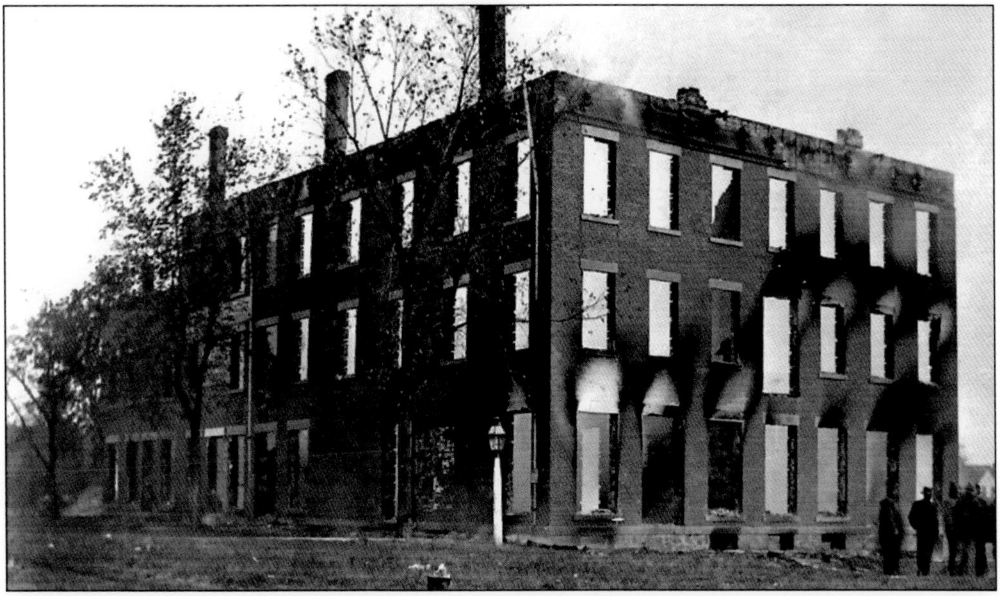

The Camanche Glove Factory fell to fire on October 27, 1912. The building, which would be known as "Brown's Brick" after completion, was under construction at the time of the Camanche tornado in 1860. It didn't sustain much damage; however, the architect's original plans were never completed. During the time of its existence, its many rooms were used as meeting rooms, stores, a cigar factory, and a skating rink/dance floor. (Photograph from the Clinton County Historical Society archives.)

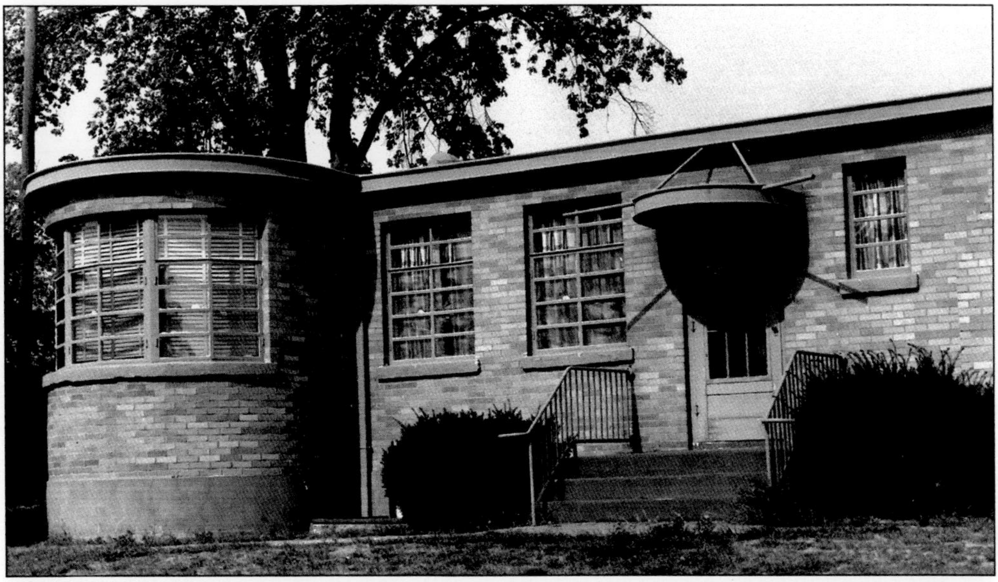

The Camanche Public Library, facing the scenic Mississippi River with its circular banks of windows, was built as a private four-bedroom, five-bathroom home on the site of the former Camanche Club by Arthur DePue, president of Central Steel Tube Co., in 1943. After Mr. DePue's death, the home was purchased for use as a library and civic center by the Camanche city officials in 1964. The purchase included a 20-foot square steel and concrete boat dock which the city still maintains. (Photograph from the Clinton County Historical Society archives.)

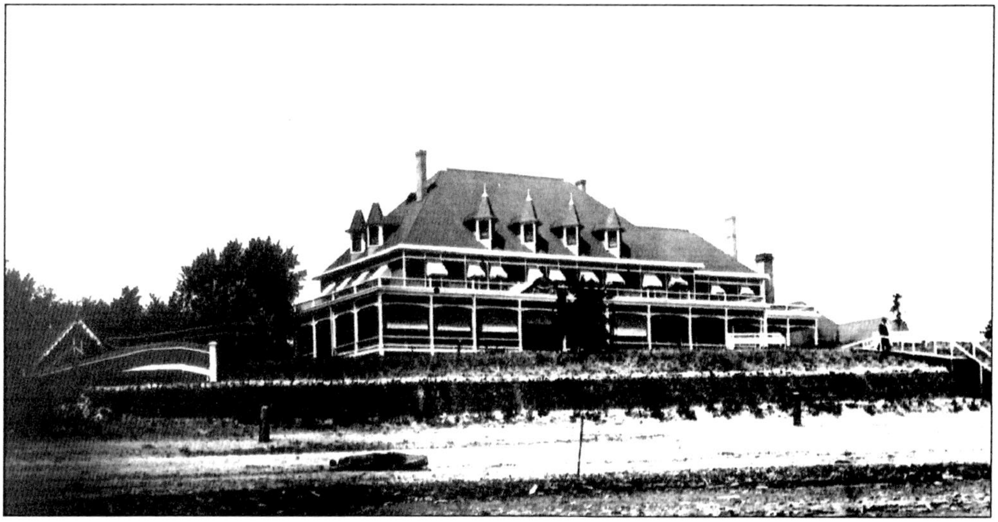

With the dream of a gathering place for Clinton's "finer society," Artemus Lamb was the financier and mover and shaker of the $100,000 Camanche (Country) Club, built in 1901 on the rolling banks of the Mississippi River. Charter members from Clinton and Chicago, as well as Boston and other east coast cities, spent their summers enjoying the club's two spacious parlors, sterling silverware in the dining halls, and 28 luxurious guest rooms. When the charter members faded, no younger people took their place and the club was sold to F. Emerson, M.D. Emerson converted the club into the River-View Sanitarium. It was advertised as an institution for the care and treatment of the sick using the "Battle Creek" methods. The sanitarium closed and the building was razed in the spring of 1941. (Photograph from the Clinton County Historical Society archives.)

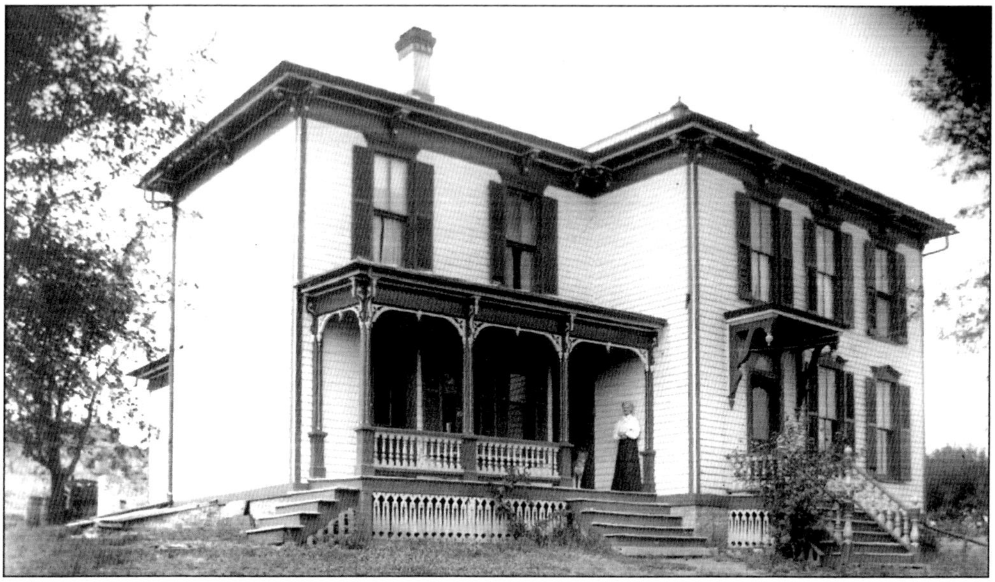

In 1878, this house on the John Thomas farm, west of Camanche, was built for $3,000 for John H. Willet, John's great-grandfather. It was copied from one near Cordova, Illinois, and the stone from the basement was quarried on the farm and laid by George Willis of Camanche. The home had 12 rooms, and although it lacked a fireplace, one was added at a later date. (Photograph from the Clinton County Historical Society archives.)

The O.A. Campbell Grocery Store in Follets was located on the corner of Highway 67 and McCausland road. Ice cream and soda were advertised and the post office was located in this store for a time. Later, the store was located several hundred feet further north and was owned by Art Carstensen for many years. It has since become a residence. (Photograph courtesy of John and Evelyn Shaff.)

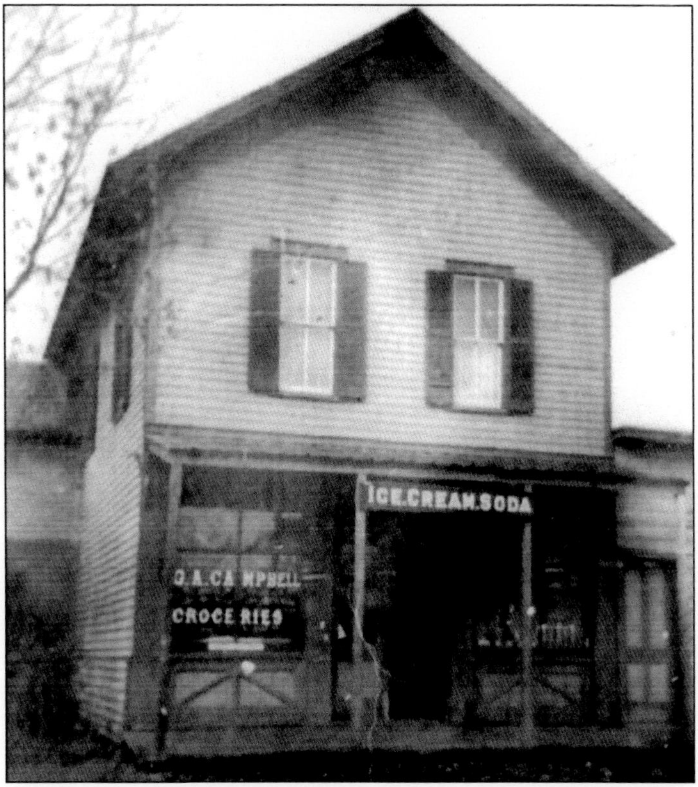

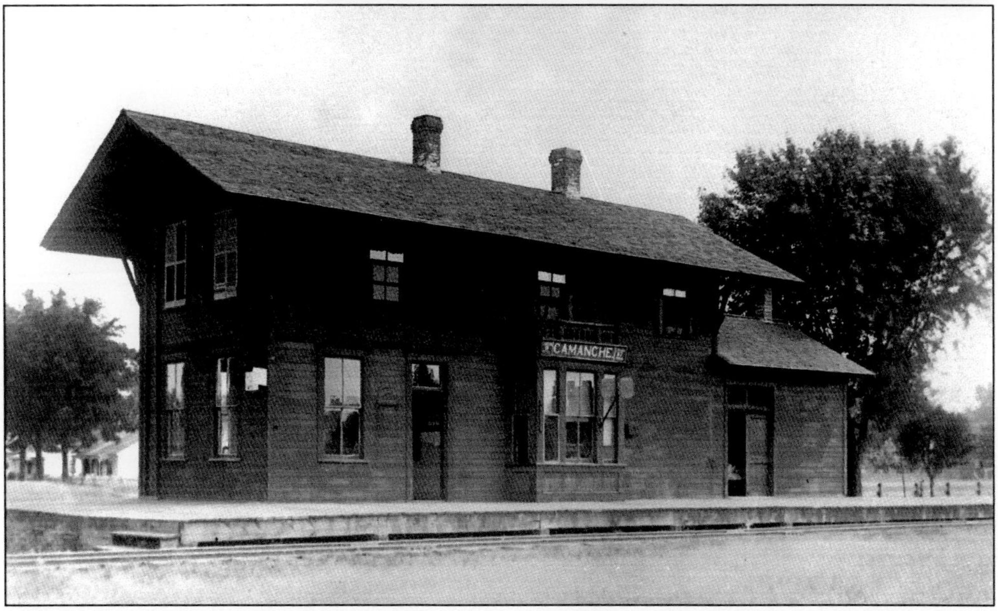

The Rock Island Lines Depot was sold at auction in 1932 to Harry Simpson for $135. It was built in the late 1800s and bustled with activity in the early days. The depot was a popular spot to meet friends before an evening's entertainment. After its sale, the depot was moved to its present location on Sixth Street and turned into a private home. (Photograph from the Clinton County Historical Society archives.)

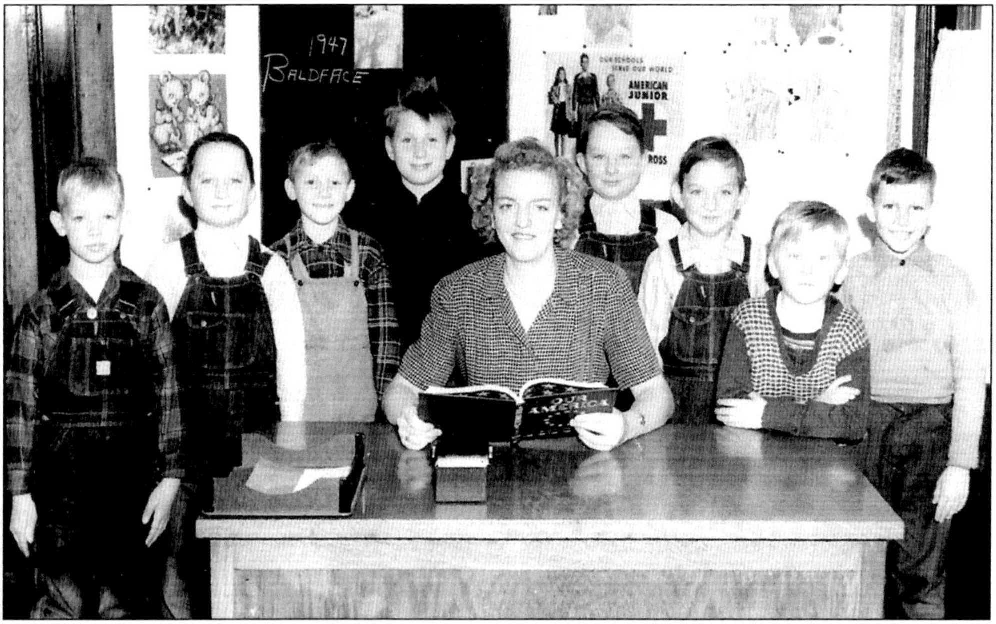

Baldface School, Eden Township #1, was 1.5 miles south of Low Moor and became a home after school consolidation. In 1947, Delores Horn Stuedeman was the teacher. These were the days when one could become a teacher with a high school diploma and a summer school course. Pictured from left to right are, John Shaff, Jack Sager, Allan Roenfeldt, George Hansen, James Sager, Lee Sager, Eugene Mess, and Jim Hansen. There were no girls in the school at this time. (Photograph courtesy of John and Evelyn Shaff.)

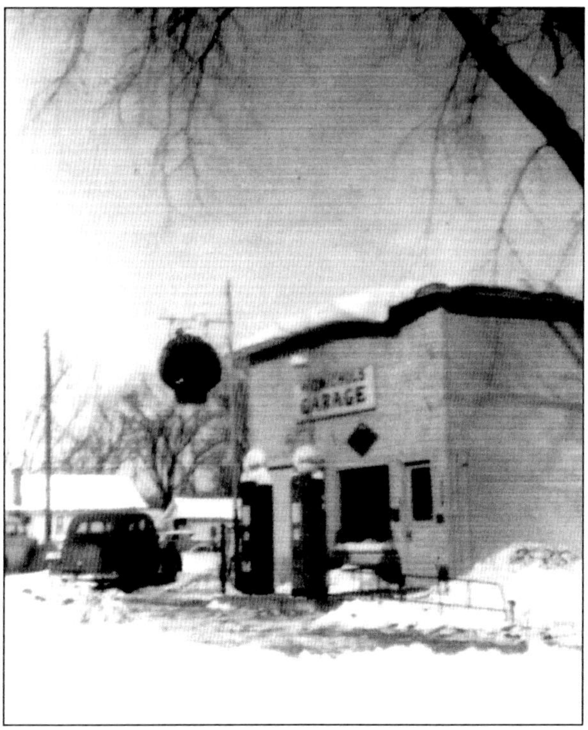

M.C. Nichols owned this Shell Station in Camanche for 40 years until his retirement in 1960. The station is shown here in snowy December of 1951. Mr. Nichols held the distinction of having the oldest Shell dealership in the state of Iowa. He also owned a Chevrolet dealership in Camanche during the 1930s. (Photograph courtesy of David Nichols.)

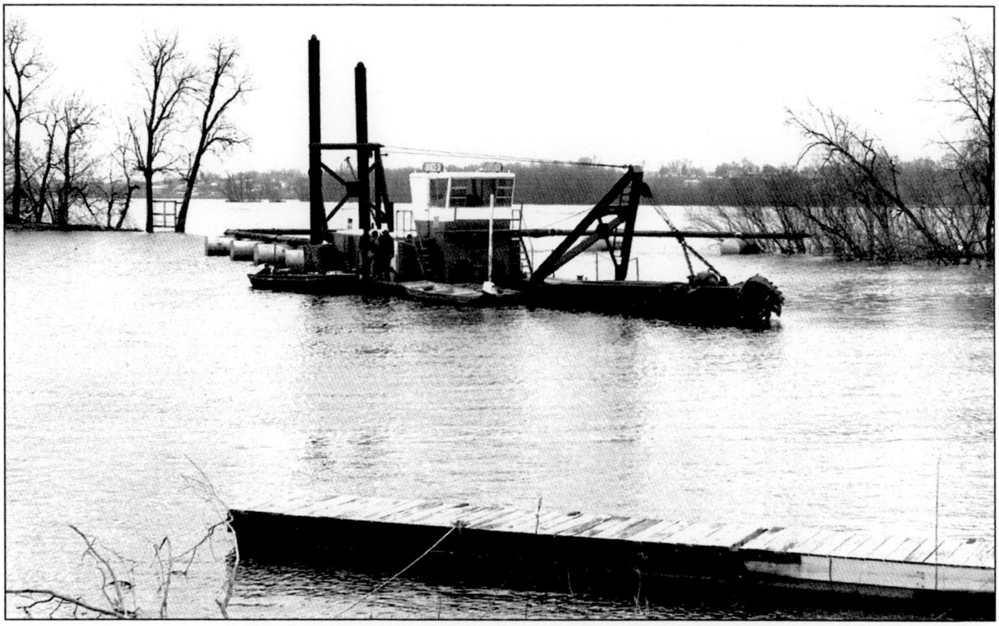

Fighting the incoming silt of the Mississippi River to keep the channel and the harbors open is an ongoing effort. This dredging of the Camanche Marina took place in the spring of 1973 in anticipation of the summer boating season. (Photograph from the Clinton County Historical Society archives.)

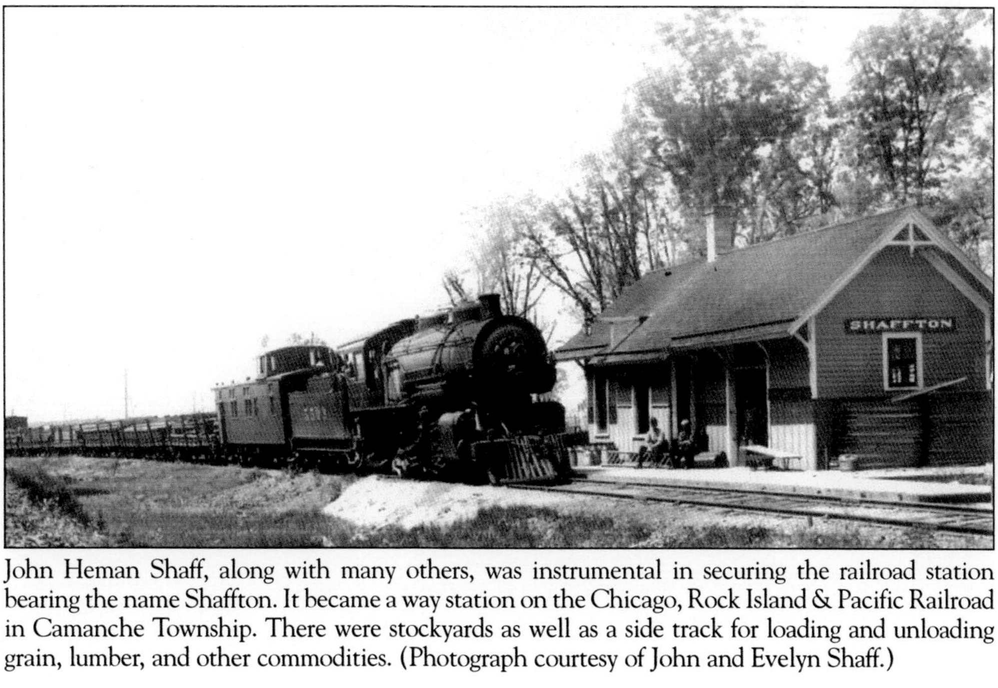

John Heman Shaff, along with many others, was instrumental in securing the railroad station bearing the name Shaffton. It became a way station on the Chicago, Rock Island & Pacific Railroad in Camanche Township. There were stockyards as well as a side track for loading and unloading grain, lumber, and other commodities. (Photograph courtesy of John and Evelyn Shaff.)

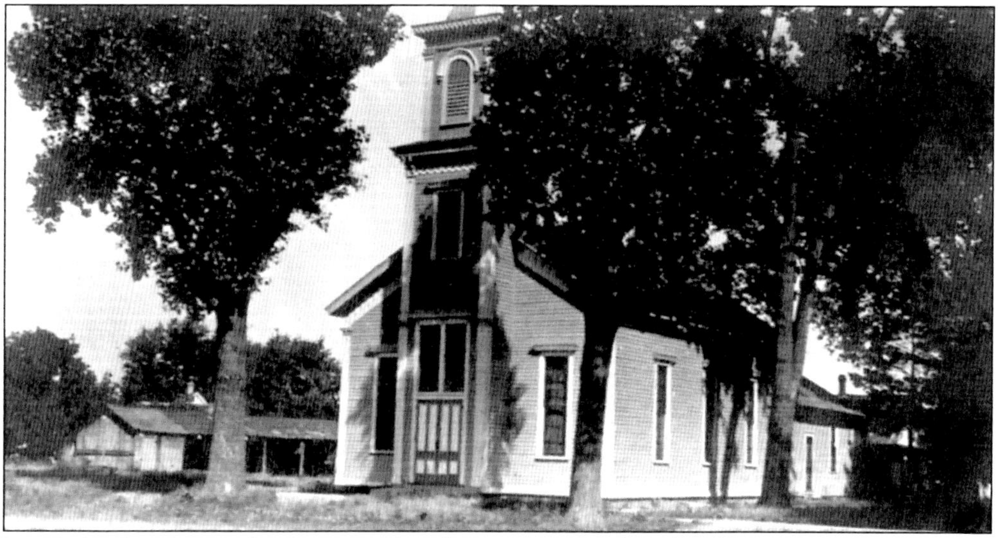

In 1843, the Camanche Baptist Church was organized with about 12 members. Their membership grew and by 1856 they were able to build their church. That church was destroyed in the June 3, 1860, tornado. Within eight months, a new church had been built to the west of the original church. The church was expanded when 13 classrooms, a pastor's study, and a chapel were added in 1968. (Photograph from the Clinton County Historical Society archives.)

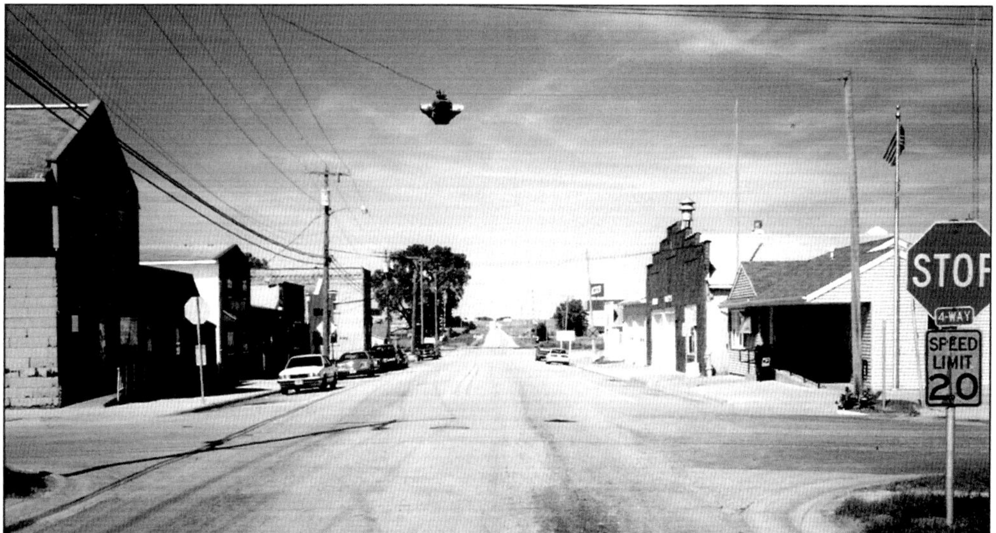

Low Moor, Eden Township, was plagued by fires in 1907 and 1924 which destroyed most of the business district each time. The residents in 1907 were awakened around one o'clock in the morning by cries of "Fire!" The east side of Main Street was in flames and sparks were starting fires all over town. By the time it was over, both sides of Main Street had burned to the ground, with the exception of the Lumber Company. The damage was estimated at $60,000; however, most of the loss was covered by insurance and the town was re-built. In 1924, fire again burned down the east side of Main Street. Again, the town re-built. Today, Low Moor remains a vibrant community and prides itself on being Iowa's "Biggest Little Town." (Photograph courtesy of Don Dethmann.)

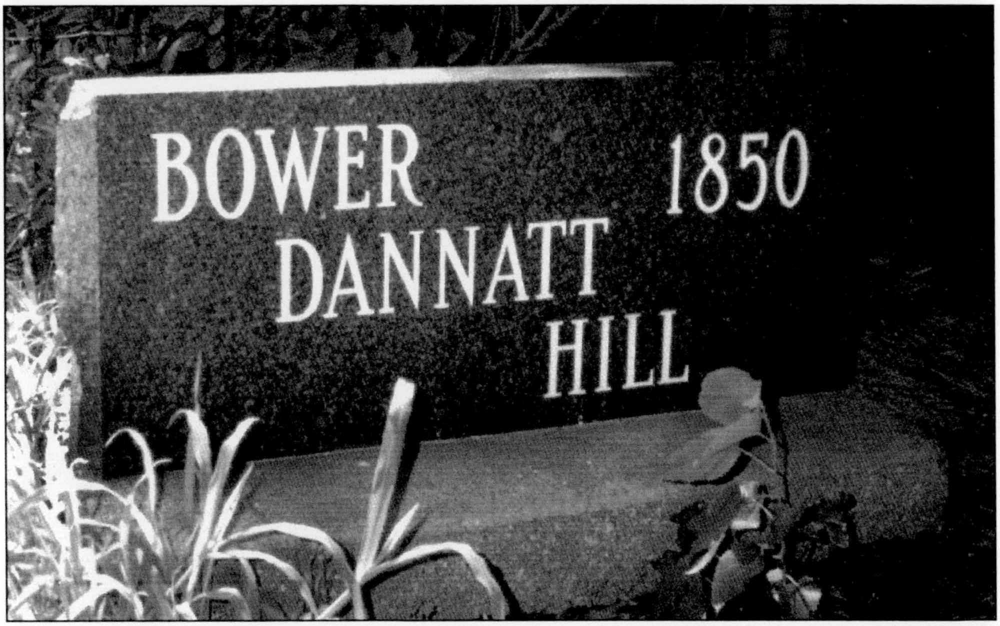

The Bower Dannatt Hill Cemetery, Eden Township, was established in 1850 by immigrants from Lincolnshire, England. They were lured to America with the promise of cheap land. The first burial was Ann Dannatt on October 31, 1851. Her grave marker states she was 6 months old and the daughter of T. and H. Dannatt. There are 49 burials in the cemetery and all are the original immigrants and their families. (Photograph courtesy of Richard Carstensen.)

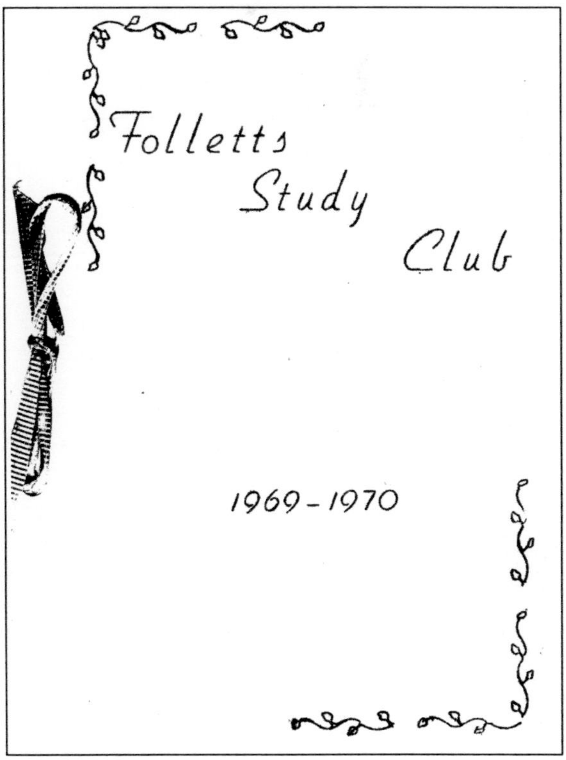

Fourteen women in the Follets, Eden Township, area met in November of 1901 and organized a club named "Circle 26 of the Progressive Women of America" sponsored by *The Housekeeper*, a popular women's magazine. Membership was restricted to women with a farm connection. Over the years, the women incorporated and reorganized as the "Progressive Woman's Club 368" and bought the Woodman's Hall in Follets to hold their many social events. By 1943, the club had sold their building and dissolved their corporation, renaming their club "Follets Study Club" and limiting their membership to 18. The secretary published a booklet of the events of the club. These booklets are now on file at the Clinton County Historical Society Library. (Photograph from the Clinton County Historical Society archives.)

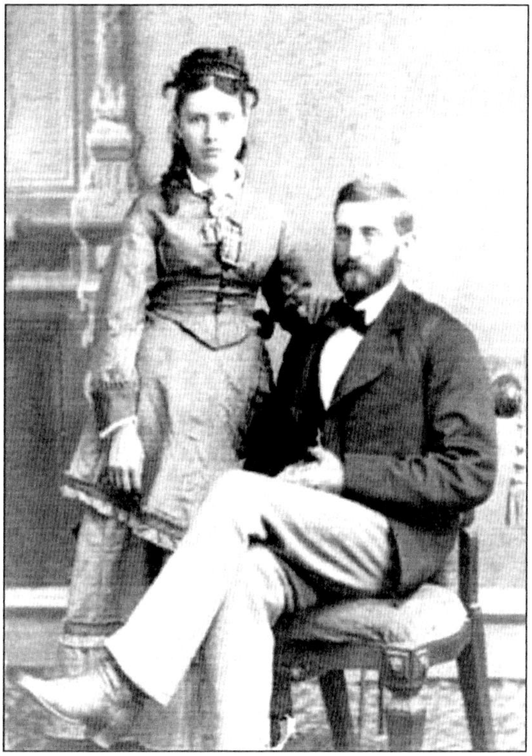

Heman Blakely Shaff was born in Sodus, New York, in 1817. He came to Clinton County in 1837 with his widowed mother, his brother, Joseph, and several of his sisters. The year of 1840 was notable for Heman as he returned to New York and took Mary Russell as his bride. That same year, when registration and purchase of land in Iowa became available, Heman and several of his neighbors went to Dubuque to buy land for $3 an acre which was paid in gold. Paul Shaff and his sons, Jon and Sam, are farming the original tract of land while Roger Shaff and his son, John, and grandson, Peter, are farming adjacent land purchased a few years later. Peter is the sixth generation to be farming this ground. (Photograph courtesy of John and Evelyn Shaff.)

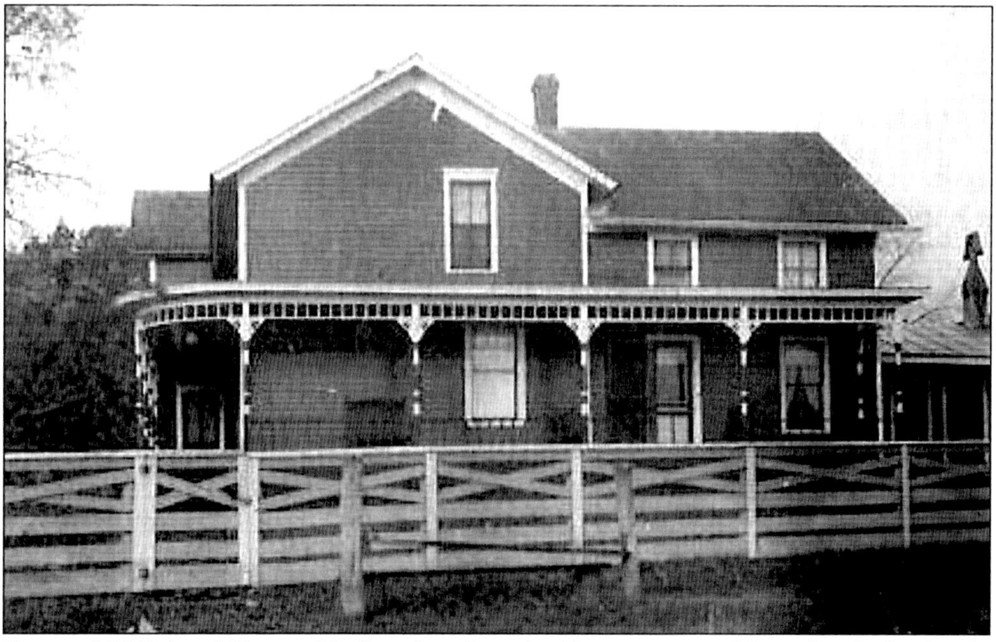

Spring of 1840 found Heman Shaff, on his claim, building a stone and log cabin for his family close to the river. Because of the risk of water-borne disease, Heman soon built a stone house on higher ground. After a number of years, this house was built around some of the earlier stone walls. In 1950, the house was remodeled into a modern ranch house that still used some of the original stone on the southeast corner. (Photograph courtesy of John and Evelyn Shaff.)

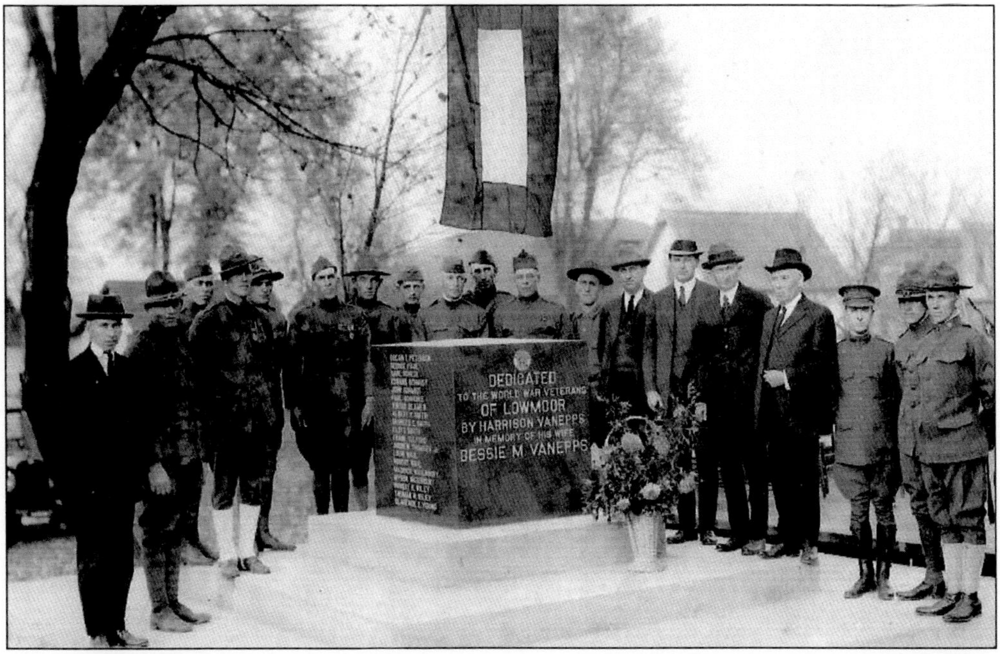

The memorial monument to honor the town's veterans of World War I became a reality for Low Moor, Eden Township, in 1923, when Harrison Van Epps offered to pay for the monument in memory of his wife, Bessie, who died in 1922. The monument is located in the Low Moor City Park. (Photograph from the Clinton County Historical Society archives.)

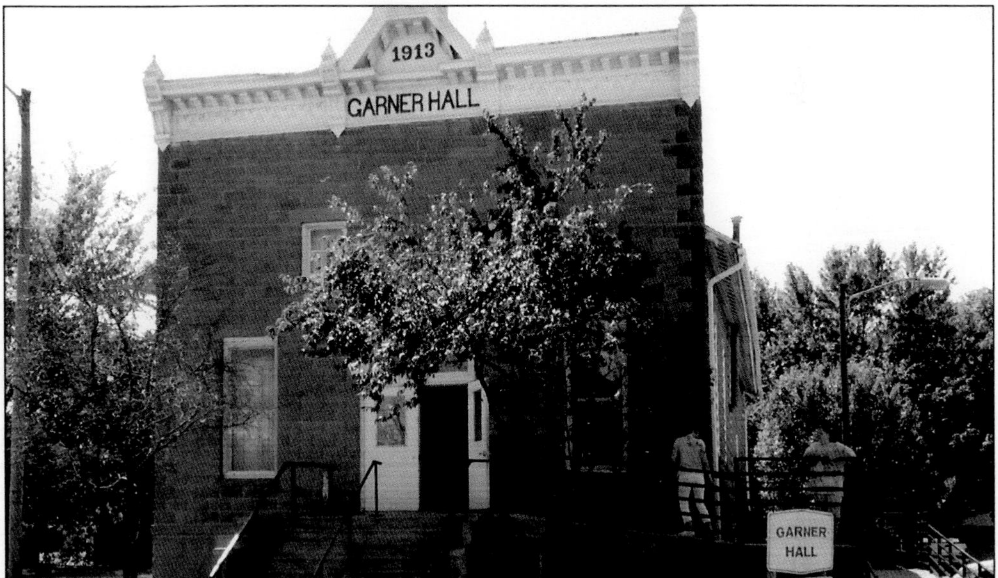

Garner Hall in Camanche, Eden Township, was built in 1913 at a cost of $3,000 with volunteer help; otherwise, the cost would have been at least $5,000. The men of the McKenrick family excavated the basement while several other families helped build the building. Garner Hall is used for public meetings, lodges, dances, movies, receptions, and was used as a polling place until City Hall was built. (Photograph courtesy of Don Dethmann.)

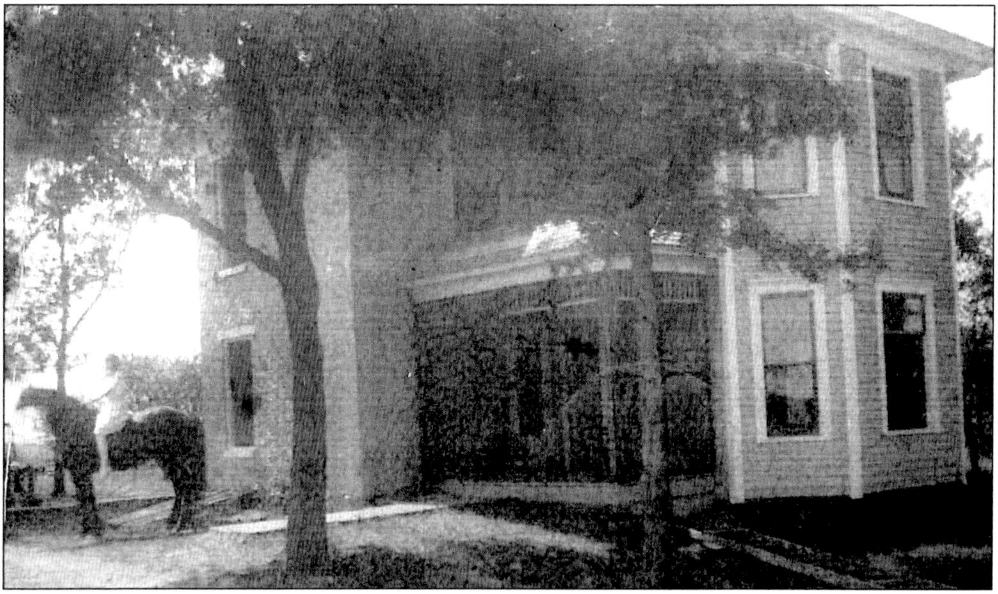

When immigrants came to Eden Township in 1851 from Lincolnshire, England, George Hill and his son, Thomas, were among them. By 1855, George had built his family the stone house, shown above, with walls a foot thick. In 1913, a frame addition was added. Robert Earl Hill, George's great-grandson, was a pioneer of electrical service in rural Clinton County. A private Delco Power Plant was built on the Hill farm in the early 1930s with appliance and light wires at 32 volts. REA funds for Clinton County were obtained in the mid-1930s and the Eastern Iowa Light and Power Co-Op was formed at that time. REA electricity to the Hill farm was completed in 1939. Ruby Hill Wallace is shown on her horse. (Photograph courtesy of Thomas George Hill.)

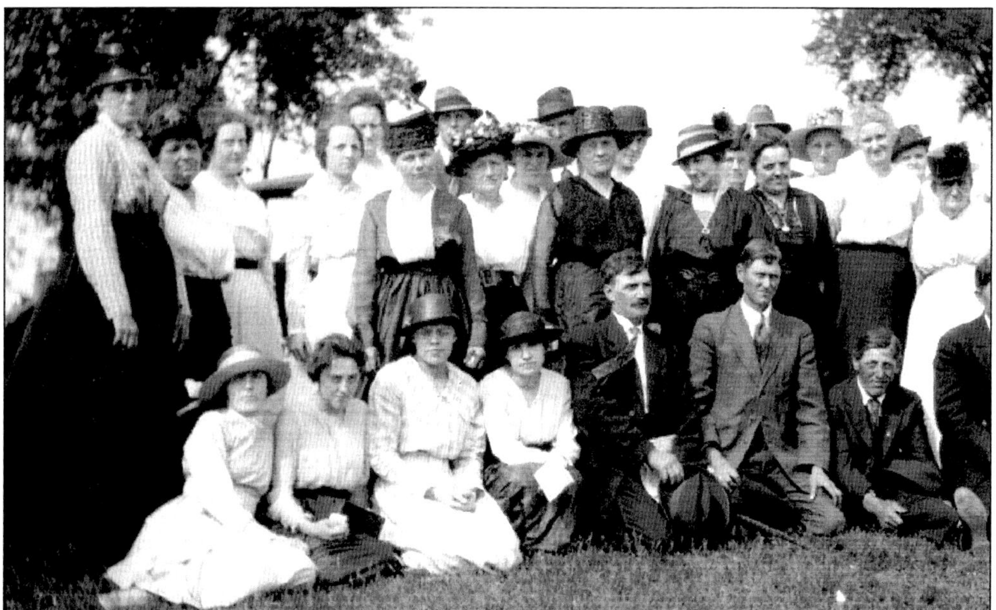

The annual Beckwith School Parents' Picnic, Camanche Township, was held in the spring. This photo dates to c. 1910. (Photograph courtesy of Richard Carstensen.)

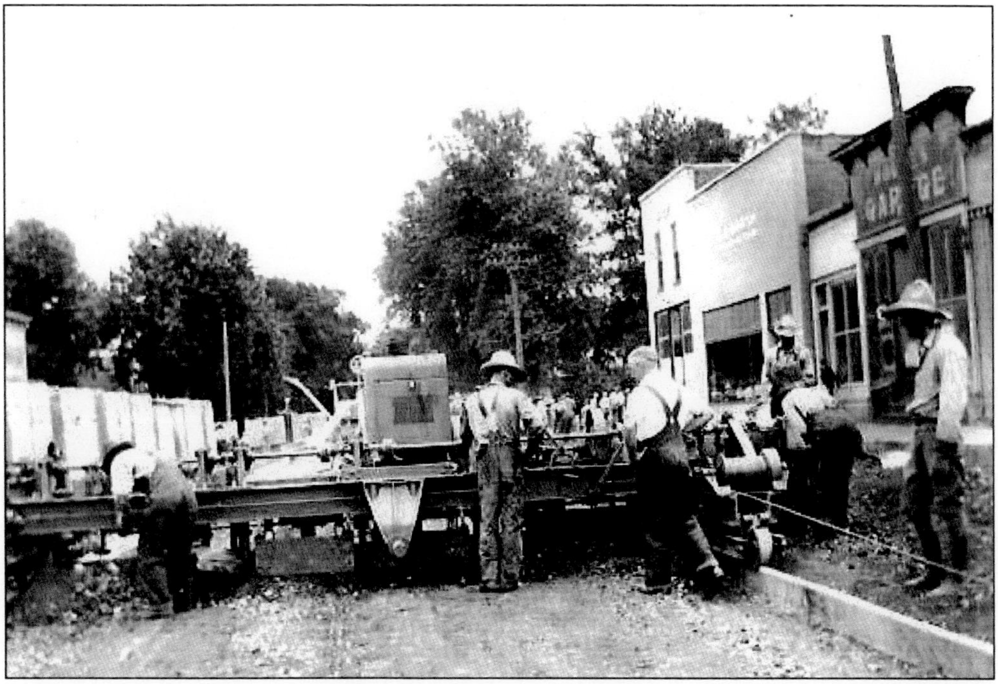

Paving the streets in Low Moor, Eden Township, was a labor-intensive job during the early part of the 20th century. (Photograph courtesy of Harold Fatchett.)

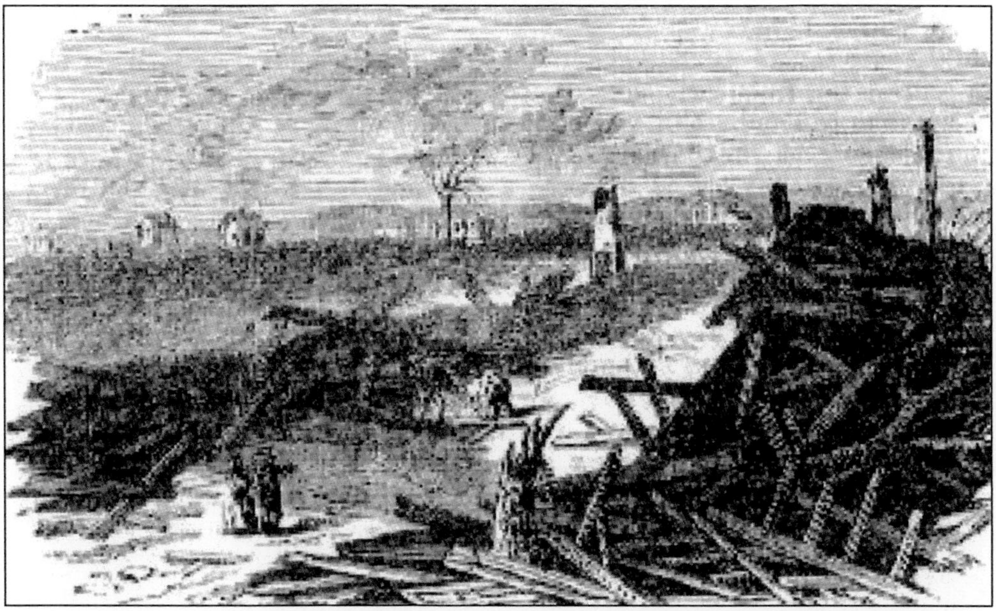

The Camanche Tornado roared through the community on Sunday, June 3, 1860, destroying most of the town and leaving 28 people dead in its wake. This 1861 engraving from *Our Whole Country: Or the Past and Present of the United States, Historical & Descriptive, Illustrated by 600 engravings, Vol. II* gave the world a chance to see the devastation and ruins following that memorable event. The Rose Hill Cemetery in Camanche has a memorial honoring those who lost their lives that evening. (Photograph from the Clinton County Historical Society archives.)

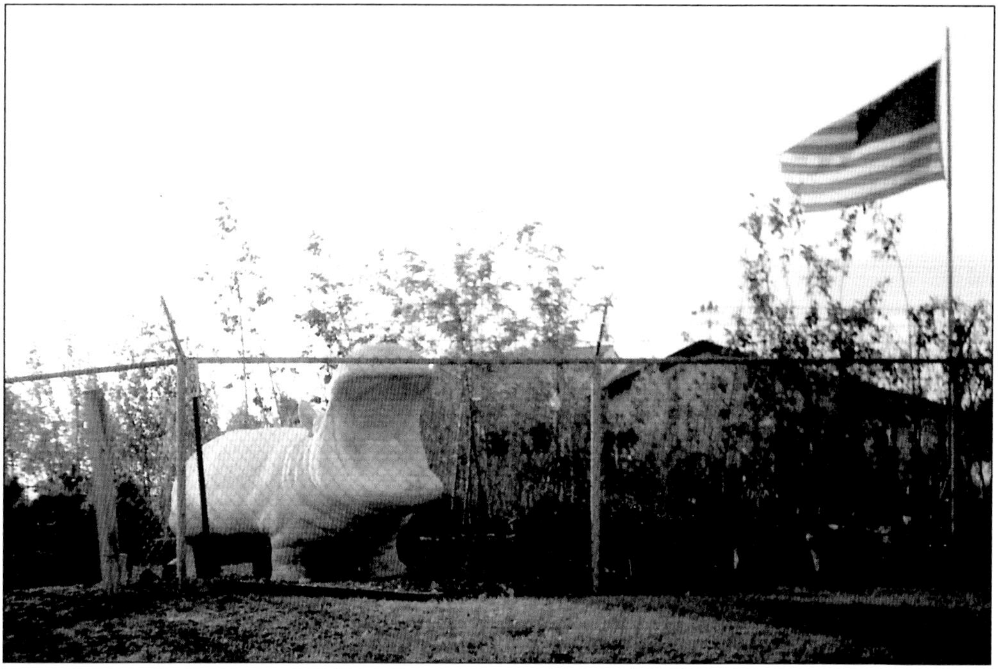

This cement hippopotamus welcomes visitors as they turn off Highway 30 onto the road that leads to Malone, Eden Township. This quiet collection of homes was once a large cattle shipping point on the Northwestern line with E. and L. Hansen operating a general store there. (Photograph from the Clinton County Historical Society archives.)

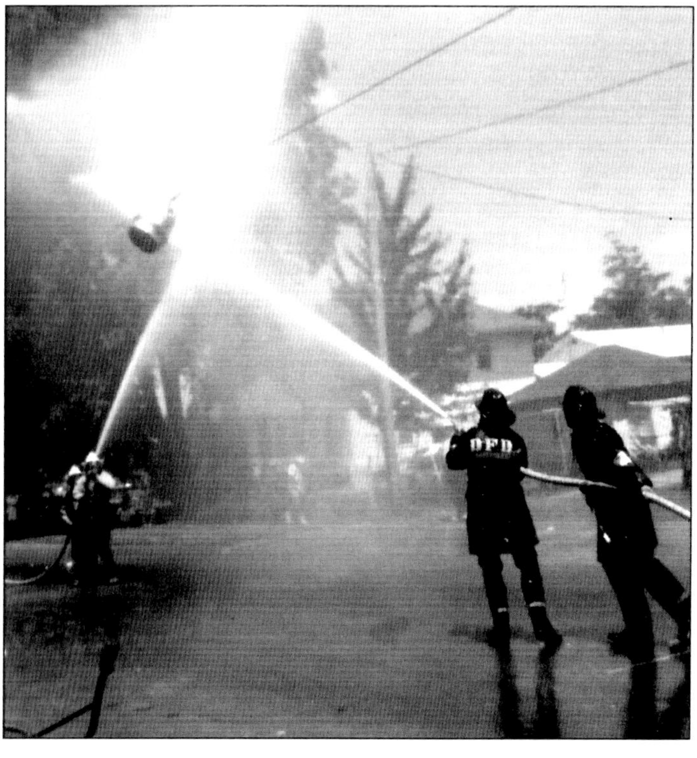

During the June 1976 Bicentennial Celebration held in Camanche, the Camanche Volunteer Fire Department Waterfight Team challenged the DeWitt Fire Department to a water-ball fight. Ben Vogel, 86, and Floral Lind, 80, served as king and queen during the festivities. (Photograph from the Clinton County Historical Society archives.)

Three

DeWitt

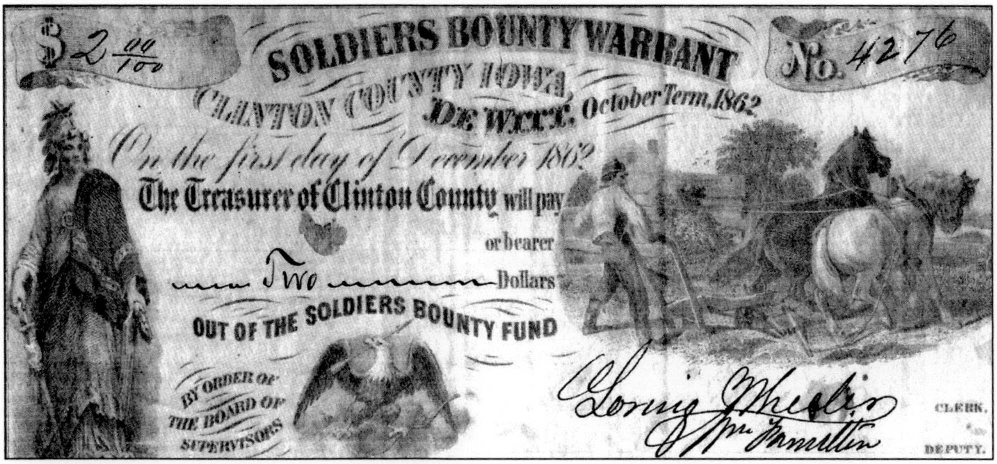

In October of 1862, the State Legislature met in Des Moines and passed a resolution allowing the Clinton County supervisors to issue and pay a bounty to the soldiers of the Twenty-sixth Regiment which had just taken to the field. Under this resolution, about $75,000 was distributed. (Photograph from the Clinton County Historical Society archives.)

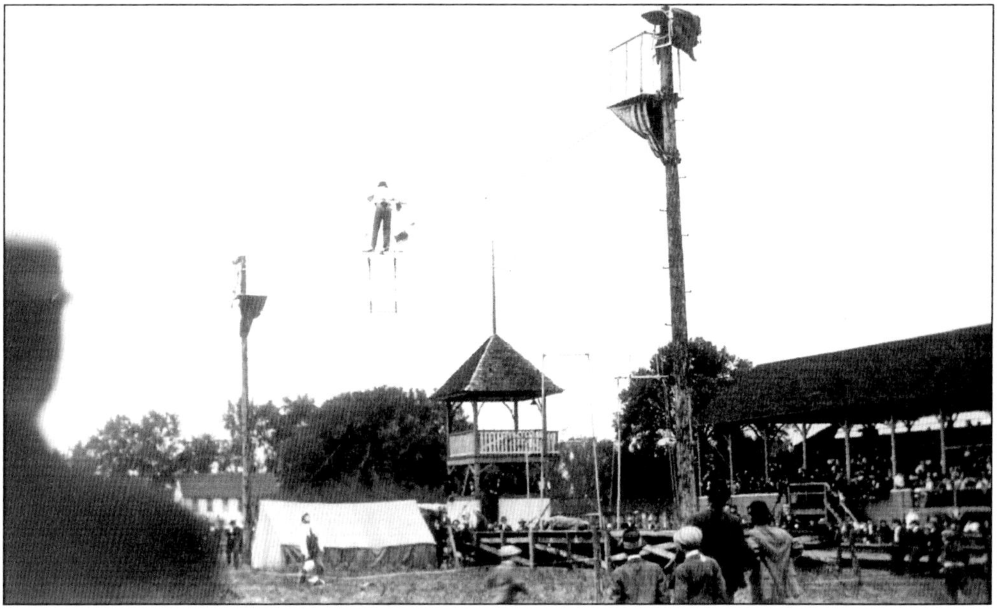

On February 19, 1881, the DeWitt Fair Association adopted its constitution and took the name of "The Clinton County Agricultural Society." The object was to improve the condition of agriculture along with the mechanical and household arts. In anticipation of the pleasant week that was to come, many farmers scheduled the week of the fair as "a week off." Old friendships were renewed while admiring the displays of Clinton County products on exhibit. (Both photographs from the Clinton County Historical Society archives.)

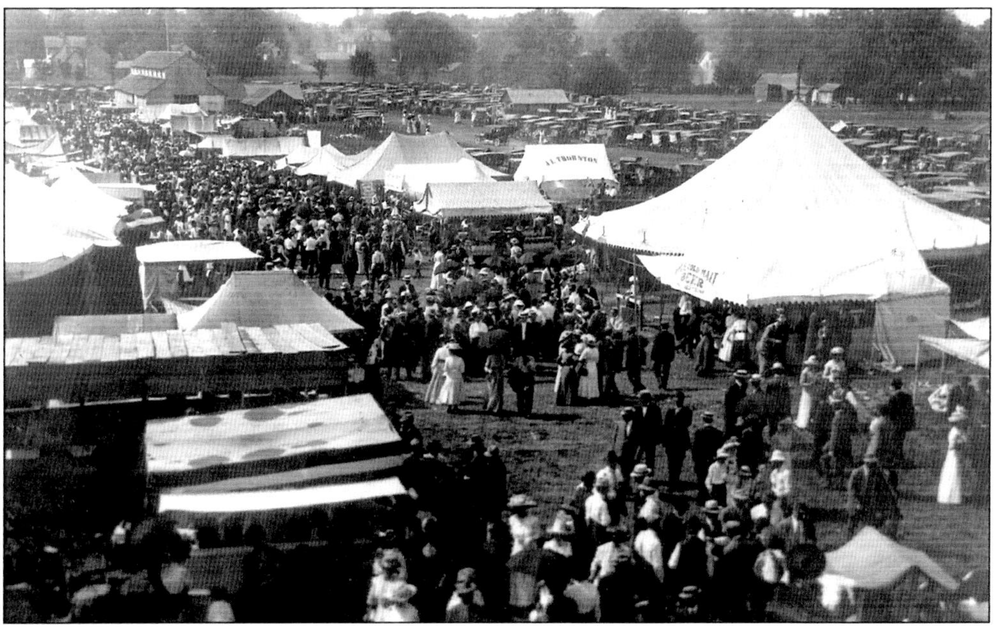

The Peropoulos Sweet Shop was located at 809 Eighth Street in DeWitt for many years. Their savory homemade candy was sold both in bulk and in take home boxes. In this popular soda shop, a lettuce sandwich on toasted bread sold for 10¢ on the Luncheon Menu, which was also the same price as their sodas and plain ice cream sundaes. It is noted on their menu that they assume no responsibility for lost apparel or parasols. (Photograph from the Clinton County Historical Society archives.)

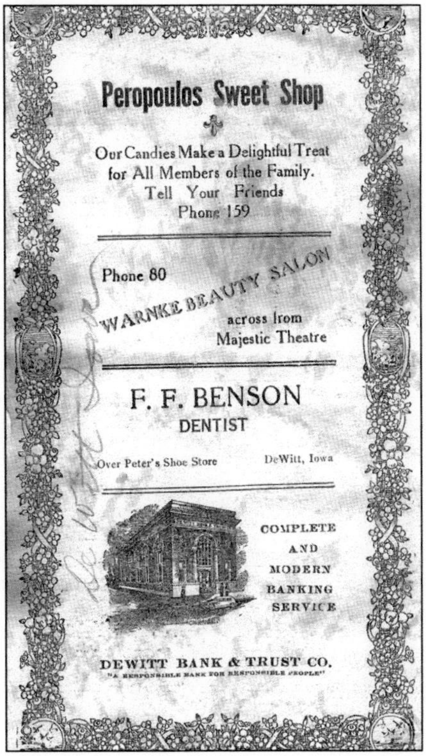

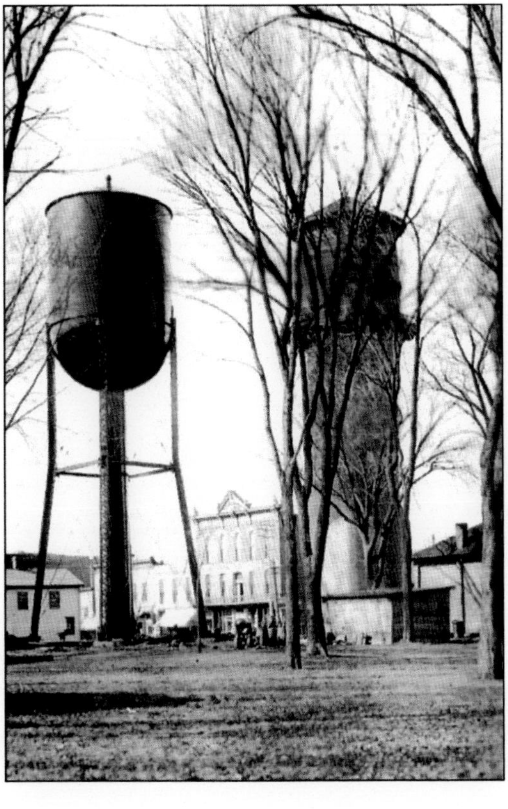

The original brick-based water tower, along with an early steel tower, remained a DeWitt landmark until 1955 in Lincoln Park. Cracks had developed in the old tower's base and additional water storage capacity was also needed. A new 300,000 gallon waterspheroid replaced the old towers. This mighty structure announcing that you are near DeWitt can be seen for miles around. (Photograph from the Clinton County Historical Society archives.)

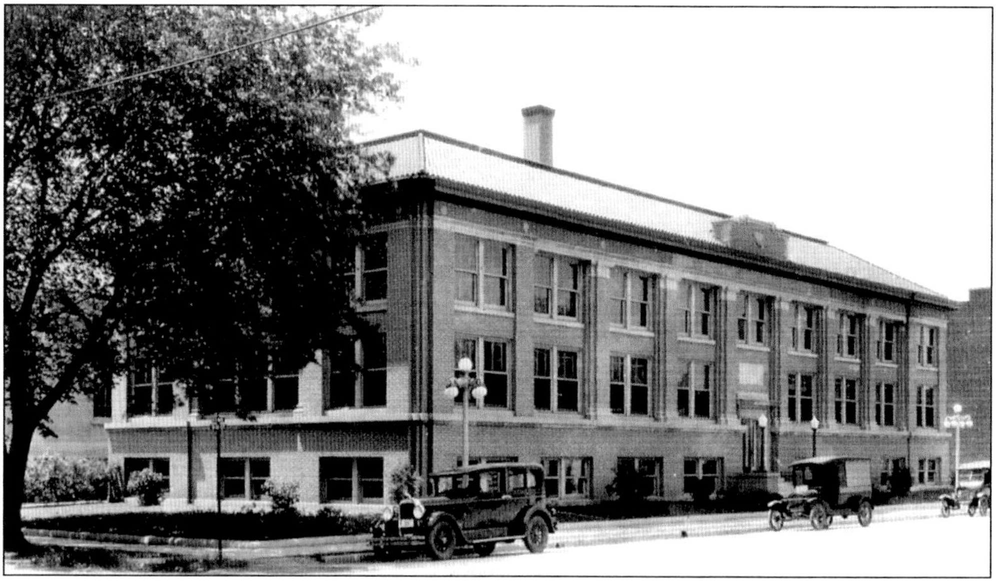

By 1900, George Morris Smith, former teacher and farmer, had brought together a group of investors to raise the $100,000 necessary to fund the Iowa Assessment Mutual Fire Insurance Association. The first office was Smith's own kitchen, and the kitchen table served as a desk. By 1924, the company had prospered and built a prestigious two-story building to accommodate their 30 employees. The company still prospers and the headquarters remains in the same building in DeWitt. (Photograph from the Clinton County Historical Society archives.)

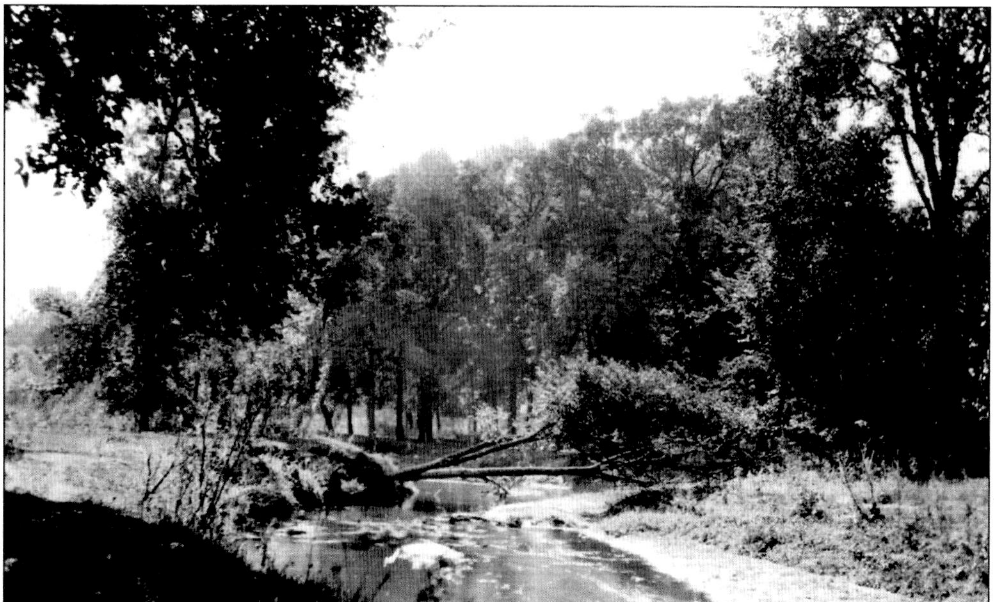

This is an early view of Silver Creek, *c.* 1908, which winds its way through the entire western section of DeWitt Township from north to south and finally empties into the Wapsipinicon River. Around 1837, J.W. Keithley claimed 400 acres and built a mill on Silver Creek which he later sold to Dr. G.W.H. Turner. (Photograph from the Clinton County Historical Society archives.)

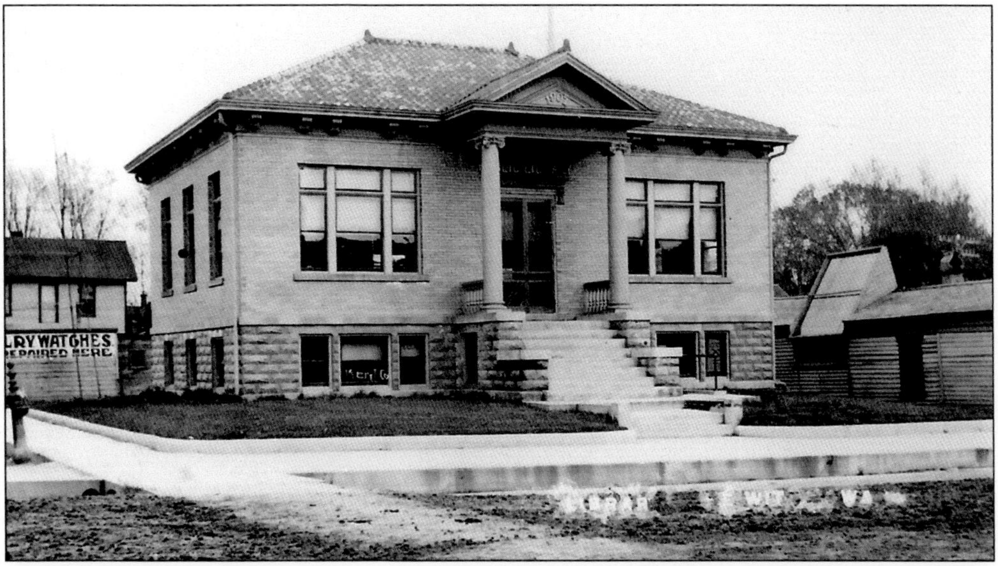

The first DeWitt Public Library was housed in the Craig Building and was opened for the loan of books on March 18, 1897. By 1905, a campaign began to raise funds for a new library. When the necessary funds couldn't be raised, Mayor L.S. Harrington succeeded in obtaining a Carnegie endowment totaling $7,100. In 1907, the new brick library opened and was the pride of the city, where Miss Elsie Saxton worked as city librarian for 50 years. The library was moved to a new facility in 1989 and the old library became City Hall until the city offices were moved into the renovated old post office in 2003. (Photograph from the Clinton County Historical Society archives.)

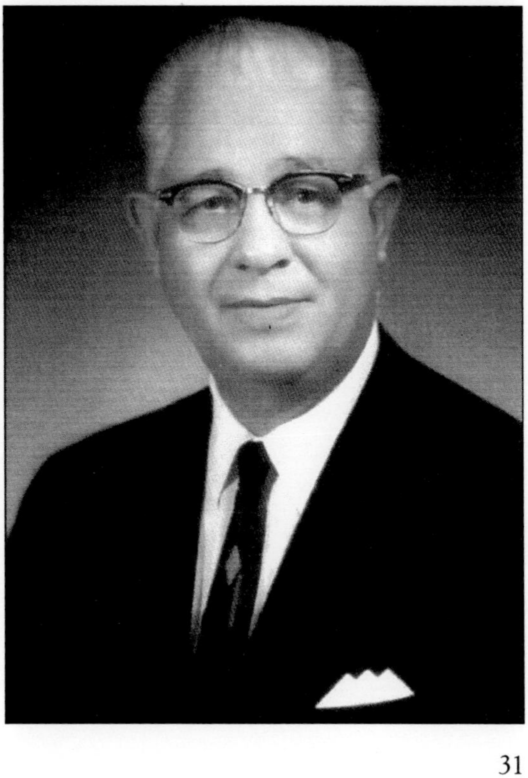

In July 1926, Dr. Clarence J. Christensen graduated from the Palmer College of Chiropractic in Davenport, Iowa, and immediately established a practice in DeWitt. He maintained an active chiropractic office until he retired in 1969. During those years, Dr. Christensen established a life of public service and served on many church, civic, and professional boards helping to make DeWitt the progressive community it has become today. (Photograph courtesy of Jayne Christensen McElfresh.)

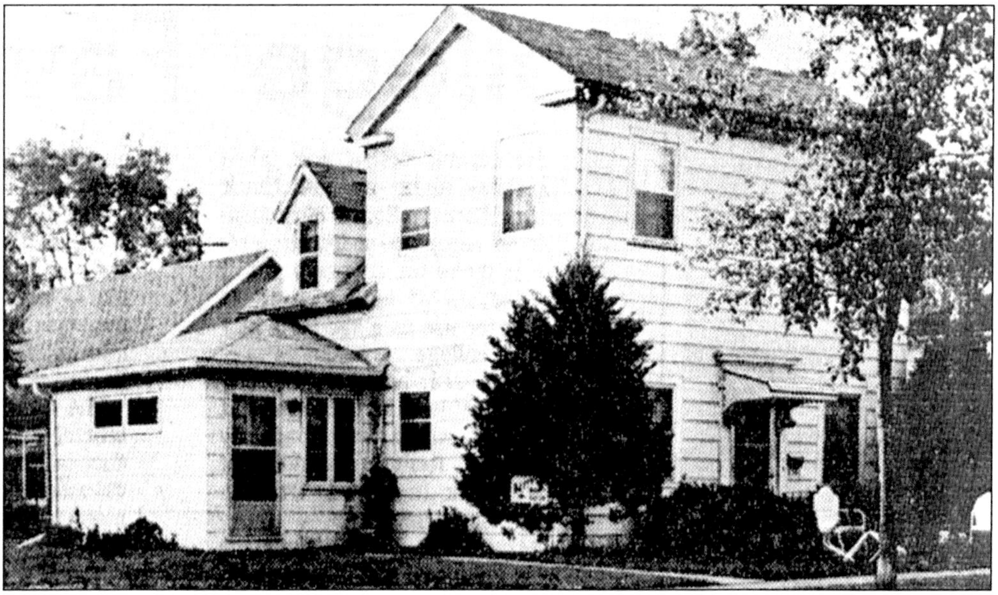

J.D. Bourne, Clinton County's first sheriff, built the first frame home in DeWitt in the summer of 1842. The house was built at a site just south of where it stands today and has been remodeled over the years. However, it is still in use as a family home and is located on the corner of Fourth Avenue and Eleventh Street. (Photograph from the Central Community Historical Society archives.)

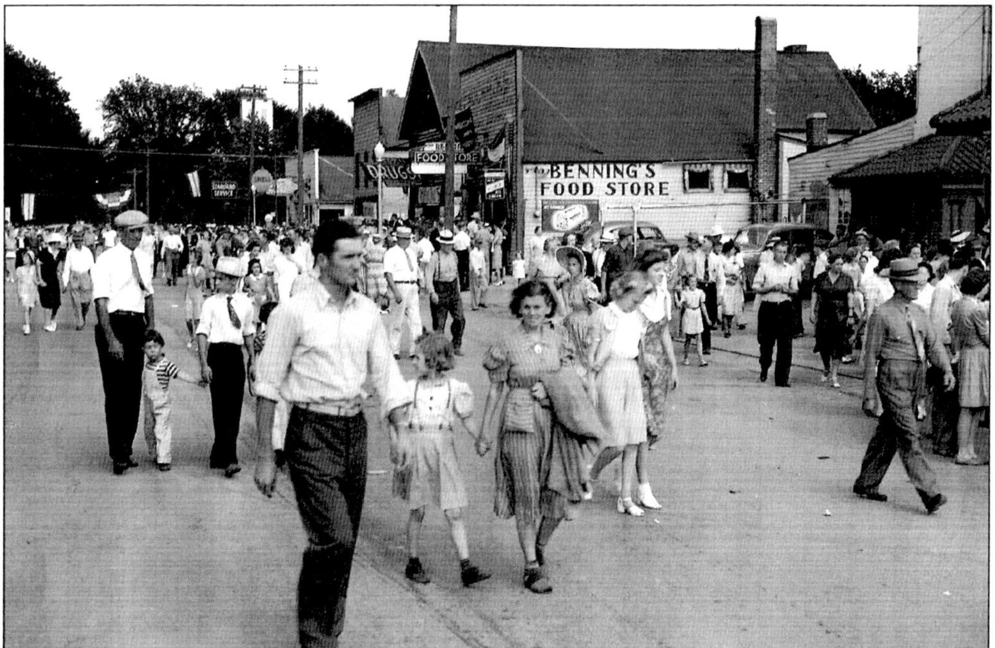

The DeWitt Centennial in 1941 brought out droves of people for the celebration. This was still the era when women wore dresses and skirts for every special occasion. The photographer took this picture looking east on Tenth Street as people were heading for the parade. (Photograph from the Central Community Historical Society archives.)

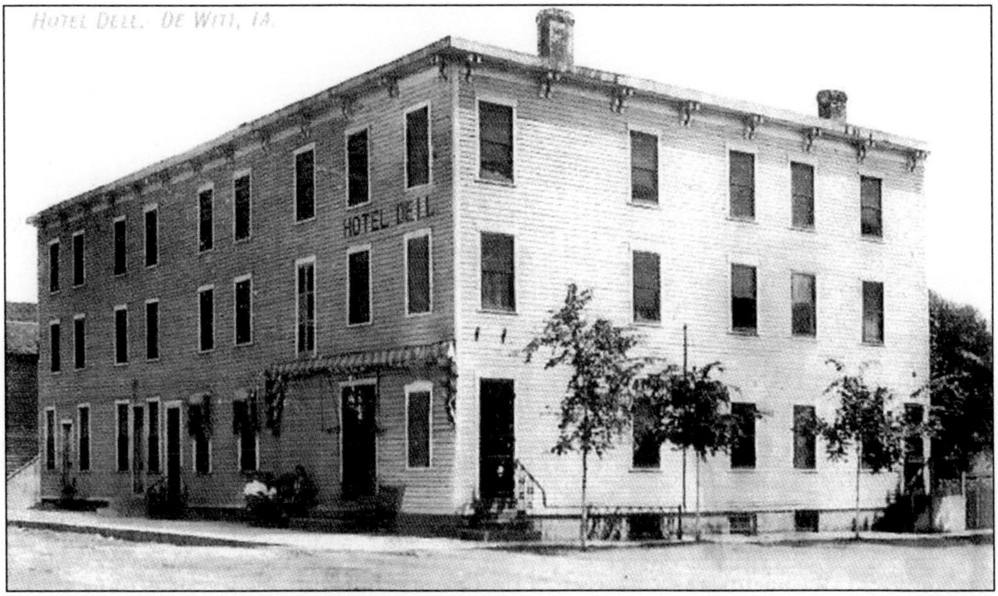

The frame three-story Hotel Dell was built in 1855 on the northeast corner of Sixth Avenue and Seventh Street in DeWitt. The rock for the foundation was quarried in Anamosa and the lumber was brought in by horse-drawn wagons from Camanche. This photo was taken c. 1917. (Photograph from the Central Community Historical Society archives.)

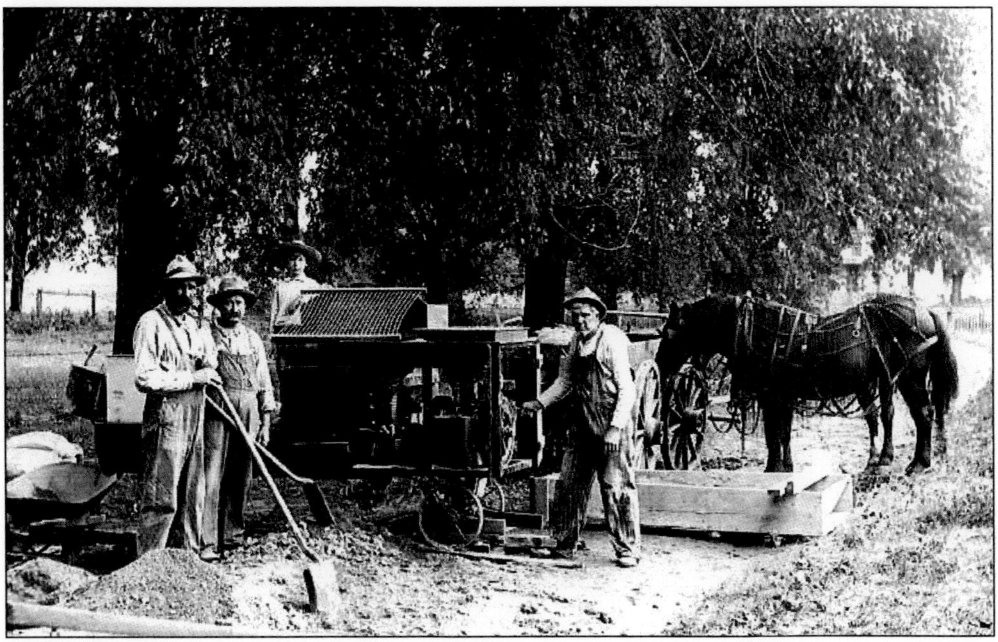

During the summer of 1911, the city of DeWitt committed to installing cement sidewalks. W.E. Lambertson and his crew are shown building those sidewalks with their early horse-drawn equipment. (Photograph from the Central Community Historical Society archives.)

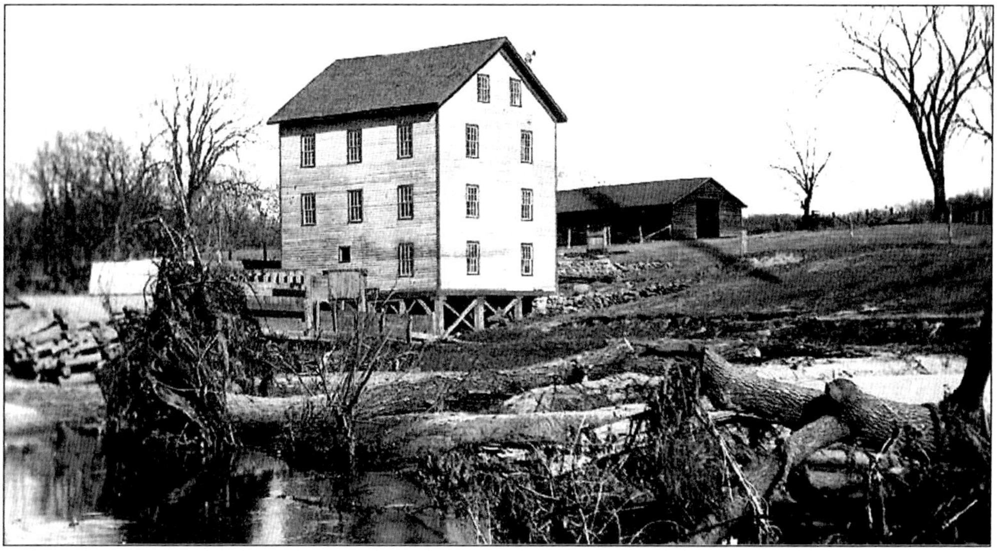

In 1840, Dr. G.W.H. Turner brought his family to Silver Creek, near Crystal Lake, and bought the mill business of J.W. Kirtley. His son, Thomas, erected a sawmill on the site of the Silver Creek Mills which was later owned by Captain W.H. Hall and remains known as Hall's Mill today. (Photograph from the Central Community Historical Society archives.)

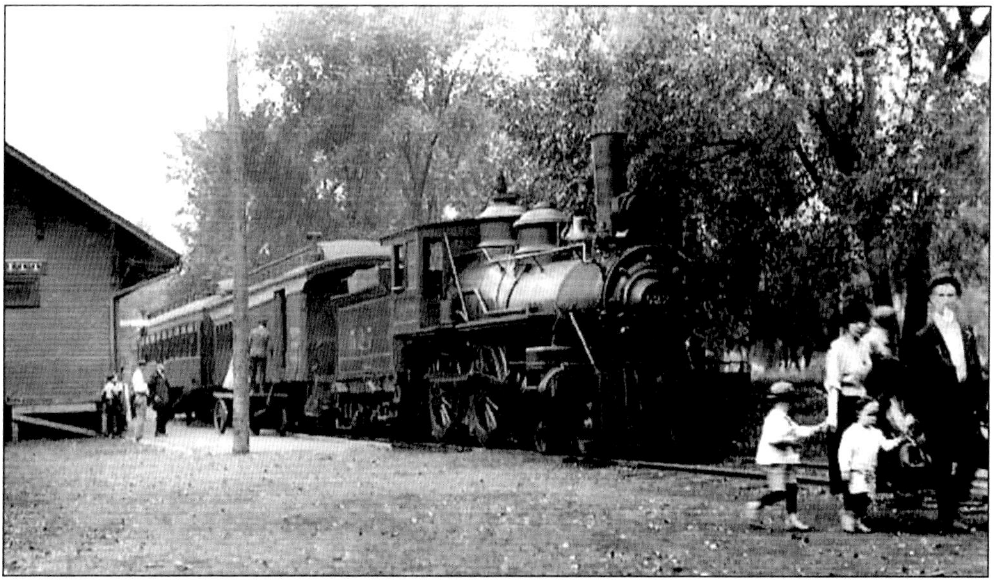

In 1870, DeWitt businessmen raised $65,000 so that the Davenport & St. Paul Railroad (later named the Milwaukee Railroad) could secure a branch from Davenport to DeWitt and then on to Maquoketa. The tracks ran where the Hardee's restaurant is located. By 1971, the railroad ceased operation and the tracks were closed. (Photograph from the Central Community Historical Society archives.)

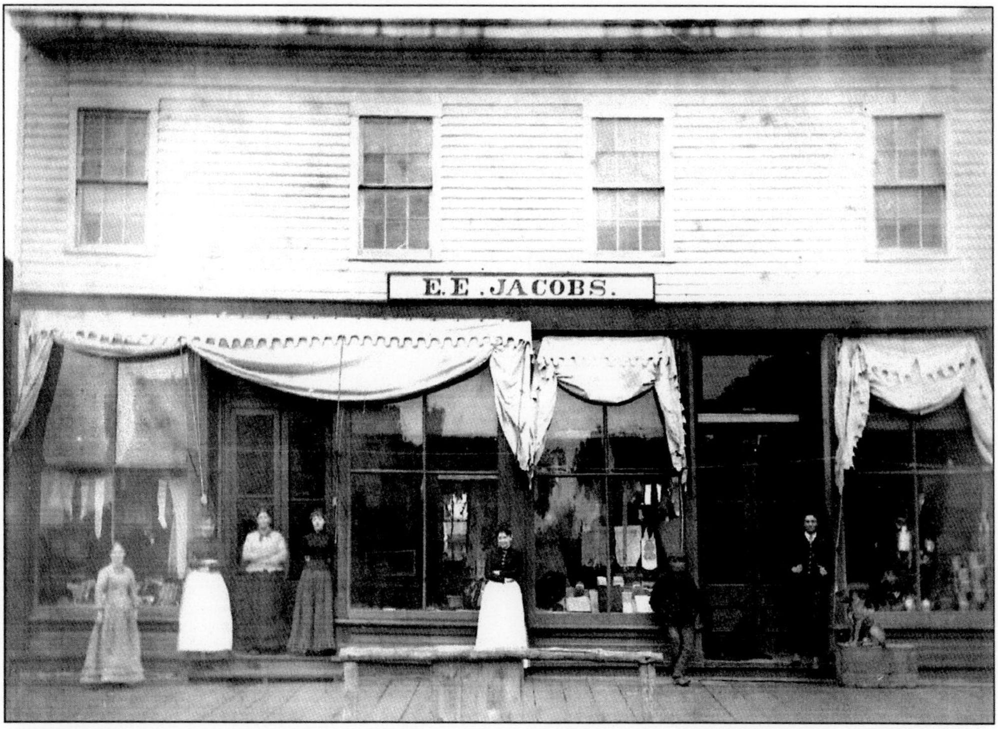

From 1880 to 1910, the E.E. Jacobs Store, located south of the Pacific House on Main Street in DeWitt, sold the ladies of the community their millinery and other clothing. This photo was taken *c.* 1875. (Photograph from the Central Community Historical Society.)

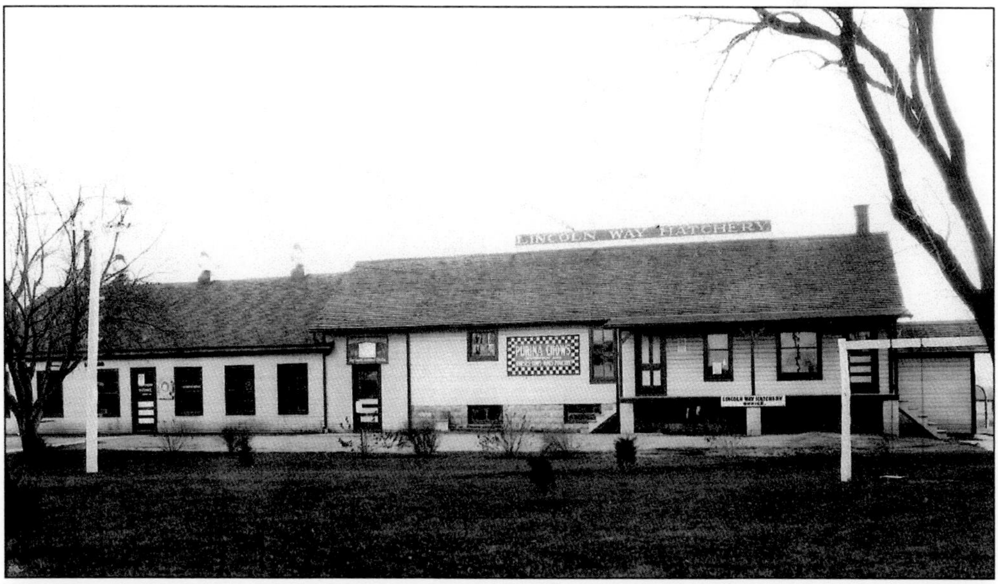

The Lincoln Hatchery, started in 1922, was located on Highway 30 east. It was one of three hatcheries owned by Carl J. Smith and all chicks were sold locally. (Photograph from the Central Community Historical Society archives.)

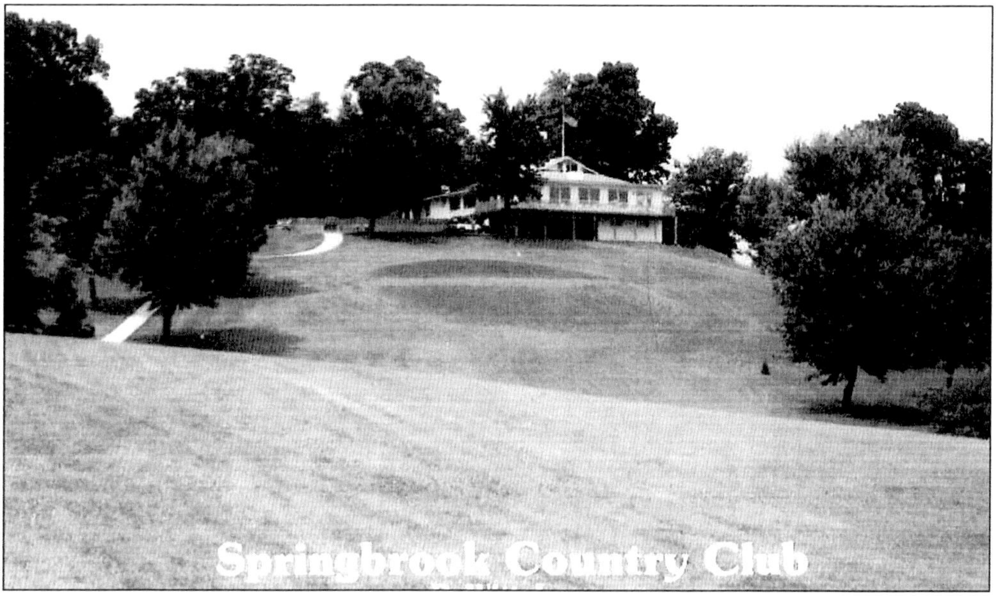

In 1915, several DeWitt businessmen bought Desmond's Pasture from Sheriff William Desmond to establish the Spring Brook County Club. By 1917, a nine-hole golf course was laid out and the brush and berry bushes were cleared. Sheep were brought in to complete the landscaping. It remains one of the most beautiful and challenging courses in eastern Iowa today. (Photograph from the Central Community Historical Society.)

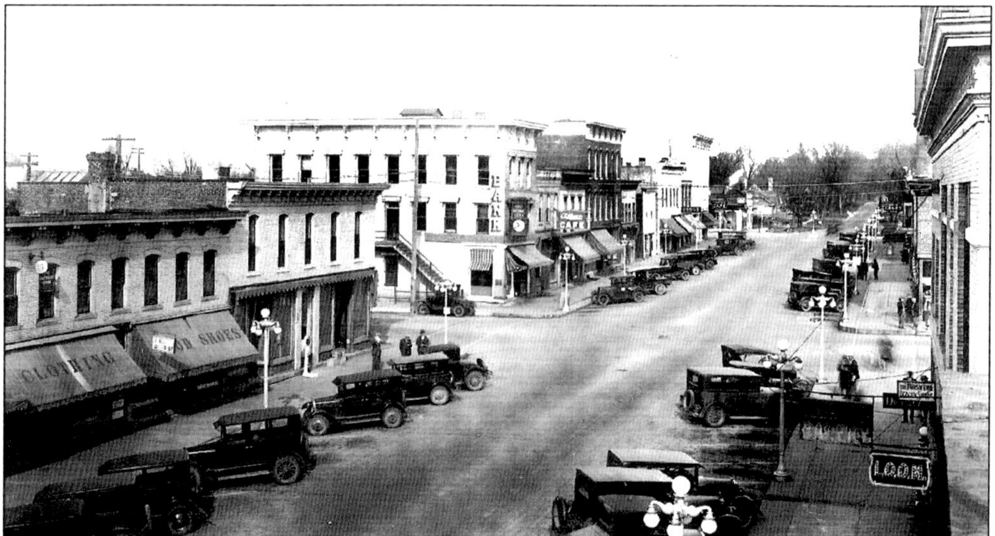

This 1925 downtown DeWitt scene, looking north on across Ninth and Tenth Streets, shows that the arc lights are now gone and the street lamps are in position to light up the nights. The clock on the bank reveals that this photograph was taken at 10:40 on a cool morning. (Photograph from the Central Community Historical Society archives.)

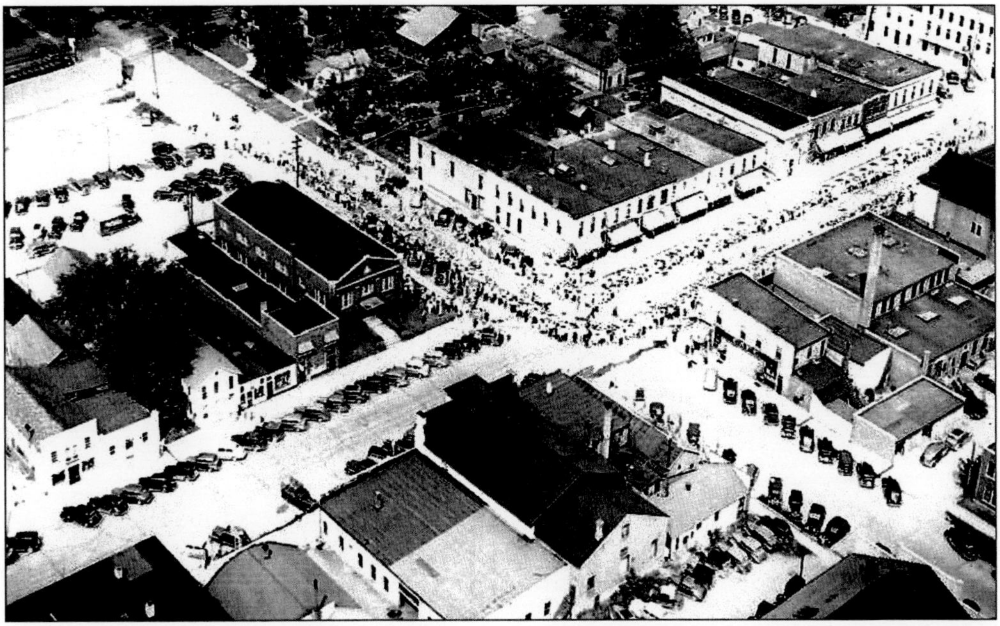

The Farmers' & Merchants' Picnic was started in 1933 by a group of DeWitt businessmen. This aerial view shows the 1939 Farmers' & Merchants' Parade, at the intersection of Sixth Avenue and Eighth Street, which always preceded the picnic. Thousands of people then converged on Fairyland Park where an afternoon of games, entertainment, and dancing awaited them. (Photograph from the Central Community Historical Society archives.)

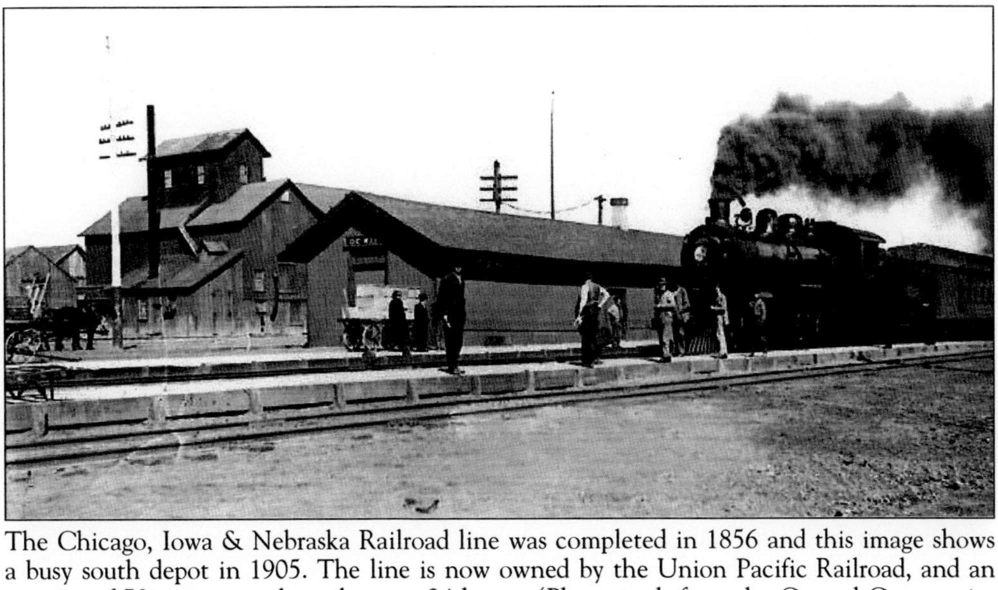

The Chicago, Iowa & Nebraska Railroad line was completed in 1856 and this image shows a busy south depot in 1905. The line is now owned by the Union Pacific Railroad, and an average of 70 trains run through every 24 hours. (Photograph from the Central Community Historical Society archives.)

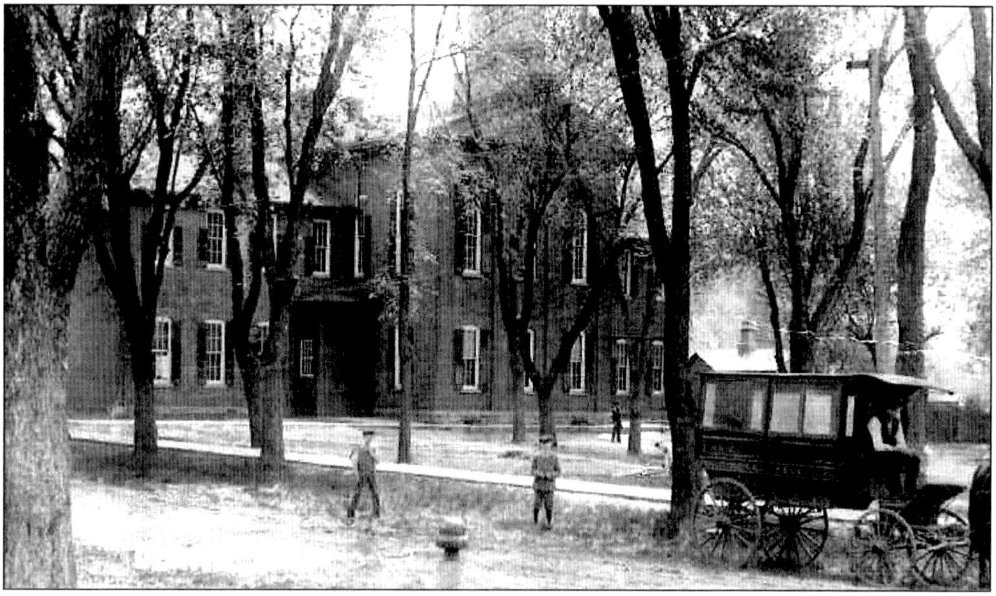

This early school in DeWitt was built in 1868 and was first occupied that fall. Built of brick, it was comprised of a main building with two wings containing rooms, halls, wardrobes, and closets for 370 pupils under the supervision of Mr. Charles Robinson. The impressive building had extensive landscaped grounds, graveled walks, and imposing shade trees at a total cost of $20,000. It later was used as the St. Joseph Catholic School. (Photograph from the Central Historical Society archives.)

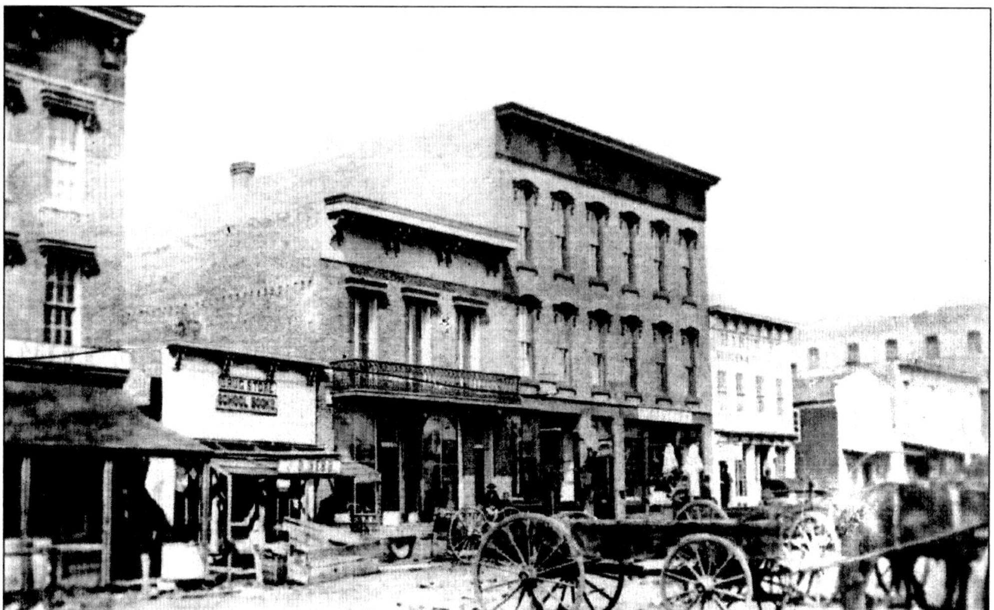

DeWitt was settled in 1841 and by 1868, when this photograph was taken, the town had become a bustling, vibrant city. In 1868, 396,998 bushels of grain and 150,160 pounds of butter were shipped from the DeWitt railroad station. J.B. Webb's Drug Store is shown advertising the sale of school books. (Photograph from the Central Community Historical Society archives.)

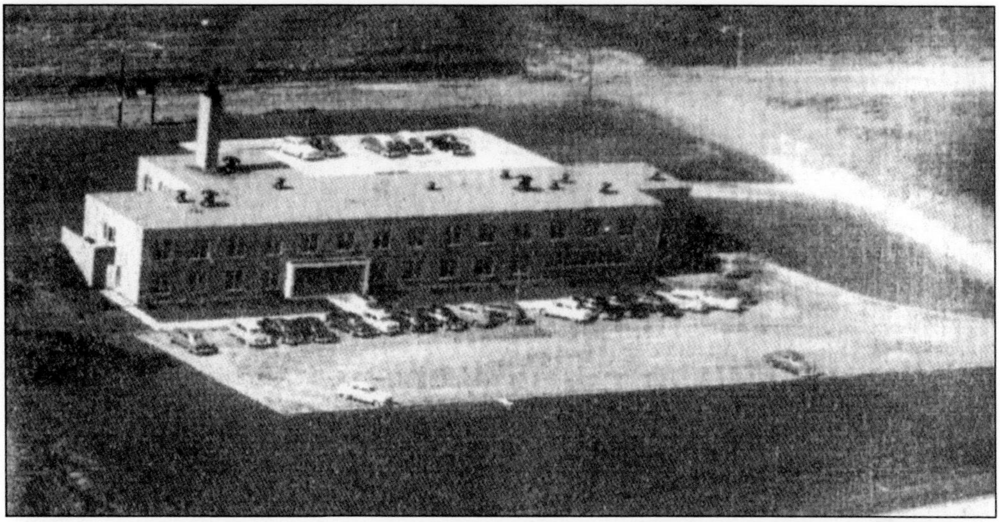

In 1952, after five fundraising drives, the DeWitt Community Hospital, located at 1118 Eleventh Street, opened to serve the area with health care close to home. Even with much of the land donated, the fundraisers still found themselves facing a five-year battle to raise the money necessary to make their dream happen. Westwing Place was added in 1972 to provide long-term care for the community. (Photograph from the Central Community Historical Society archives.)

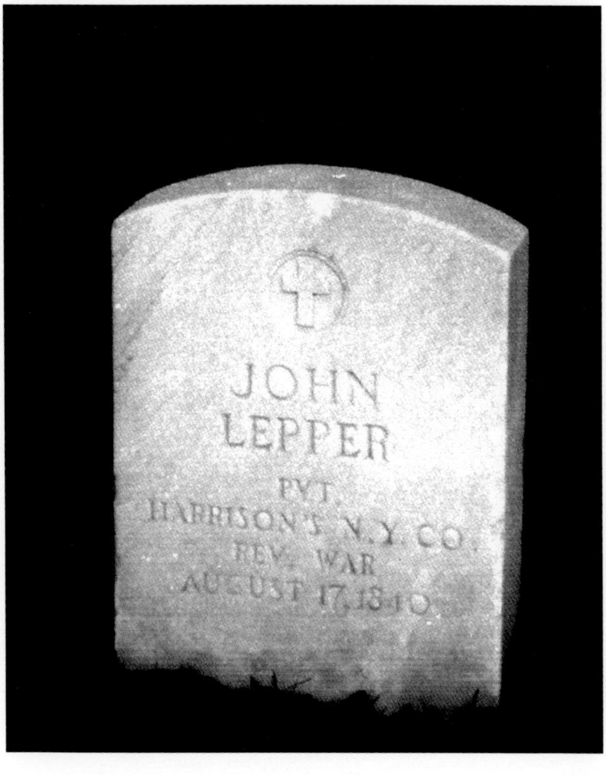

John Lepper, the only Revolutionary soldier buried in Clinton County, is buried in Elmwood Cemetery, DeWitt. He was an early settler who lived in a grove north of town with his wife and three sons. He died in 1840, and his body was moved to its permanent resting place in 1941. (Photograph from the Clinton County Historical Society archives.)

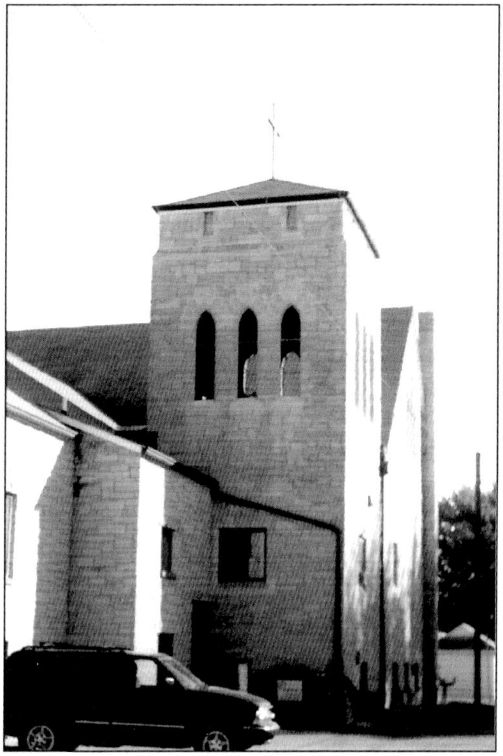

When the county seat was to be moved to Clinton, the word spread that the DeWitt courthouse bell would be moved to the new courthouse. Late the next Sunday evening, ten local men quietly went to the courthouse, and after earlier loosening the bolts, sawed a hole in the ceiling of the room below the bell. They lowered the bell and moved it out to a waiting wagon. The wagon was driven to the old DeWitt Cemetery where a grave had recently been opened and the disturbed dirt would not be noticed. The bell was placed in the grave and the cemetery was the keeper of the bell until the Campbellite Church was built without a bell. Another midnight trip to the cemetery by several of the original conspirators unearthed the bell and the next Sunday it rang out from the belfry of the new church. Later, it was used by the United Presbyterian Church congregation. Today, the bell peals the welcome of worship at the Grace Lutheran Church. (Photograph courtesy of Don Ketelsen.)

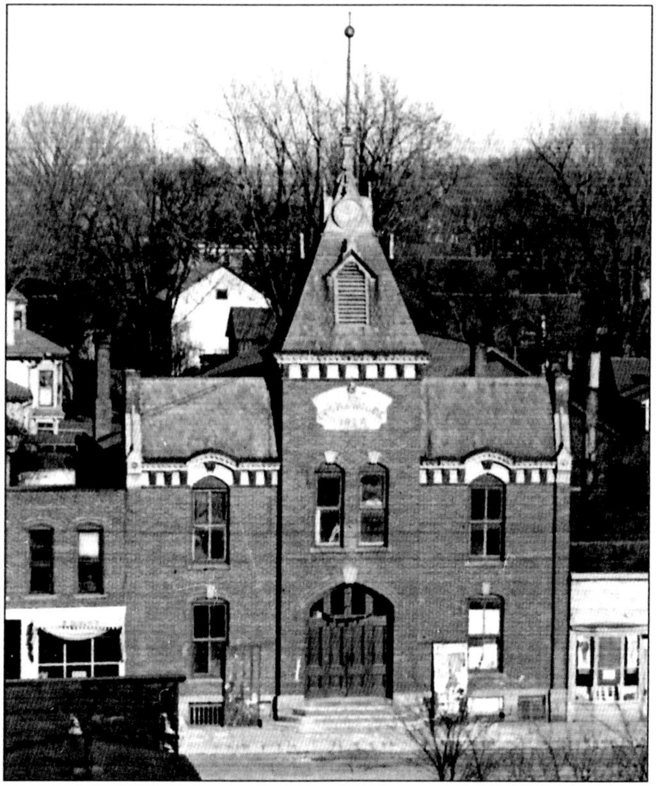

The Opera House in DeWitt opened in 1878 and was considered a model of its time for convenience and architecture. It advertised a capacity for 900 people using both the gallery and auditorium. After 125 years, the Opera House, minus its cupola and lightening rod, is still in use today by the citizens of the community. (Photograph from the Clinton County Historical Society archives.)

In 1858, a petition was presented asking that the necessary steps be taken for the incorporation of the town of DeWitt. An election was ordered to be held on January 7, 1859, and N.A. Merrell was elected the first mayor of DeWitt for the term of 1859–1860. Mayor Merrell was born in New York in 1827, died in 1894, and became a Captain in the Civil War before settling in DeWitt. (Photograph from the Clinton County Historical Society archives.)

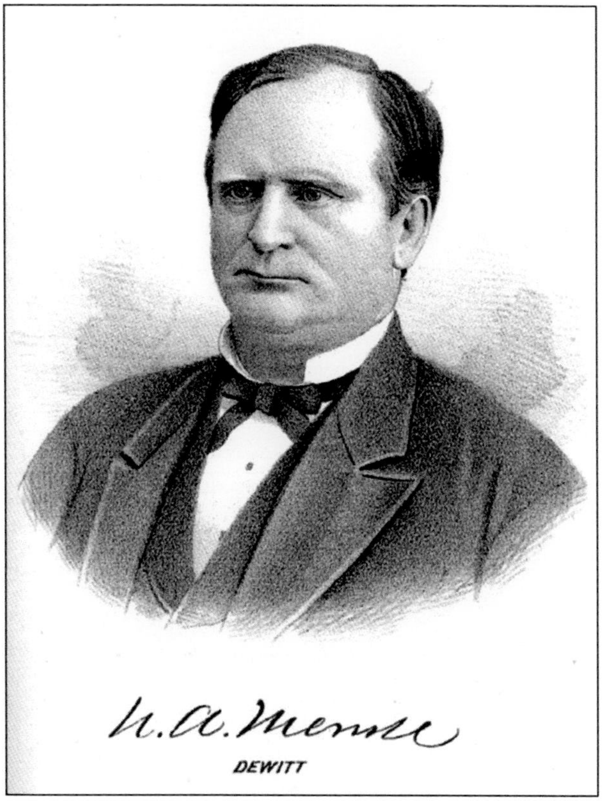

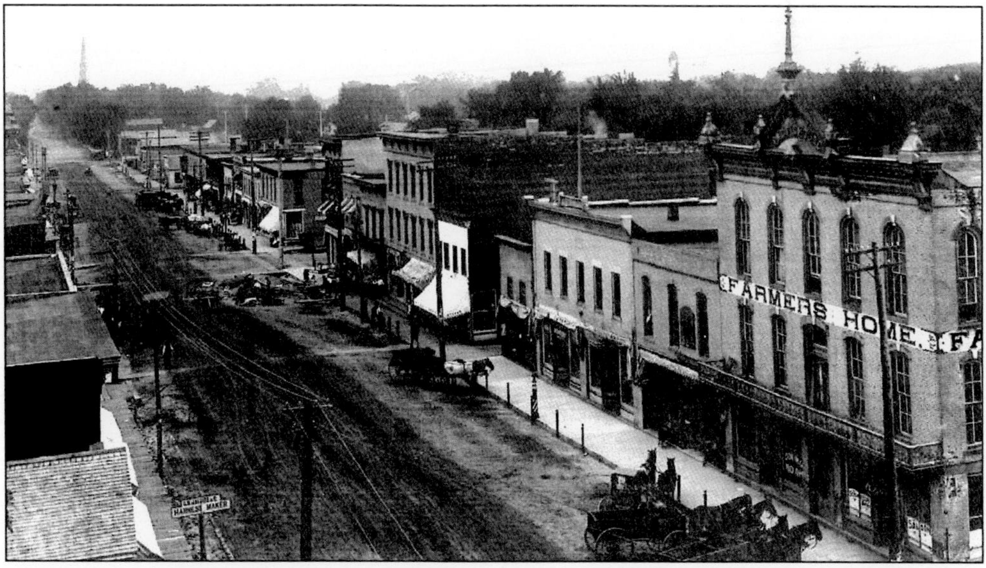

The length of Jefferson Street, now Sixth Avenue, in DeWitt could be seen from the water tower in Lincoln Park where this photograph was taken in 1902. The first floor of the Farmer's Home Building advertises a saloon in the corner window and a dining room on the other side of the doorway. Across the street, E. Jacobs advertised his expertise as a harness maker. (Photograph from the Central Community Historical Society archives.)

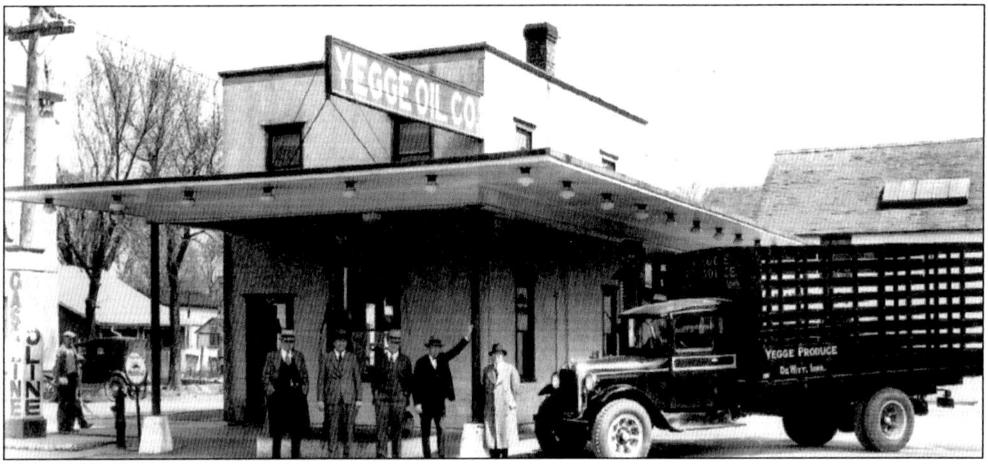

The Yegge Oil Company was located on the southeast corner of Sixth Avenue and Seventh Street in DeWitt. In an unfortunate accident, an explosion occurred there and five people were killed. It was after this event that a drive was started to build a local hospital as the injured had to be moved to Davenport and Clinton. (Photograph from the Central Community Historical Society archives.)

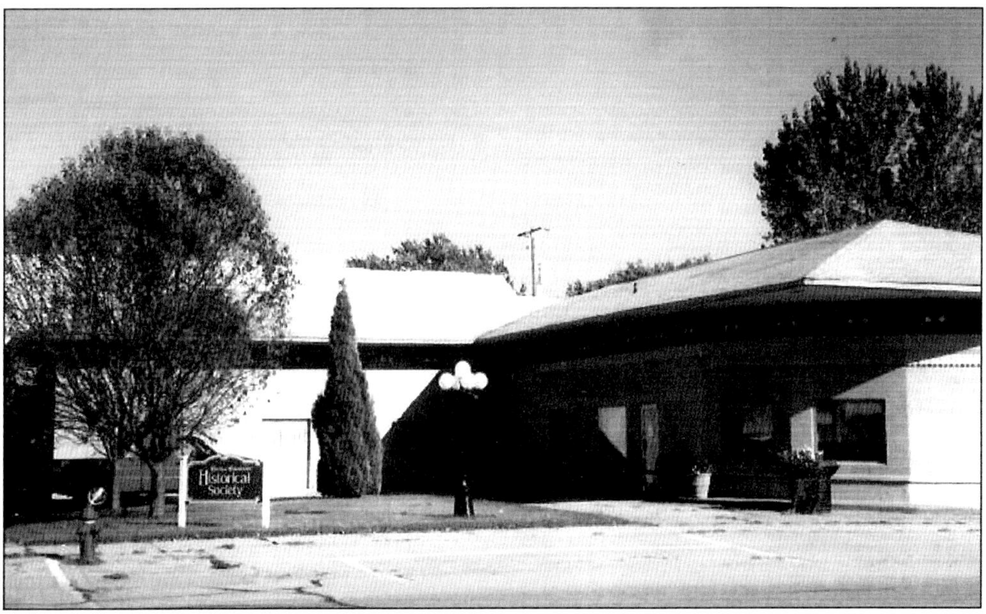

The Central Community Historical Society in DeWitt was organized in 1977 and located, in 1987, at 628 Sixth Avenue. Extensive remodeling has been completed to make this engaging location into a vibrant museum. The museum preserves a cross-section of Midwestern life—from the tools of the Sauk and Fox Indians to the possessions of hearty Midwestern families. (Photograph from the Central Community Historical Society archives.)

Four

LOOKING SOUTHWEST

ORANGE, OLIVE, SPRING ROCK, GRANT, AND WELTON TOWNSHIPS

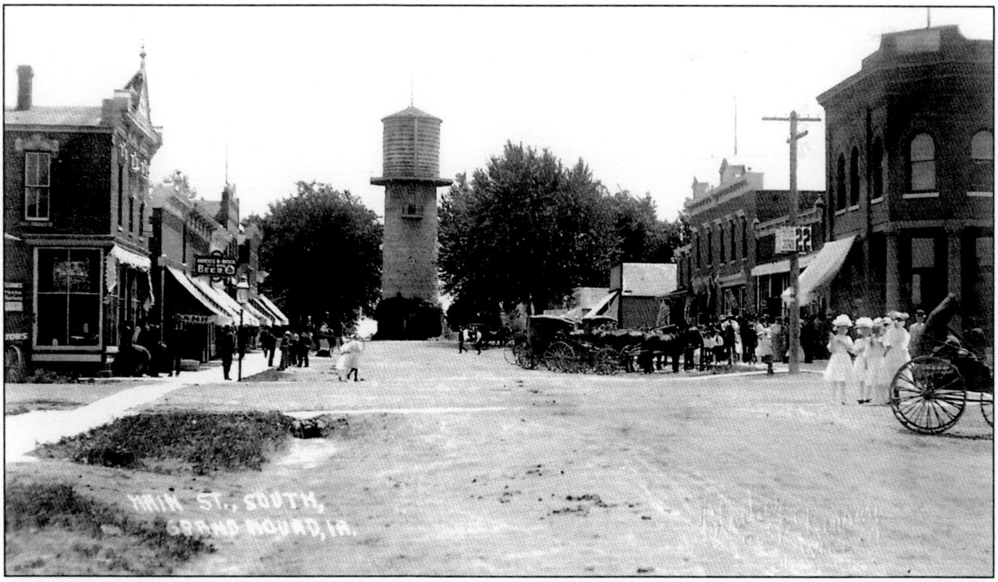

One of the earliest settlers of the village of Grand Mound, Orange Township, was Nathaniel Barber who arrived in 1837. His original log cabin was eventually enlarged and by 1848 was serving as an inn for immigrants heading west. At first, the settlement was named "Sand Mound," however, when the railroad selected it as the site of a depot, it was officially named "Grand Mound." The village developed slowly, but by the 1860s a spurt in the farming population encouraged numerous new businesses to open and Grand Mound became a vital shipping and trading center. The water works system was installed in 1889 and the stone water tower on Main Street served as a landmark for many years. (Photograph courtesy of Bill and Lucille Wharff.)

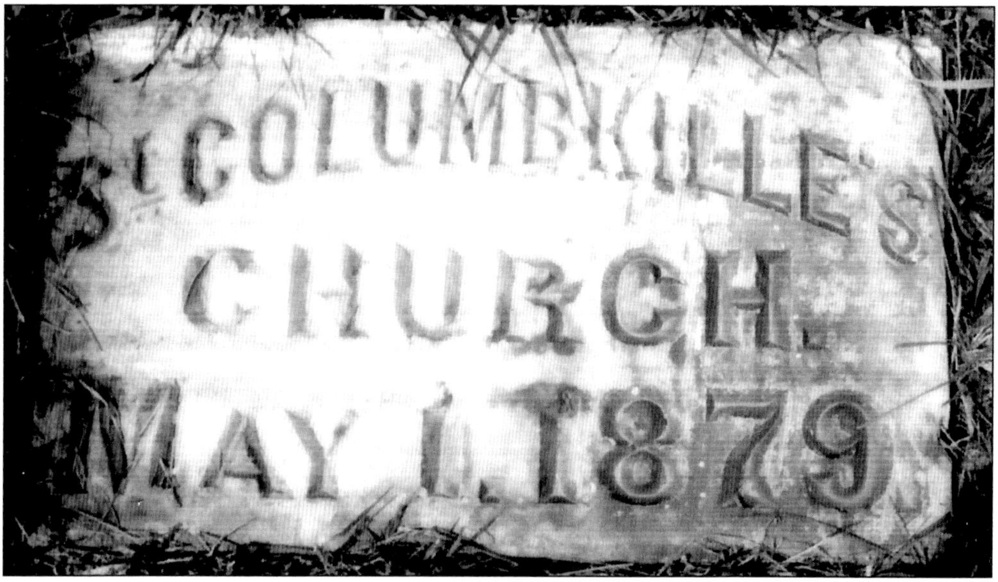

St. Columbkille's Catholic Church, part of the Hughes Settlement, is situated in the northwest corner of Grant, formerly Berlin Township, on a high eminence overlooking the fertile valleys below. The land for a church was donated by Richard and Esther Hughes and the cornerstone of the church was laid in May of 1879. Richard's father gave land near the church for a cemetery and the first burial dates back to 1880. The church was served at times by pastors of Toronto and Delmar, but had not been used since 1962. In 1972, the church was sold to a nearby farmer to use as a farm building. The cornerstone was removed from the church and placed in front of the Hughes family monument in the cemetery. (Photograph from the Clinton County Historical Society archives.)

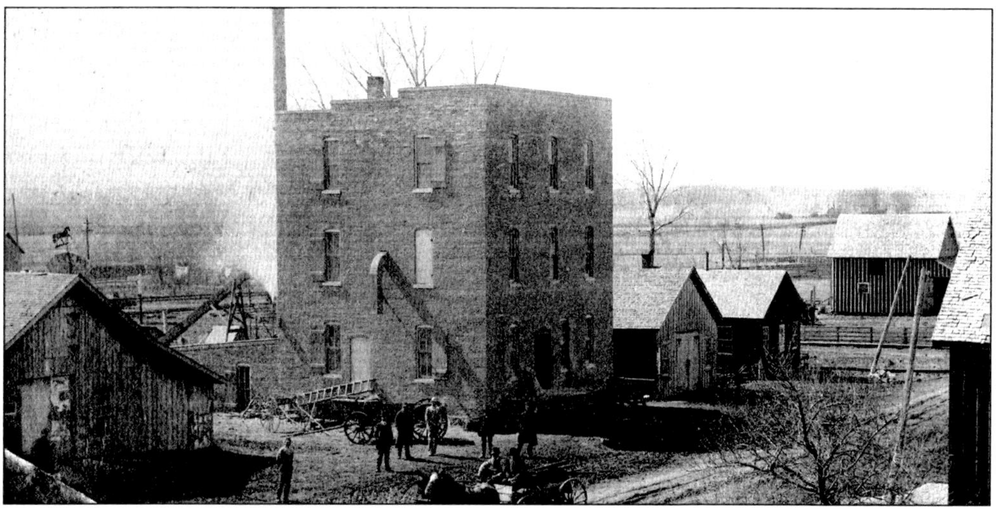

The mill on Jefferson Street in Wheatland, Spring Rock Township, was owned by the Homrighausen family in 1887. It operated with a steam boiler and ground wheat, oats, and barley both for animal feed and home baking. At times, the mill was so busy that people had to wait in line to get their grain processed. Families came and camped on the river bank while waiting. They made an outing of the day by fishing and swimming. (Photograph courtesy of Don and Ethel Hamdorf.)

The first settlers in Calamus, Olive Township, found *acorus calamus* (sweet flag) growing profusely along a stream which they promptly named Calamus Creek. The *acorus calamus* is mentioned in four books of the Bible, as the root was used in biblical days for the preparation of holy oil. It has a long history of use with the American Indian tribes as an anesthetic for headaches and toothaches. Some years ago, a plant was dug up and given to the Bickelhaupt Arboretum in Clinton. It was planted along a creek but did survive. (Photograph from the Clinton County Historical Society archives.)

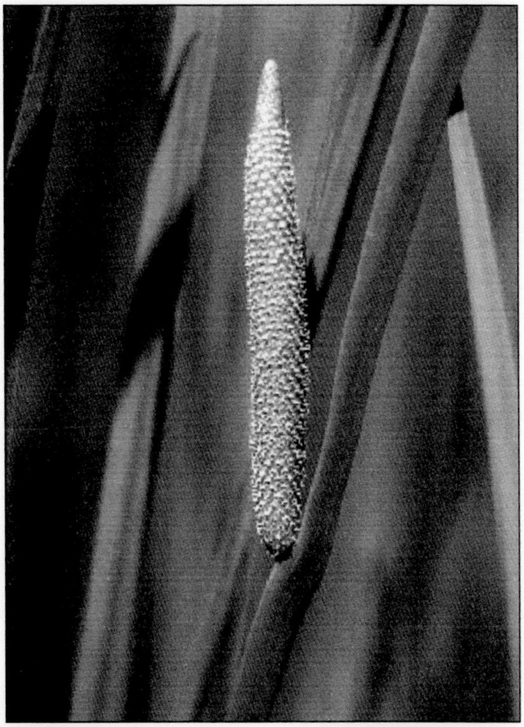

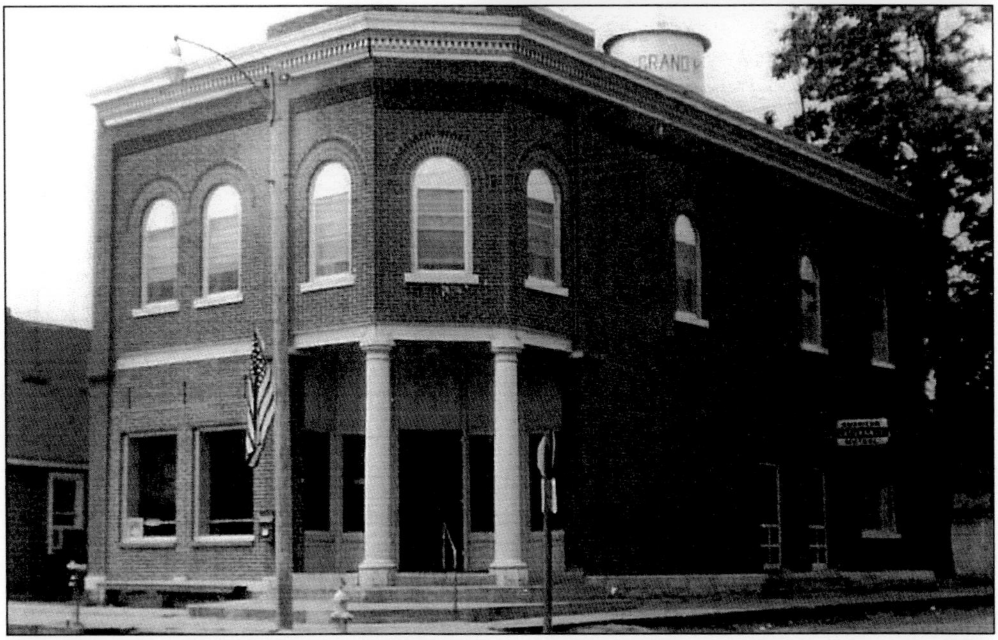

The W.M. Dugan Building at 516 Main Street, Grand Mound, Orange Township, was built in 1905. It was sold in 1955 for a price of $10,500 and the front half was remodeled into the post office. The back half of the building was used by the American Mutual Insurance Association. In 1967, it was again remodeled for the full use of American Mutual. The Dugan Building is on the National Register of Historic Places. (Photograph from the Central Community Historical Society archives.)

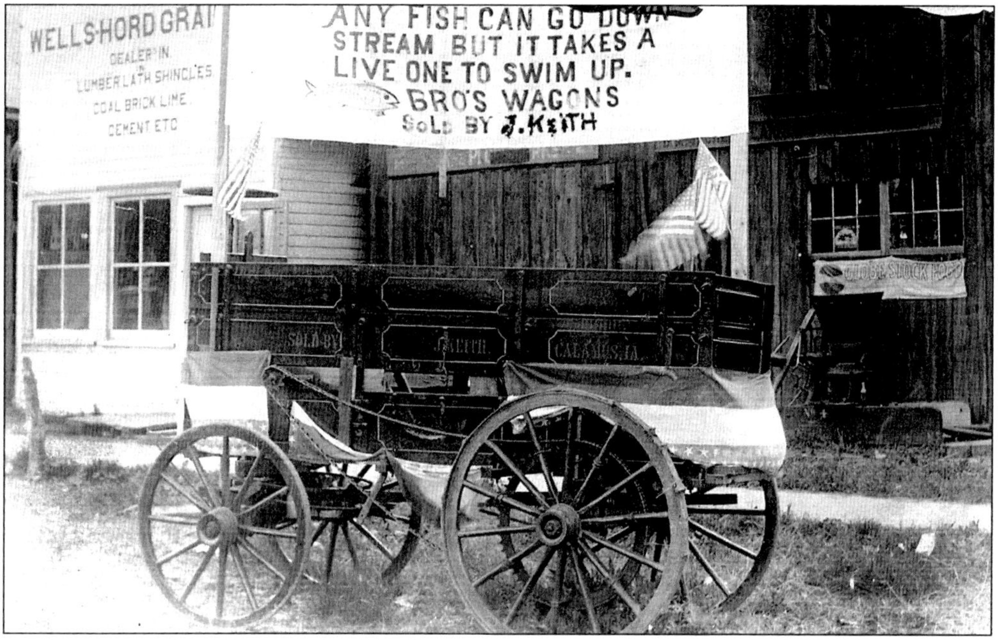

The Fish Brothers Wagon Company in Calamus, Olive Township, flourished next to the Dosland Lumber Company. Later, this building would be bought by the Doslands to enlarge their lumber business. Wagon wheels made of wood were in demand as they would break easily in the muddy roads. J. Keith, salesman, was an early resident of Calamus. (Photograph courtesy of Elmer Ketelsen.)

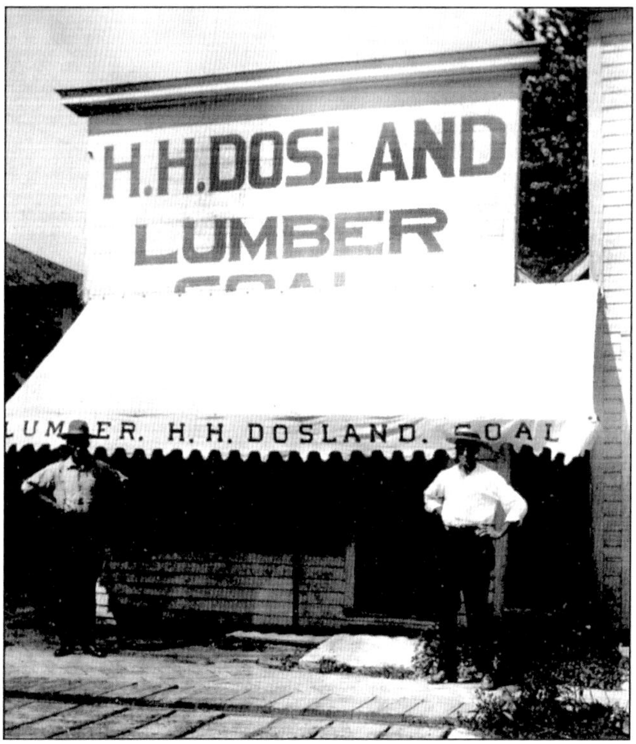

The H.H. Dosland Company was founded in 1908. Mr. Dosland died in 1918 in the flu epidemic, along with his brother and his wife. The lumber company was managed by the Dosland sons, Arnold, Wilbur, and Max. Before trucks, the lumber was hauled by farmers with teams of horses and wagons. In 1990, the business was sold to the Witte Ready Mix Company in DeWitt and is now called the Witte-Dosland Lumber Company. (Photograph courtesy of Elmer Ketelsen.)

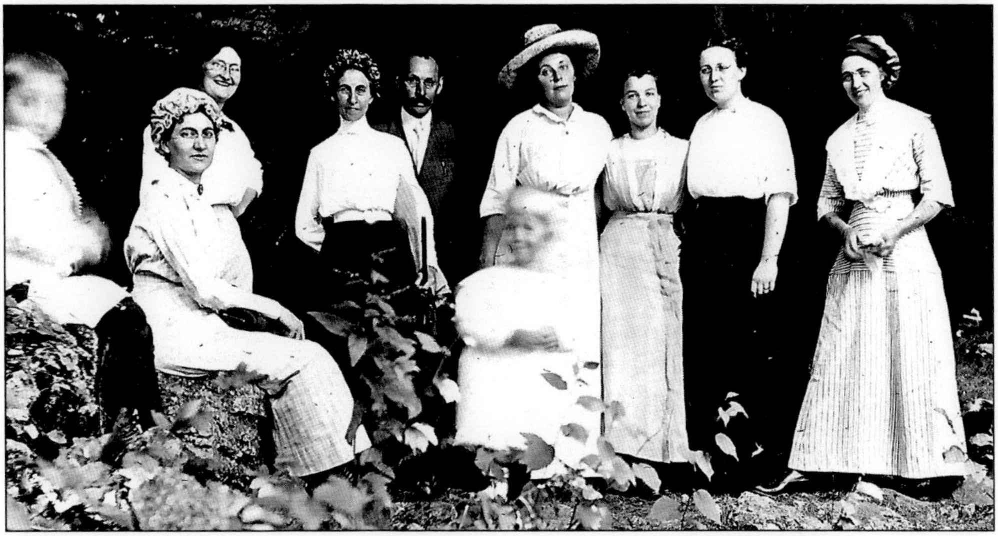

These Wheatland women are shown at the Maquoketa Caves, Jackson County, Iowa, on a day's outing. Henry Guenther is the only man in the photograph; however, Henry was not the driver of the group as he never drove a car. He purchased a new one every couple of years and was a Commissioner on the Clinton County Board for the Lincoln Highway construction through Clinton County. Pictured from left to right are Harold Lohman, Lena Peningroth, Minnie Lohman, Ida Guenther, Henry Guenther, Norman Guenther, Elizabeth Guenther, Mrs. Carl Lohman, unknown, and Ella Guenther. (Photograph courtesy of Don and Ethel Hamdorf.)

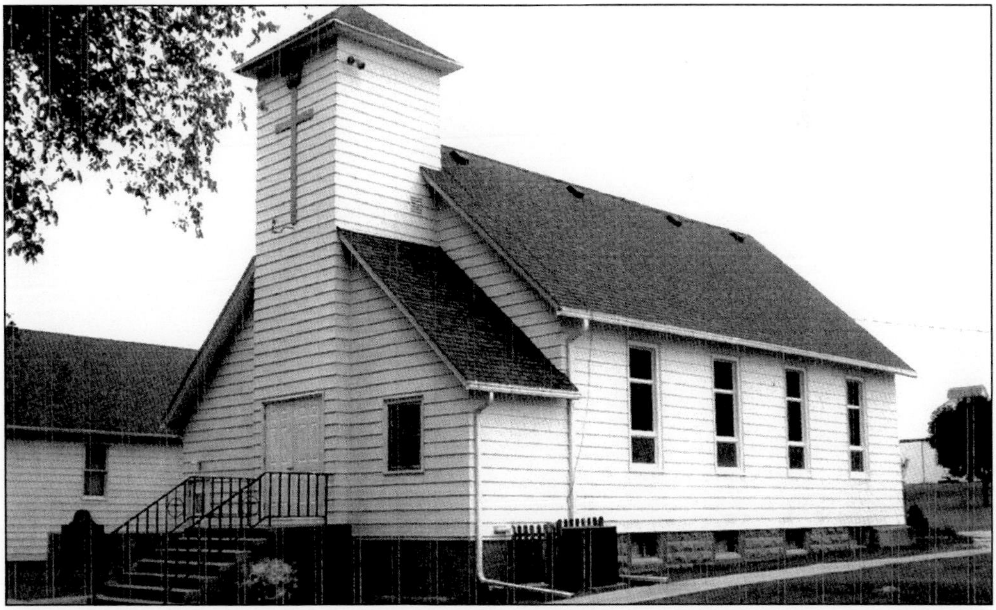

Bliedorn Church (St. John's Lutheran) in Grant Township was built in 1879 on land donated by Wm. Bliedorn. Until that time, St. John's parishioners had held services at the Cornell School. Mr. Bliedorn was a general merchant who was appointed postmaster at Bliedorn in 1898. In 1928, a basement was built under the church and other improvements made in 1949. In 1957, a new 28-by-40-foot educational unit was built on the northwest side of the church. (Photograph courtesy of Jule and Jean Luckritz.)

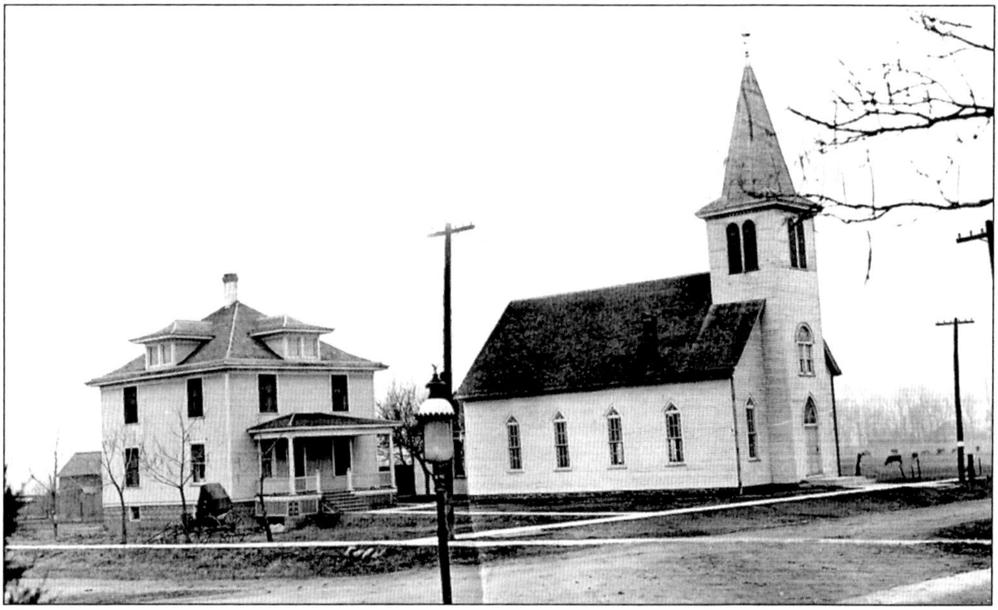

On July 29, 1872, a meeting was held in Clinton's Presbyterian Church to organize the Swedish Evangelical Lutheran Immanuel Church. By August 22nd of that year, another meeting was held to select a site for the proposed church with dimensions of 60 by 36 feet. Once the church was built, it was difficult to secure a permanent pastor and services were not held regularly. The church was rented to the German Lutherans for $2 per Sunday, provided their services did not conflict with the Swedish Lutherans. In 1944, Rev. Roy F. Thelander came and by 1948, new pews were installed into a recently remodeled interior. A modern two-story parish house was completed, and in 1967, the exterior of the church was bricked and new doors and a steeple installed. (Photograph courtesy of Bill and Lucille Wharff.)

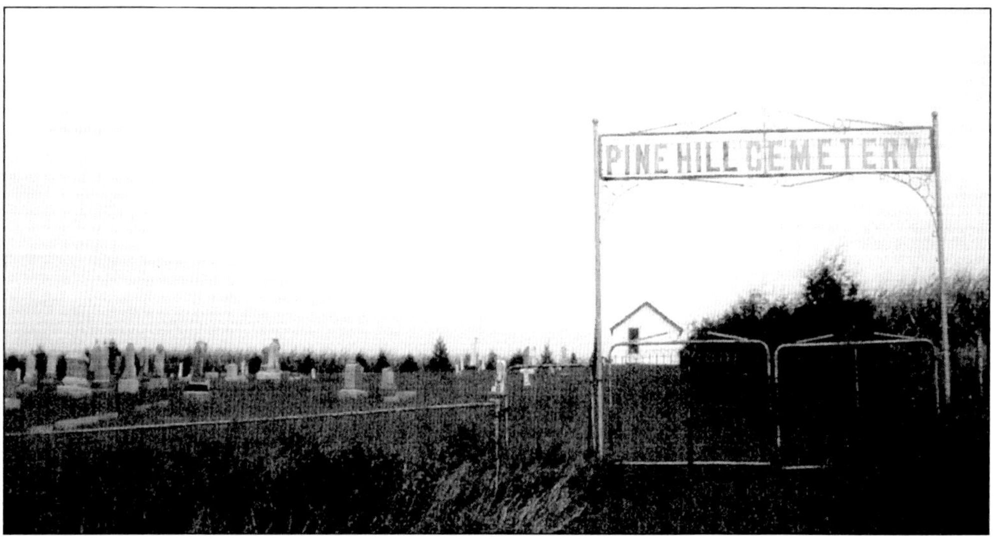

Pine Hill Cemetery, originally Berlin and now Grant Township, is located about two miles north of Bliedorn Church. The first recorded burial was Mary A. Hierche who died on June 3, 1867, at the age of 75 years. Pine Hill is a pioneer cemetery that is still being used today. (Photograph from the Clinton County Historical Society archives.)

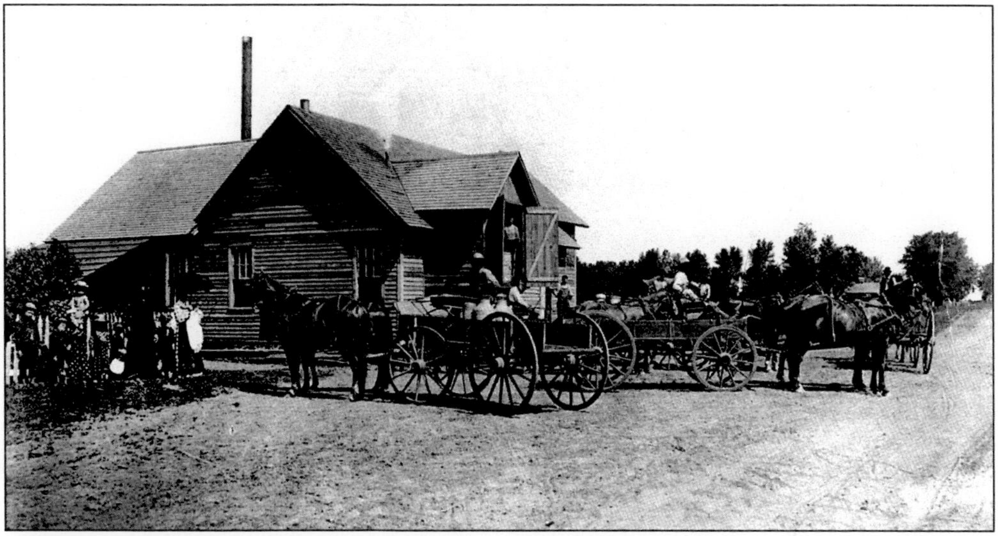

Every community had a creamery center where farmers could bring in cream to be made into butter and then take butter home to their families, while also receiving a cream check at the end of the month. In 1892, the creamery station in Calamus, Olive Township, was located south of the water tower. Farmers competed to see who would be the highest producers of cream and Calamus farmers were delighted in being among the champion producers. (Photograph courtesy of Elmer Ketelsen.)

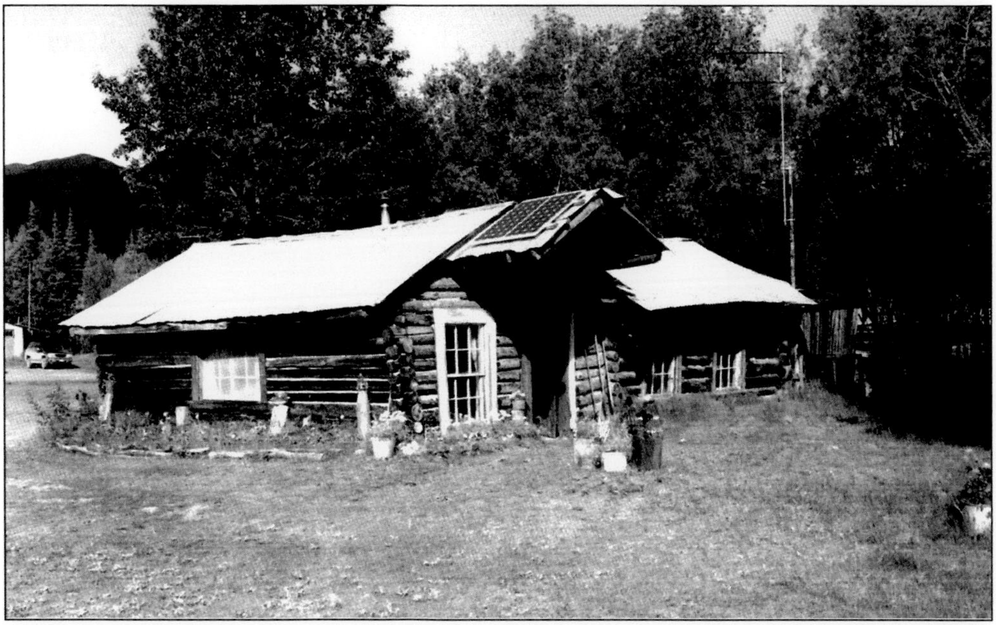

Henry Pingel was born and spent his youth in Wheatland, Spring Rock Township. He left in 1890 to mine gold in Alaska and ended up with gold mines in Coldfoot on Nolan Creek and built the cabin at Wiseman, Alaska, shown above, as his home. In 1930, Henry and his wife, Fredericke, a missionary and cook for the mining crews, retired to the Wheatland home which had been purchased by his family in 1898. Today, the cabin is a retreat and educational center. (Photograph courtesy of Dorothy Pingel.)

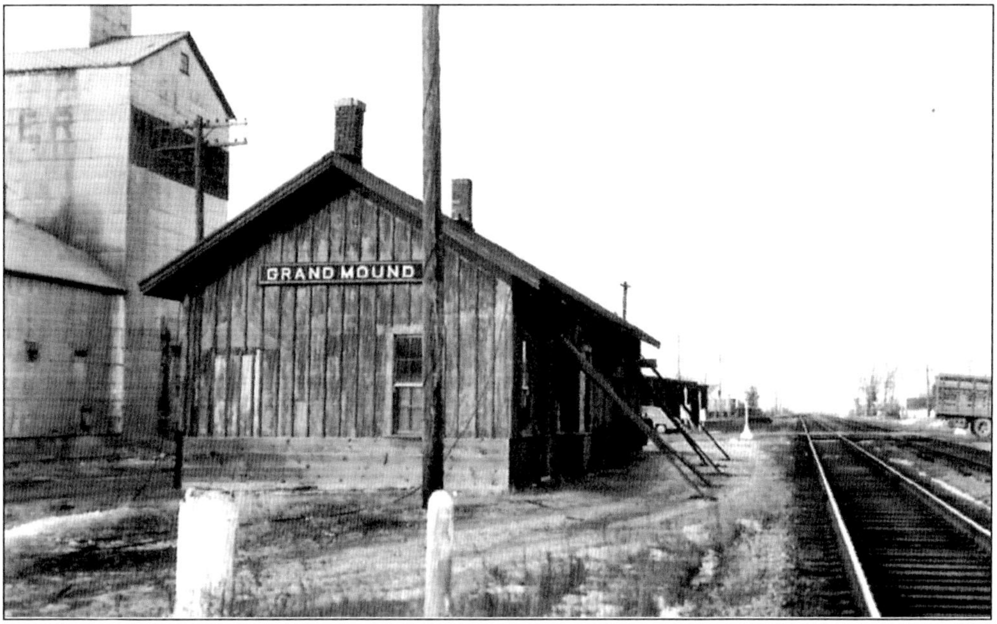

The Grand Mound, Orange Township, depot was closed in 1958 when Bill Lambert was the last agent. In January of 1959, the Chicago & Northwestern Railroad razed the depot as part of their program to eliminate a number of stations in Iowa. The Grand Mound sign was placed over the door of Mae Gest's Nursing Home in Grand Mound. It is now at the Central Community Historical Society in DeWitt. (Photograph from the Central Community Historical Society archives.)

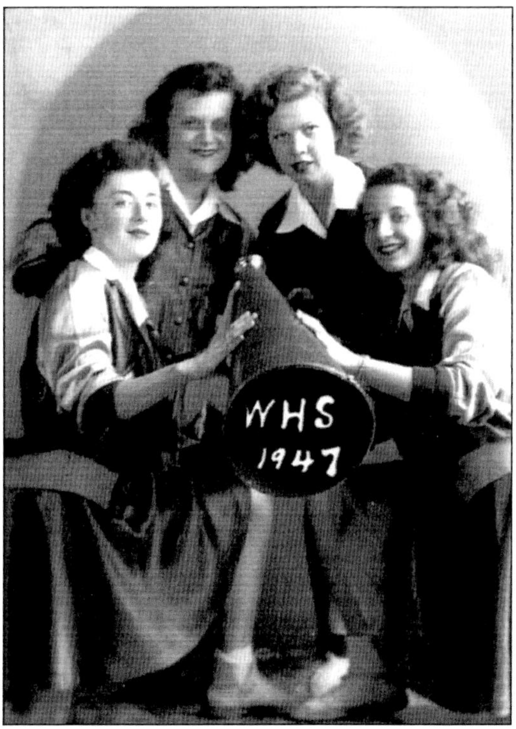

The 1947 Wheatland High School, Spring Rock Township, basketball season was spurred on to victory by their lively cheerleaders. Pictured left to right are LaVonne Smith, Betty Cavey, Ethel Bouchante, and LaDon Riedesel. (Photograph courtesy of Steve Roling.)

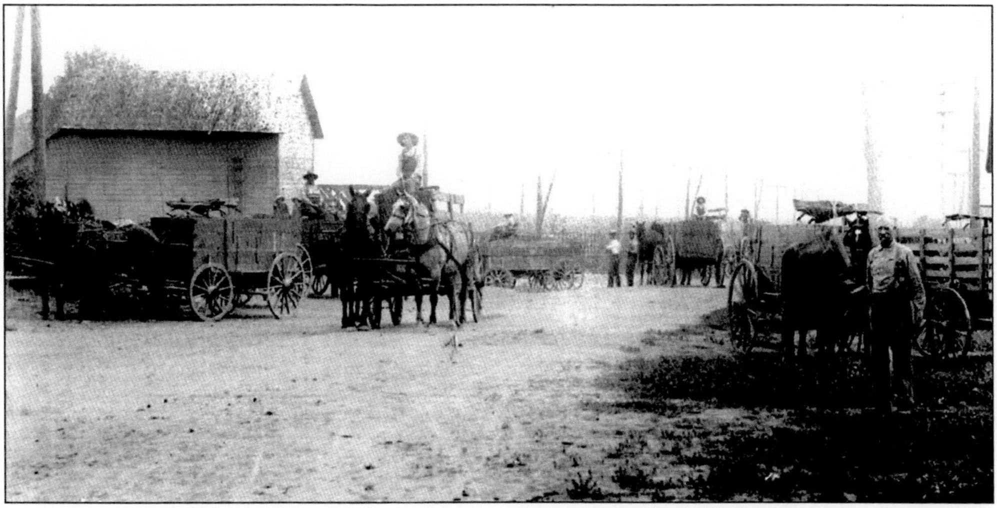

This 1907 photograph of Hog Day in Welton, Welton Township, shows how busy market day can be in small communities. Farmers brought their hogs to town for shipping or slaughter. With the location of the Milwaukee & St. Paul Railroad in the center of the township, it became the shipping point for the vicinity. (Photograph from the Central Community Historical Society archives.)

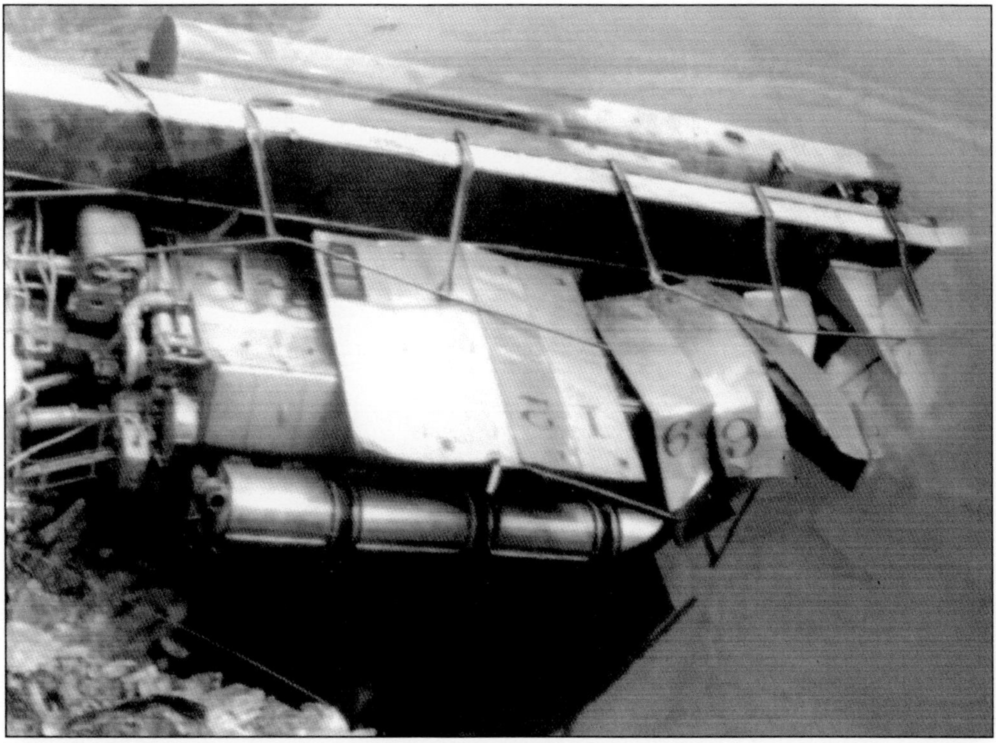

In July of 1976, a bridge over the Wapsipinicon River in Spring Rock Township gave way. When the train running with engine #6912 came through, the men on the train were unable to stop in time and the engine dropped into the river. The engineer was killed and a brakeman was injured. (Photograph courtesy of Jule and Jean Luckritz.)

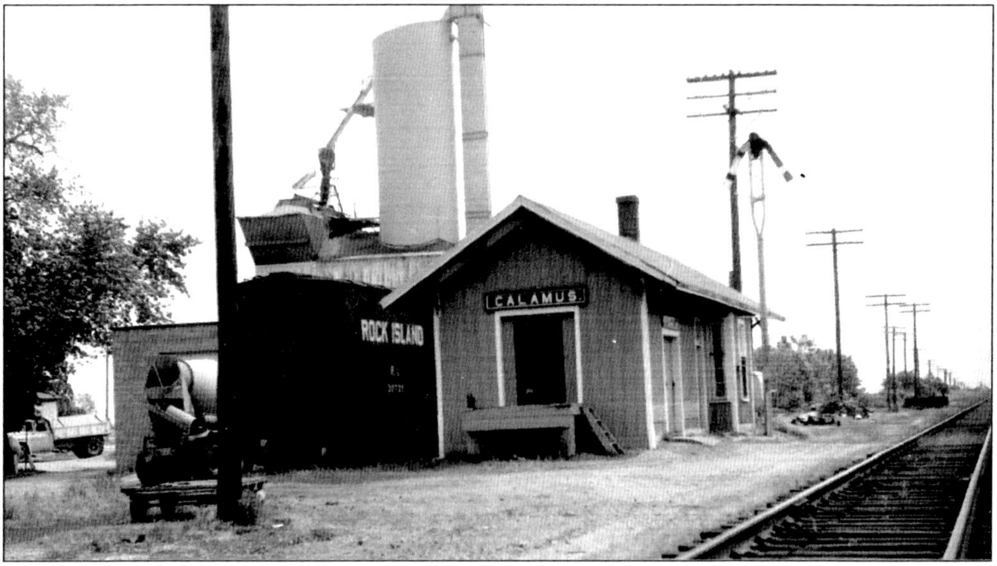

In 1860, R.S. Dickinson settled Calamus, Olive Township, which was not laid out as a town until 1864. By 1866, the settlement began to grow on the north side of the railroad tracks. John Richolson erected an elevator near the railroad track and, along with Mr. Dickinson and Mr. Houck, put together store rooms from which they commenced an extensive trade with the surrounding country. In a few years, the business center found its way to the more favorable south side of the railroad tracks and the town developed from there. By 1871, Calamus had become a farming community of over 250 residents and remains a farming community today. (Photograph from the Clinton County Historical Society archives.)

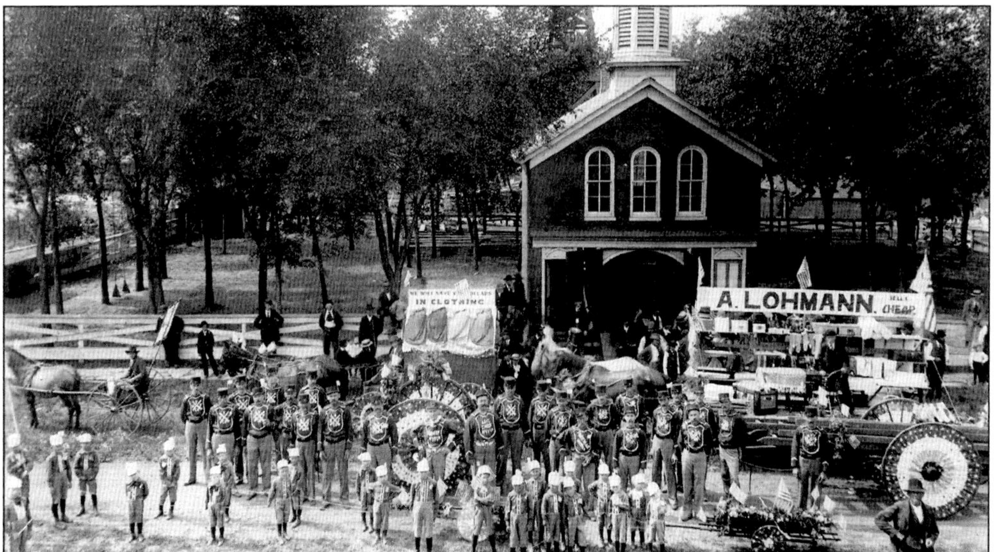

The 4th of July celebration in Wheatland, Spring Rock Township, in 1895 started early that morning. At 5:00 a.m., Johnnie Thompsen, one of the local blacksmiths, placed gun powder under the anvil and blew it up in the air with a big "bang." Later, the floats and the Wheatland Volunteer Fire Department assembled for the parade in front of the town hall located at the park. (Photograph from the Clinton County Historical Society archives.)

As one of Clinton County's earliest pioneers, Nathaniel Barber, a New York native, came to Grand mound, Orange Township, in 1837 and settled near a creek which came to be known as Barber's Creek. He built a cabin 18 feet square and during the first winter 29 people lived together in that small space. Nathaniel and Mary Pearsall Barber eventually owned and successfully farmed 350 acres while raising their family of 5 children. (Photograph from the Clinton County Historical Society archives.)

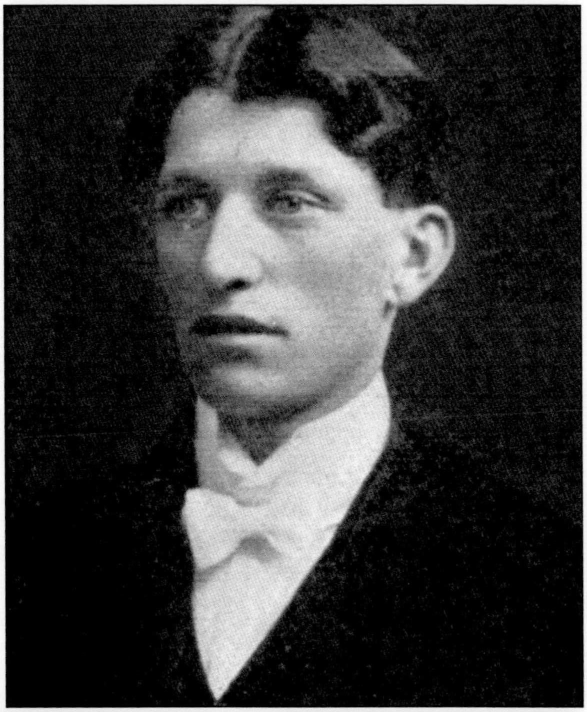

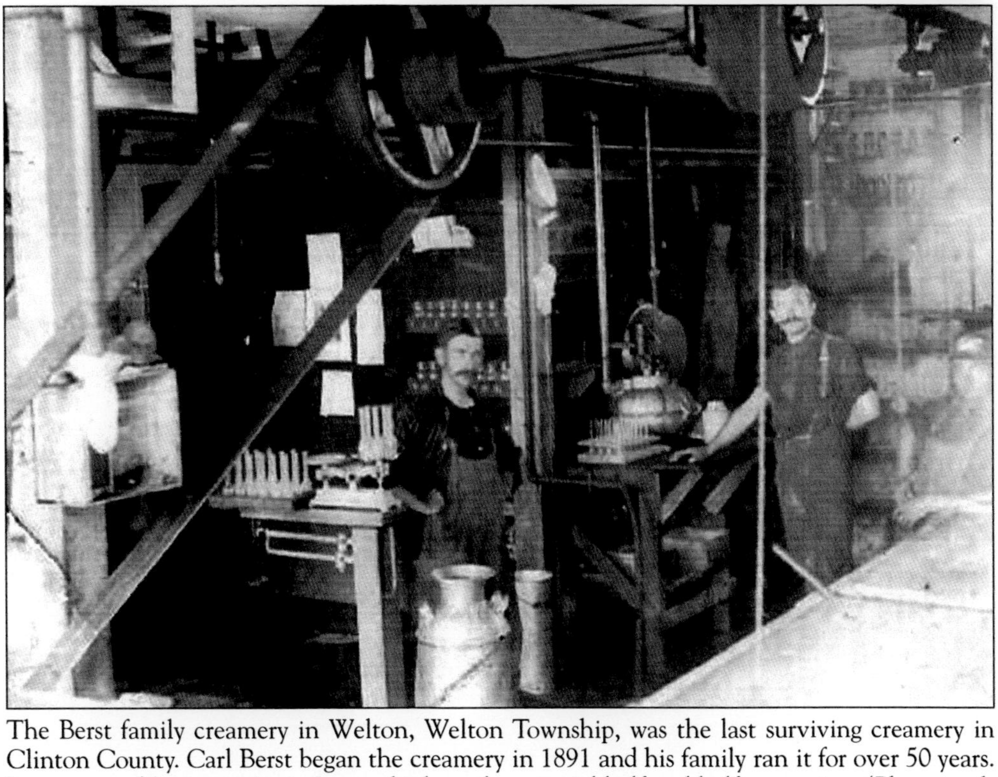

The Berst family creamery in Welton, Welton Township, was the last surviving creamery in Clinton County. Carl Berst began the creamery in 1891 and his family ran it for over 50 years. It was one of 3 creameries in Iowa which made a special half and half margarine. (Photograph from the Central Community Historical Society archives.)

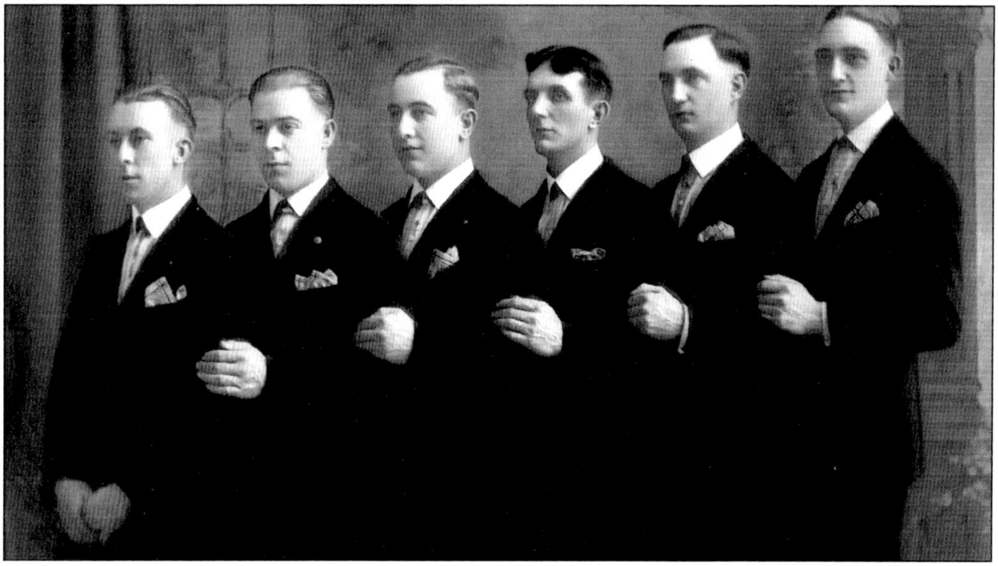

Six local musicians in Spring Rock Township organized a band, the Whizz-Bangs, just after World War I. Their first booking was a church play and dance in Big Rock. The Whizz-Bangs were a huge success and soon were in demand and booked every night of the week all over Iowa and the surrounding states. They played top ballrooms and traveled in a Model T Ford with their instruments hauled in a small truck. In 1920, they purchased a black Buick with a box built on the side for their instruments and their Whizz-Bang emblem painted on the side. (Photograph from the Clinton County Historical Society archives.)

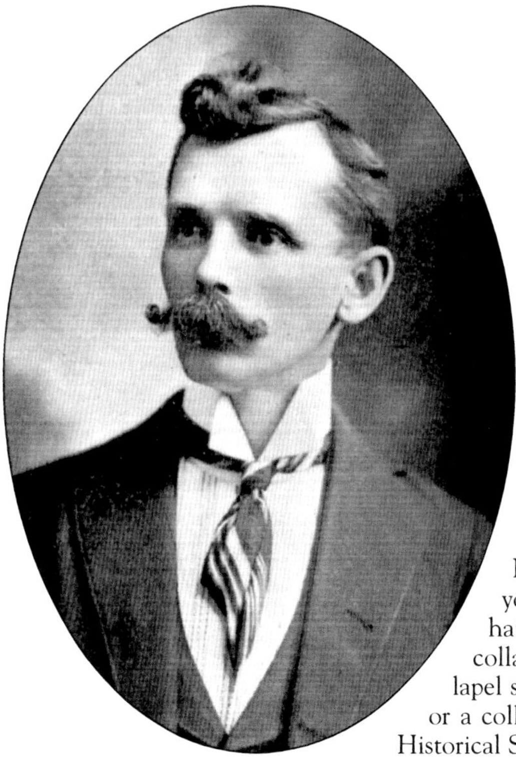

This is an 1890 photograph of J.W. Reihman, a cashier at the Grand Mound Bank, Orange Township. He was a dapper young gentleman with a full mustache, the hairstyle of the day, and a starched, upright collar with tucked-in necktie and a pin in his lapel showing his allegiance to either a local lodge or a college. (Photograph from the Clinton County Historical Society archives.)

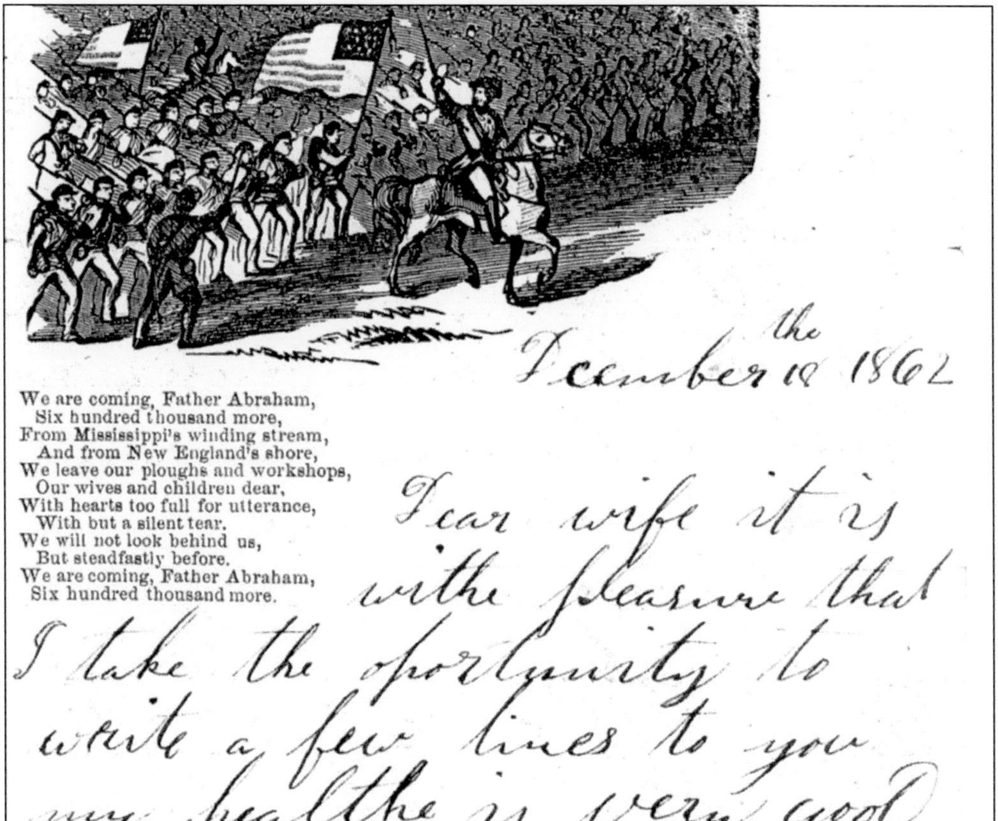

December 18the 1862

We are coming, Father Abraham,
Six hundred thousand more,
From Mississippi's winding stream,
And from New England's shore,
We leave our ploughs and workshops,
Our wives and children dear,
With hearts too full for utterance,
With but a silent tear.
We will not look behind us,
But steadfastly before.
We are coming, Father Abraham,
Six hundred thousand more.

Dear wife it is withe pleasure that I take the oportunity to write a few lines to you my healthe is very good at preasant and I hope thear few lines will find you bothe in good healthe and geting along well this winter pleas write as soon as you git this leter for I

When the Civil War began, Clinton County boys answered President Lincoln's plea to protect the Union. John Phillips of Wheatland, Spring Rock Township, left his young wife, Mary, and son, Johnny, to join his fellow soldiers. His letters to Mary tell of the hardships the troops endured, his hopes of coming home soon and the worry he felt about leaving his family. Copies of these letters are on file in the Clinton County Historical Society Library and span from December of 1862 until John's death on the battlefield in December of 1863. (Photograph from the Clinton County Historical Society archives.)

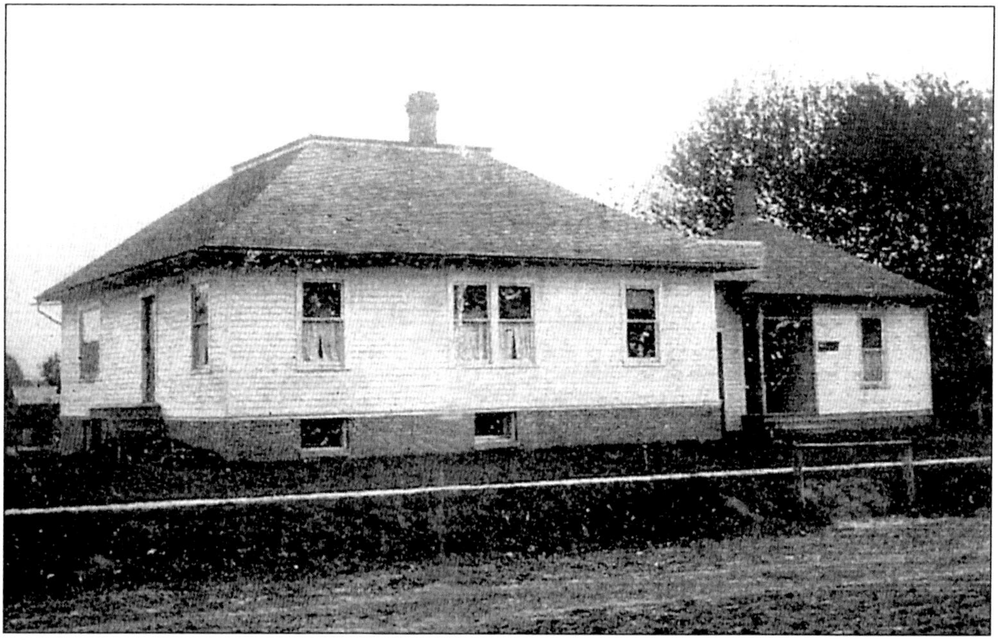

The premise of the Donald MacLean Memorial Hospital in Wheatland, Spring Rock Township, was "To Relieve the Suffering of the Afflicted Regardless of Criticism." J.S. Dean, M.D., was the proprietor and surgeon-in-chief with Frieda J. Diesel as superintendent of the facility. (Photograph courtesy of Steve Roling.)

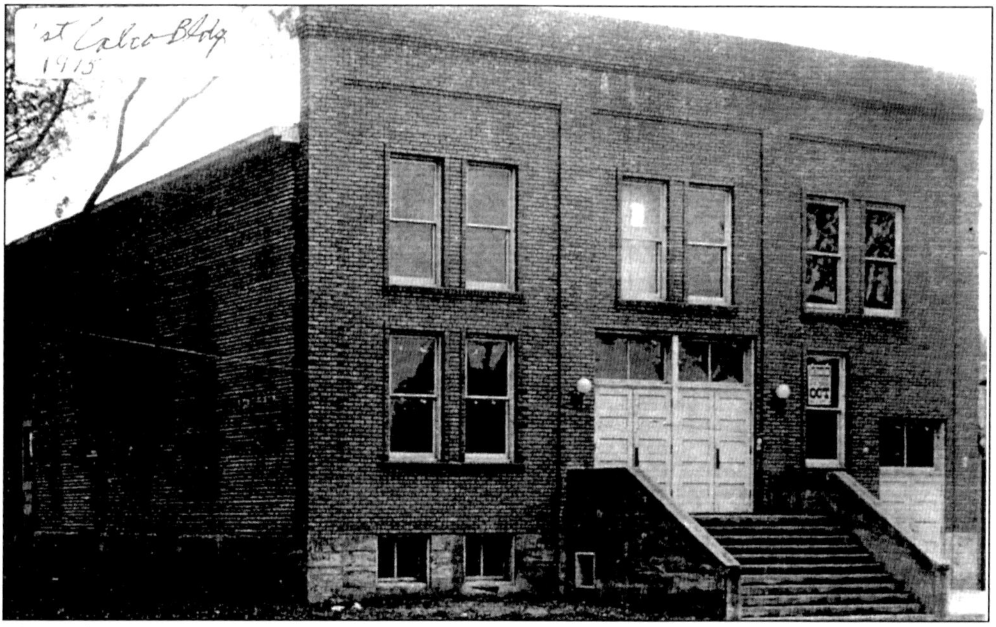

The Calamus Community Center, Olive Township, burned down in 1920. The center was an exhibition hall where the Harlem Globetrotters played against the local basketball team, Emil Flindt played for dances, and the community celebrated special events. After the fire, the foundation was in such good condition that the present Calco building was erected on the same site using the original foundation. (Photograph courtesy of Elmer Ketelsen.)

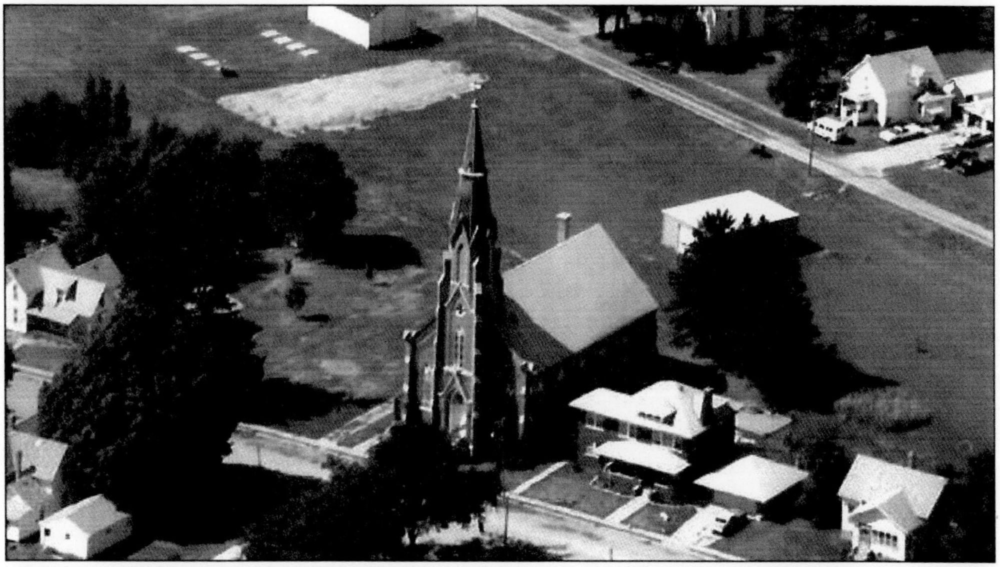

The town of Welton, Welton Township, was settled by a Mr. Shepard in 1850, about a mile from the present town. Each settler was given 40 acres, plus 2 town lots. By the early 1870s, that town had disappeared and the present town of Welton was platted around the Davenport & St. Paul Railroad station on March 28, 1871, by Nicholas and Polly Walrod. The post office was established around the same time that the railroad settled in, and the town was incorporated in 1908 when J.C. Wulf was mayor. St. Anne's Catholic Church, shown here, was established in 1909 and the church was built at a cost of $20,000. The first mass was held on Christmas day in 1912. (Photograph from the Central Community Historical Society archives.)

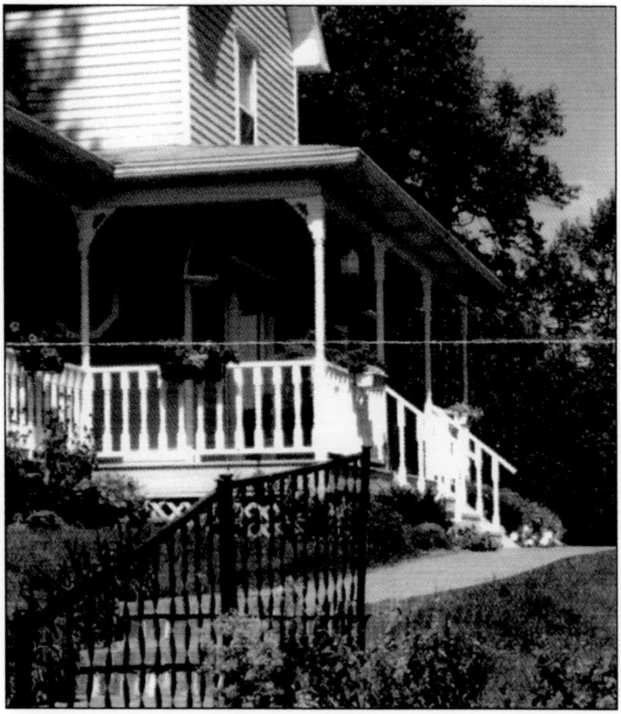

Our Lady of the Prairie Retreat house sits south of Wheatland, Spring Rock Township, on 200 acres of tall prairie grass and woodland. In the early 1990s, the Victorian farmhouse was renovated by Arlene Considine, Rita Banowetz, and Rev. Vincent Fabula of New Mellery Abbey, Peosta, Iowa. Lewis Randolph created attractive gardens, bridges, and extensive landscaping. A ministry of service and hospitality is provided by the Sisters of the Congregation of Humility of Davenport, Iowa. (Photograph from the Clinton County Historical Society archives.)

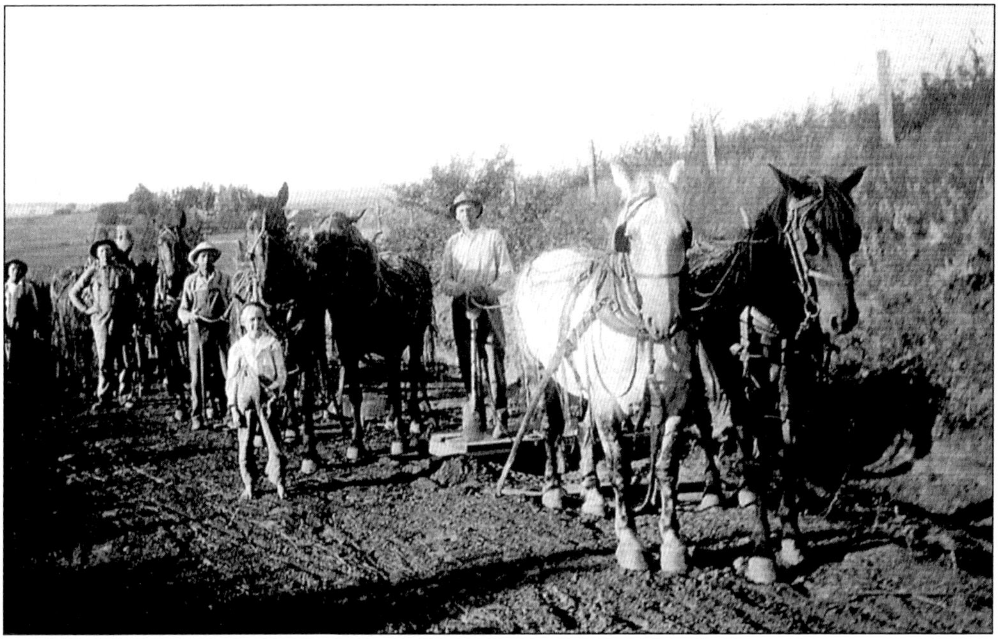

Rural road work in the county was not easy, as shown by these men working on a county road near Wheatland, Spring Rock Township. It took hard work and many men and horses to make these roads passable even in the summertime. Two of the men shown are Ray Smith and Louis Schnede; both were county employees. (Photograph courtesy of Steve Roling.)

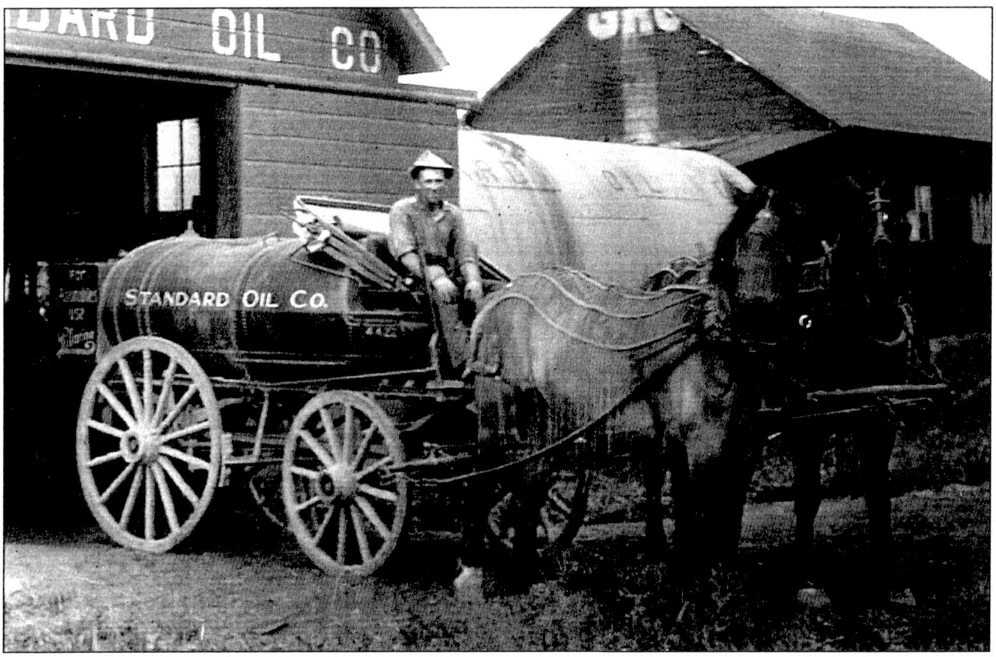

In the summer of 1914, Standard Oil was delivered in Spring Rock Township by Peter Larsen and his horse-drawn delivery cart. (Photograph courtesy of Steve Roling.)

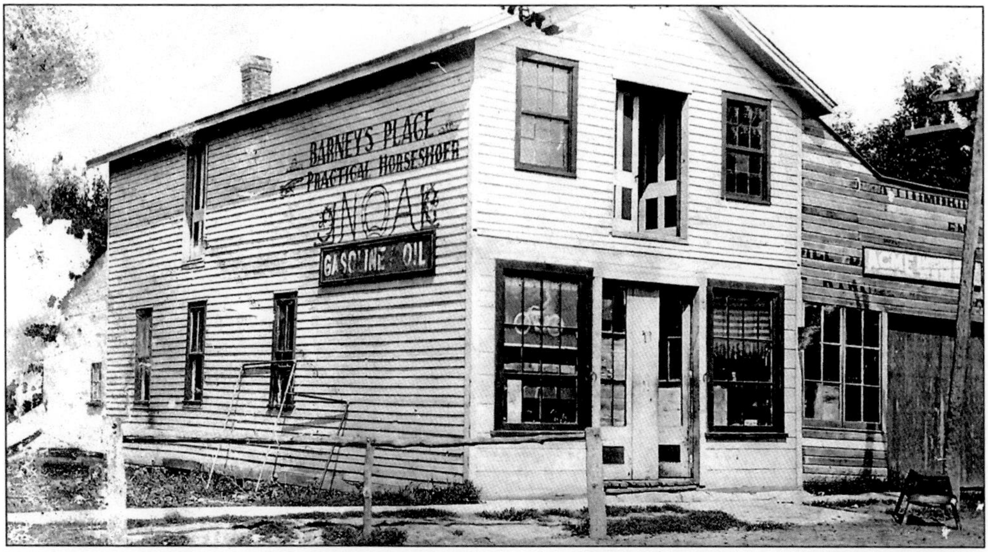

Barney advertised he was a "Practical Horseshoer" at Barney's Place in Wheatland, Spring Rock Township. He also advertised gas and oil on the side of the building, while a motorcycle is pictured in his left shop window. At one time, the building apparently had a second story landing as there are double doors opening directly onto the street. The building on the right lists ACME on its faded sign. The photo dates to c. 1920. (Photograph from the Clinton County Historical Society archives.)

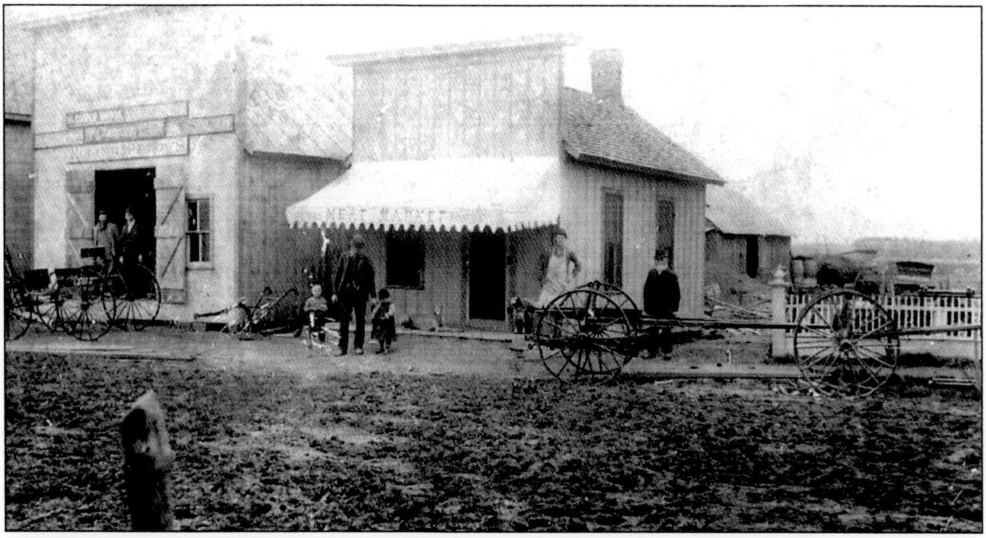

This late 1880s photograph shows the Welton Meat Market, in Welton Township, run by W.M. Wulf. Mr. Wulf also ran the harness shop next door and advertised selling Moline plows and Cooper wagons. The streets were not paved as yet, and board sidewalks were in place in some areas. (Photograph from the Central Community Historical Society archives.)

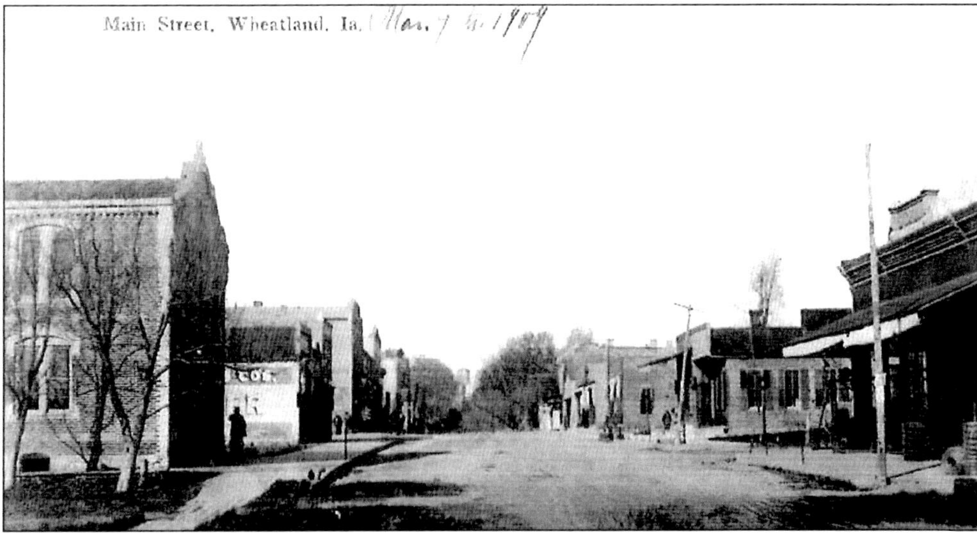

By 1858, Mr. Bennett had platted Wheatland, Spring Rock Township, and named the settlement after President Buchanan's home of Wheatland. Once the C& NW railroad extended its tracks to Wheatland, the railroad station was named "Yankee Run." A post office was also established in 1858 and, that same year, M.L. Rogers commenced mercantile operations and sold items to the railroad workers. (Photograph from the Clinton County Historical Society archives.)

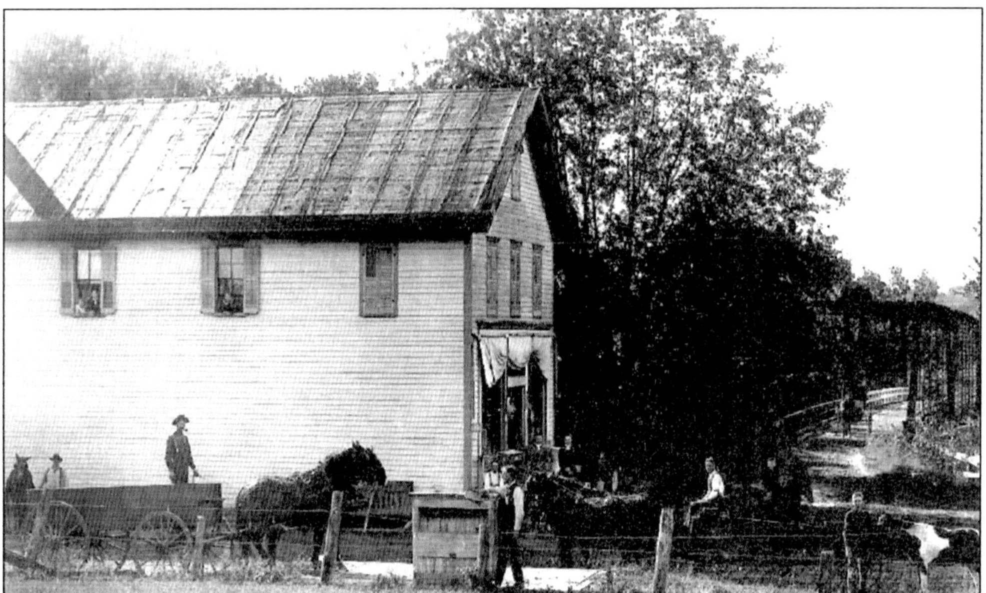

When a man named Boone began to drive cattle from Missouri to Galena, Illinois, in 1839, the trail became known as Boone's Trail. A ferry business, along with old John Shook's flatboat named the *Buena* Vista, facilitated the crossing of the Wapsipinicon River on Boone's Trail in Olive Township. The few residents were able to secure a post office there for a short time. The Boone's Trail ferry service was one of the most profitable ferries in the county until the Rothstein Bridge, shown here, was built and negated the need for a ferry. (Photograph from the Central Community Historical Society archives.)

Five

IN THE NORTHWEST LIBERTY, SHARON, BROOKFIELD, AND BLOOMFIELD TOWNSHIPS

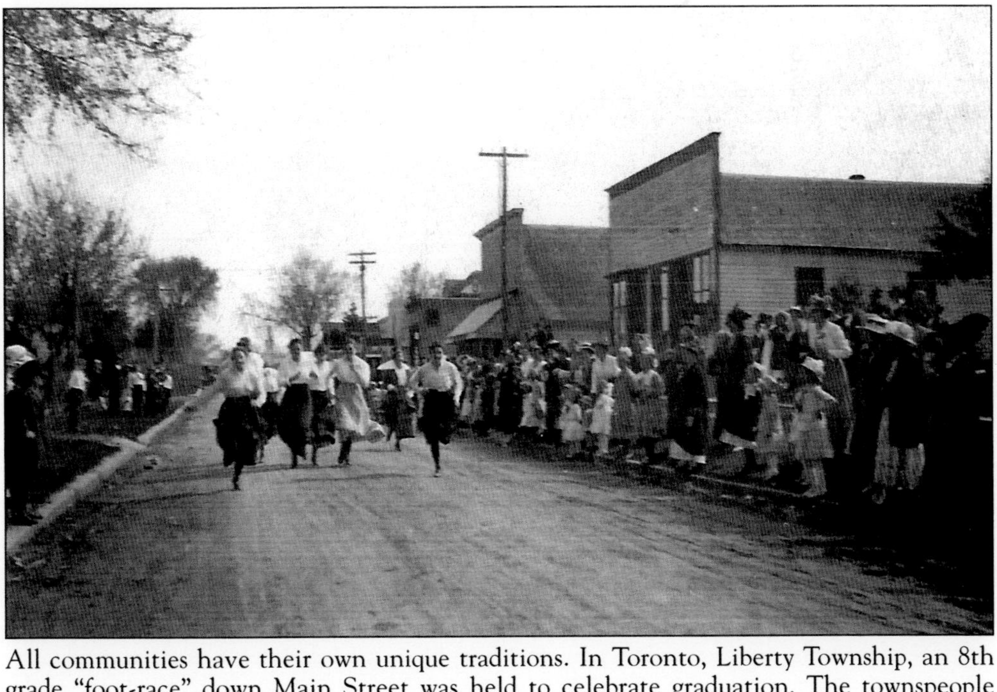

All communities have their own unique traditions. In Toronto, Liberty Township, an 8th grade "foot-race" down Main Street was held to celebrate graduation. The townspeople turned out to enjoy the festivities. This photo dates to c. 1900. (Photograph courtesy of Mr. and Mrs. Ralph Martens.)

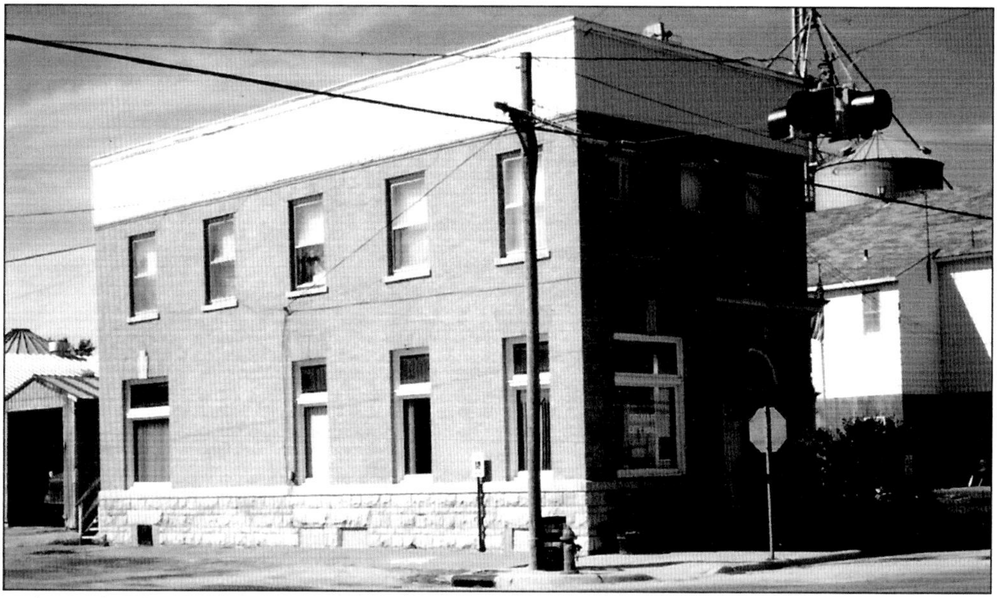

Delmar's first bank, in Bloomfield Township, was organized in the 1880s as a private bank by the firm of Hurst & Flenniker. In 1899, the People's Savings Bank was organized and remained in business until it was purchased by the Jackson State Bank of Maquoketa in March of 1945. By 1964, the bank was sold again. In 1996, the bank building became Delmar City Hall. The second story has been renovated into apartments. A temporary bank building was used until 1997, when the new bank building was completed. (Photograph courtesy of Don Ketelsen and Buss Henschel.)

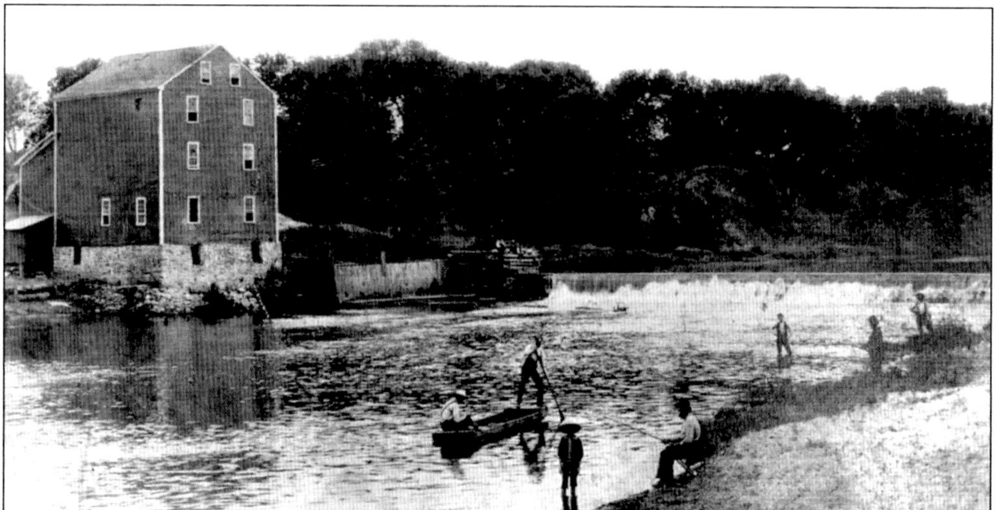

In 1848, George W. Thorn built a sawmill on the Wapsipinicon River at Toronto, Liberty Township, and in 1850 a grist mill was added. By 1853, a carding-machine was being run on the mill power by Jacob and Francis Ellis, making the settlement of Toronto a busy manufacturing site. Thorn sold his famous mill to John Heller *c.* 1868, who sold it ten years later to David O. Kidd. Mr. Kidd ran it for 30 years and then sold the mill to F.H. Pieper & Co., who owned it when it was destroyed by fire in 1909. At that time, the landmark was removed from the community. (Photograph courtesy of Mr. and Mrs. Ralph Martens.)

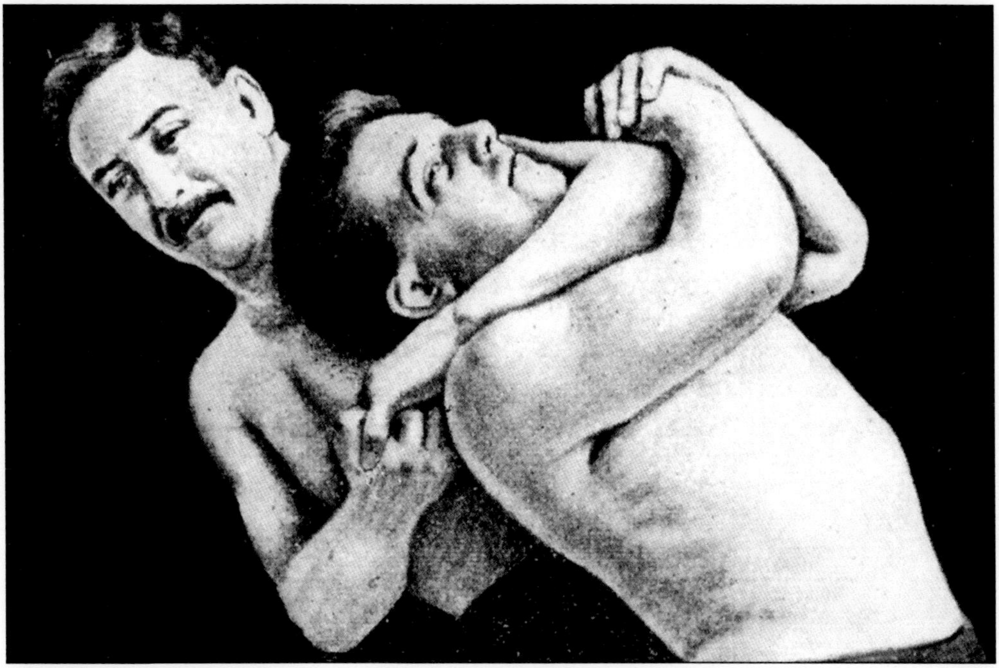

In 1900, from the small village of Big Rock in Liberty Township, a local wrestler known as Farmer Burns became the world champion wrestler on April 20, 1895, when he defeated "Lewis the Strangler." Here Farmer Burns demonstrates his own version of the strangle hold. Our sport heroes come from communities of all sizes and it is not hard to imagine the pride the people of Liberty Township felt as Farmer Burns became known in every corner of the country. (Photograph from the Clinton County Historical Society archives.)

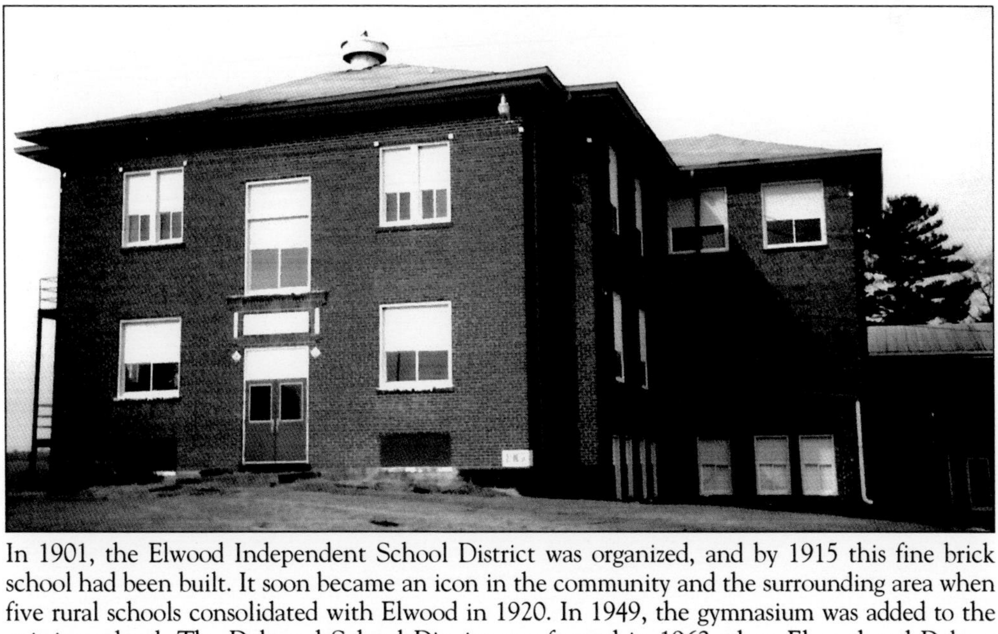

In 1901, the Elwood Independent School District was organized, and by 1915 this fine brick school had been built. It soon became an icon in the community and the surrounding area when five rural schools consolidated with Elwood in 1920. In 1949, the gymnasium was added to the existing school. The Delwood School District was formed in 1962 when Elwood and Delmar consolidated their schools. (Photograph from the Clinton County Historical Society archives.)

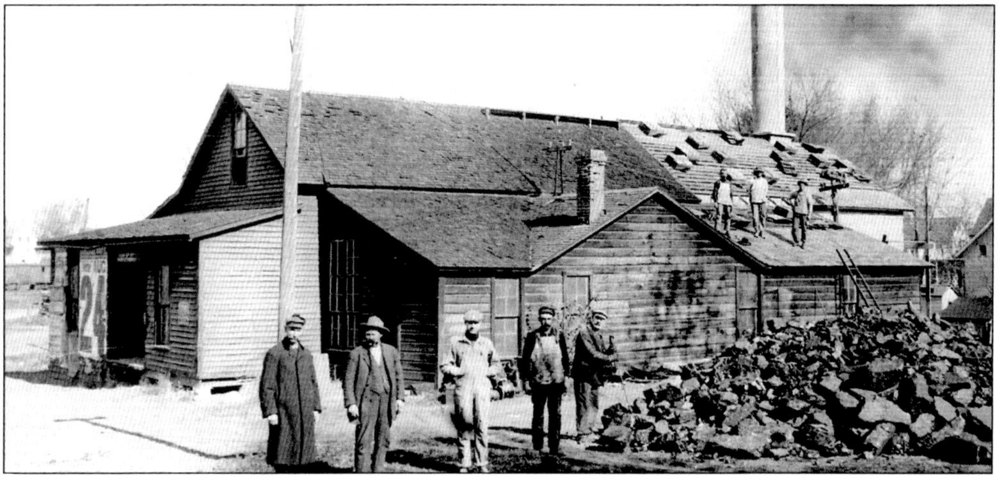

Erected in 1894, "the mill" is most likely the oldest continuously run business in Lost Nation, in Sharon Township. In 1902, Henry Dobling and Fred Daniel started an electric light plant at the steam-powered Dobling Grist Mill, which supplied electricity to subscribers in the Lost Nation area. By 1909, Iowa Electric and Power Company bought the small plant and expanded its services over a wider area. (Photograph from the Clinton County Historical Society archives.)

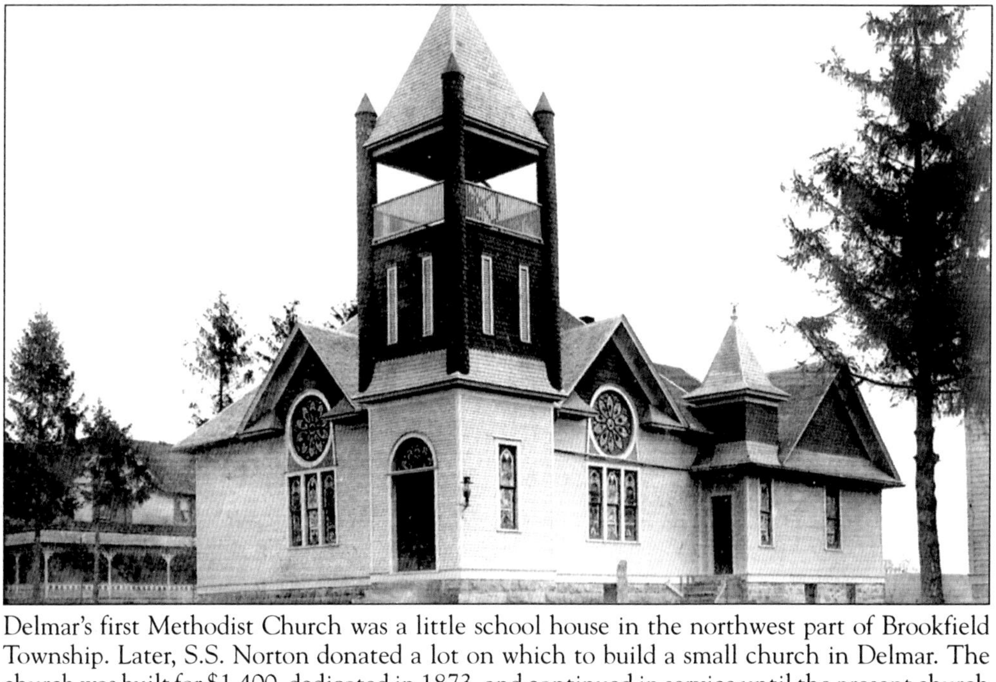

Delmar's first Methodist Church was a little school house in the northwest part of Brookfield Township. Later, S.S. Norton donated a lot on which to build a small church in Delmar. The church was built for $1,400, dedicated in 1873, and continued in service until the present church was built in 1906. By 1899, the Methodists in Welton had joined the Delmar congregation. In 1927, the church was operating as a community church, however, officially and in name it was a Methodist Church. By 1948, the Elwood congregation had joined the Delmar Church. In 1968, the Methodist Church and the Evangelical Brethren Church congregations joined and became known as the Delmar United Methodist Church. The current minister serves Methodist Churches in three Clinton County villages: Delmar, Charlotte, and Elwood. (Photograph from the Clinton County Historical Society archives.)

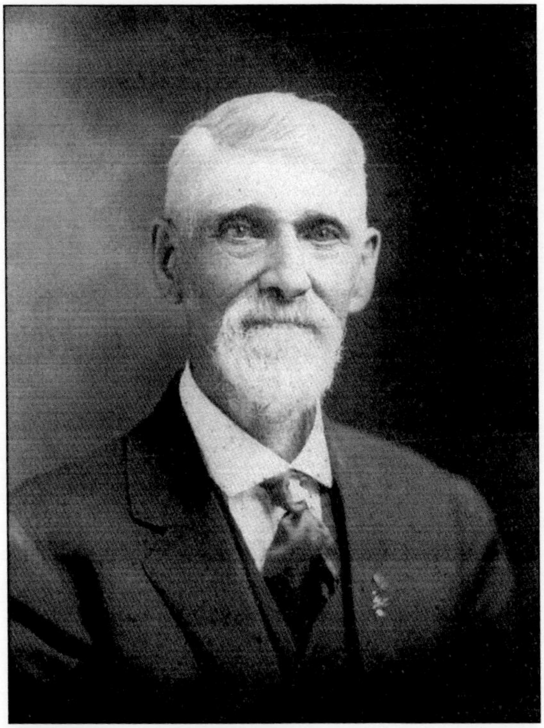

Oscar P. Cornish (1846–1931), a New York native, served in the Civil War in Co. F, 44th I.V.I. after emigrating to Elwood, Brookfield Township, in 1860. He married Miss C.C. Dobler and they raised five children. In 1877, while working as a blacksmith, he was elected Justice of the Peace. Oscar's family continued to be an essential part of Elwood as his son, Albert T. (1876–1957), owned the local lumberyard and his grandson, Buren "Brownie" (1907–1990), was a farmer/businessman who served many terms as a Clinton County supervisor. (Photograph courtesy of Thelma Wendel Kerkman.)

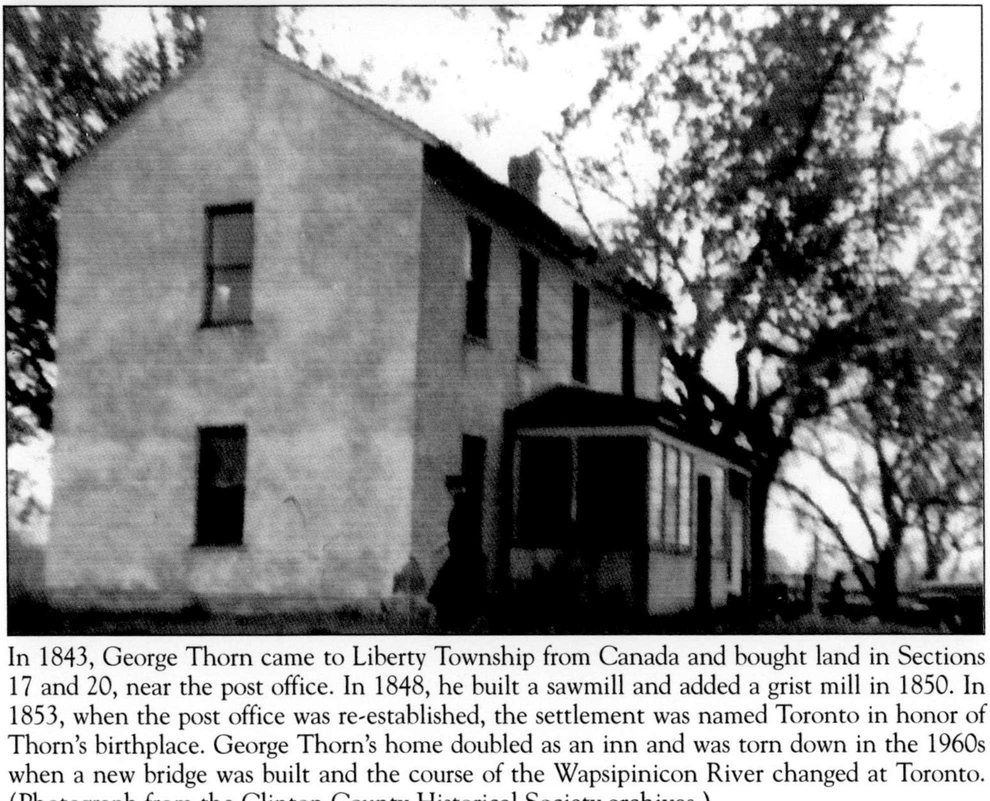

In 1843, George Thorn came to Liberty Township from Canada and bought land in Sections 17 and 20, near the post office. In 1848, he built a sawmill and added a grist mill in 1850. In 1853, when the post office was re-established, the settlement was named Toronto in honor of Thorn's birthplace. George Thorn's home doubled as an inn and was torn down in the 1960s when a new bridge was built and the course of the Wapsipinicon River changed at Toronto. (Photograph from the Clinton County Historical Society archives.)

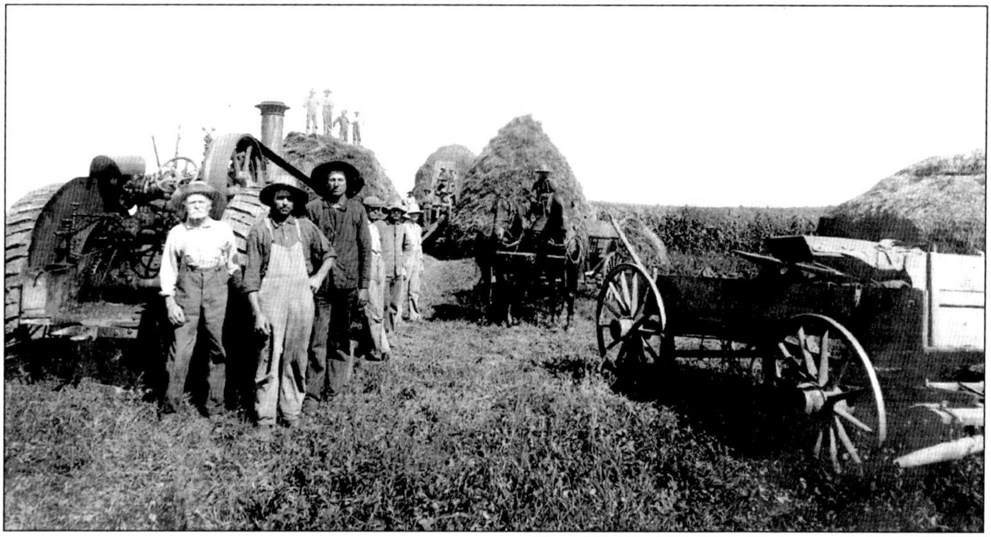

Threshing scenes were a common sight over all of Clinton County when it came time to harvest the crops. Crews went from farm to farm and made up a "threshing ring" as the machines were moved from place to place. This 1905 scene shows a crew in Sharon Township set up for harvest. The women were also involved in the work as they produced huge meals to feed the men in the fields. If you have never heard the phrase "he eats like a thresher," you have probably never experienced the cooking the women produced. (Photograph from the Clinton County Historical Society archives.

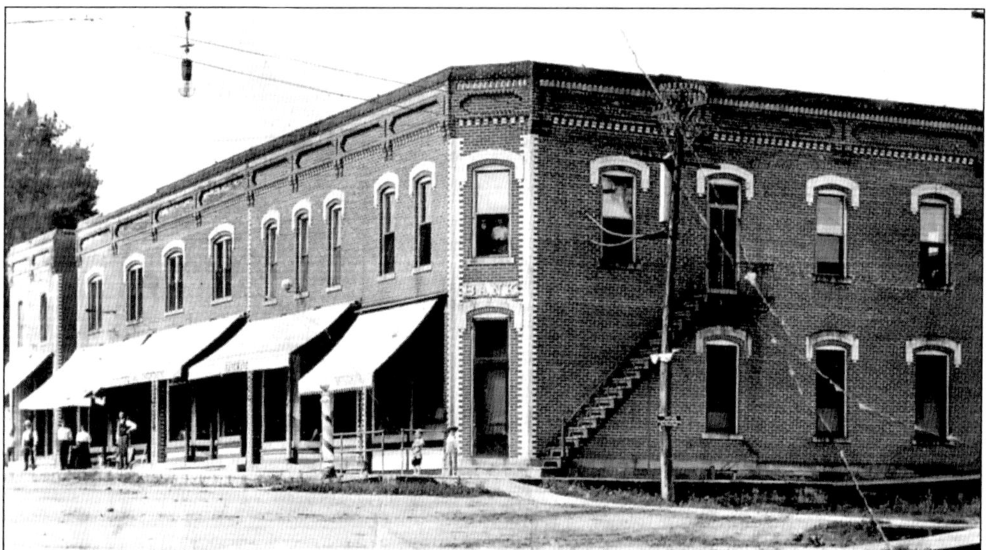

By 1871, Sharon Township had two post offices. One had been established in Burgess in 1854, which also had a blacksmith shop and store. It was closed in 1889, as most of the railroad business was then going through Lost Nation. The second post office opened in Lost Nation in 1871 and after the bank moved to another location, it was and still is located in the lower level of the bank building. The telephone office was located in the second story of the bank building, above the post office. Note the early electric street light in the photograph. (Photograph from the Clinton County Historical Society archives.)

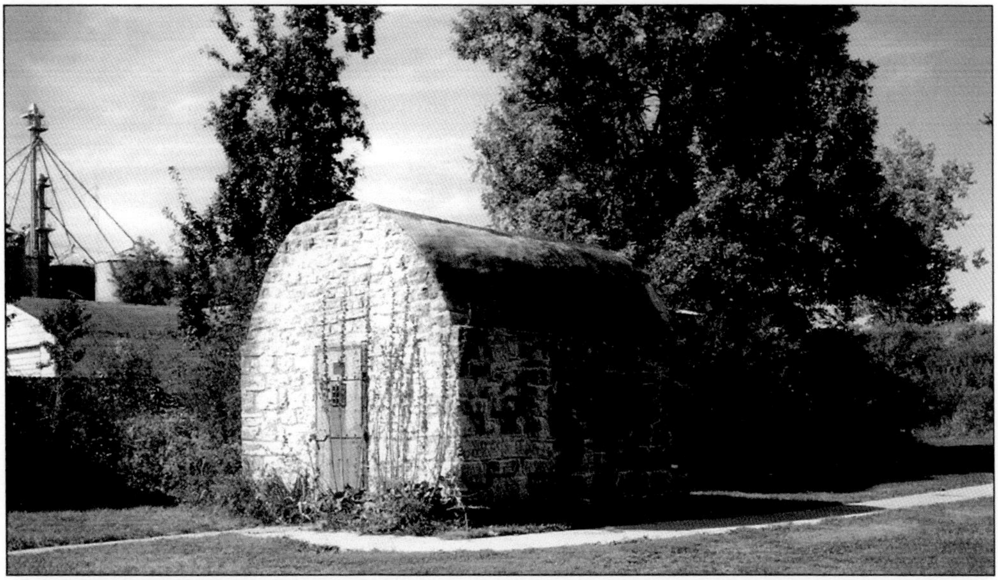

A committee in Delmar, Brookfield Township, was formed to meet on April 2, 1878, to study the problems the area faced after the railroad men received their pay. Rowdy men filled the local jail once they were paid and for two days afterward. One thought was to use the old school as a jail, however, the committee decided to build "the Calaboose," which was not referred to as a jail. By October 7, 1878, the Calaboose was ready for occupancy. It cost a total of $175 with an added cost of $7.04 for the stone. The Clinton County Historical Society salutes Delmar for placing the Calaboose on the National Register of Historic Places. (Photograph from the Clinton County Historical Society archives.)

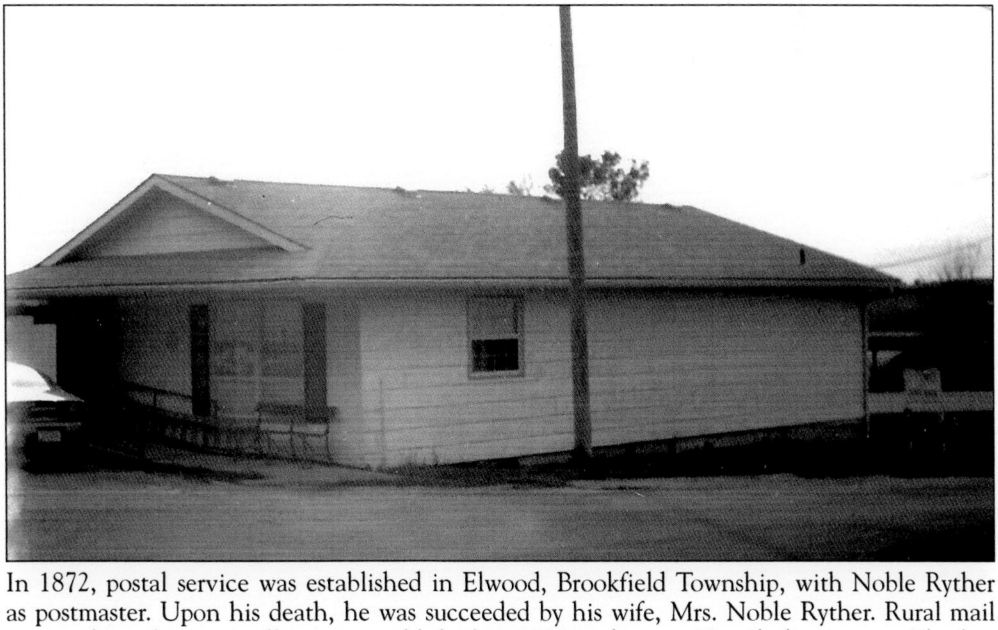

In 1872, postal service was established in Elwood, Brookfield Township, with Noble Ryther as postmaster. Upon his death, he was succeeded by his wife, Mrs. Noble Ryther. Rural mail service from that post office was established in 1907 and was a 22 mile long route. The last post office is shown above, however, local service has been discontinued and it is now a private home. (Photograph courtesy of Don Ketelsen.)

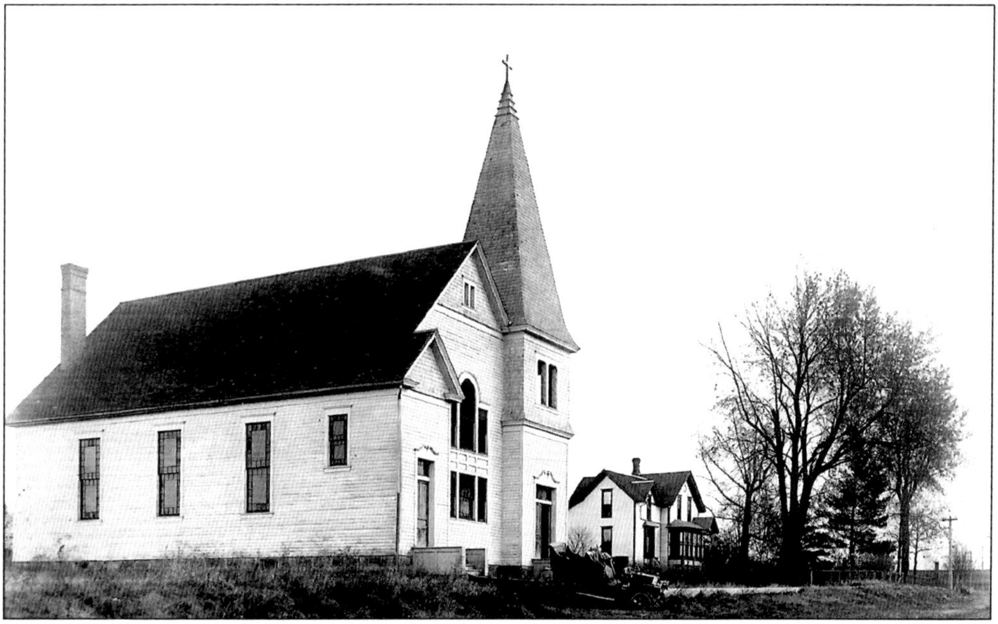

The Roman Catholics of Lost Nation built their first church, Sacred Heart, in 1895. Before that time, members of the faith attended mass at either Toronto or Hughes Settlement, five to seven miles from Lost Nation. In 1965 and 1966, a new church was built across the street from the church shown here. Both churches were built on property bought from Simon Seng. Jim McAndrews, major league baseball pitcher, had his early beginnings in this Sacred Heart Church. (Photograph from the Clinton County Historical Society archives.)

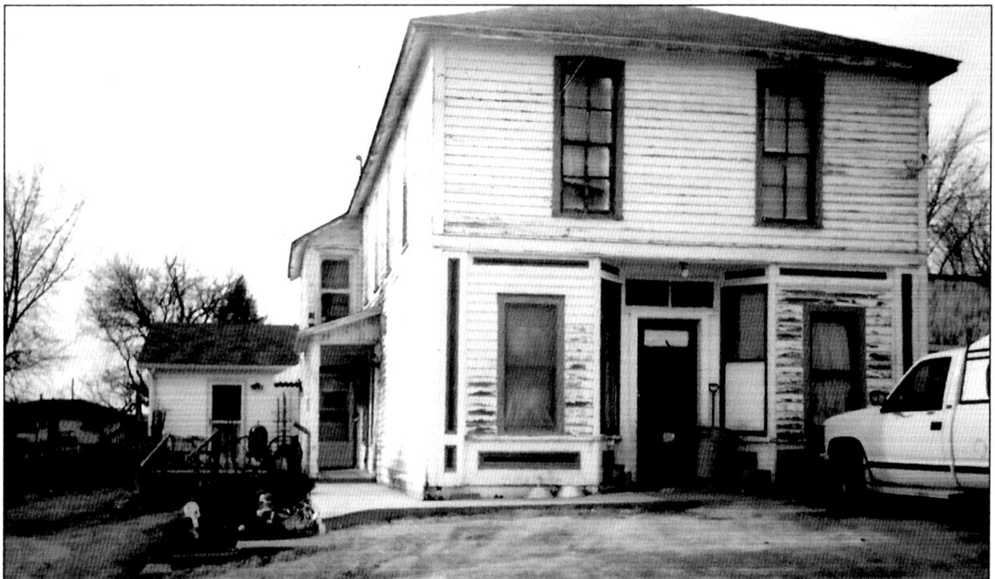

Ben and Emma Hamilton's grocery store in Elwood, Brookfield Township, was not only their place of business, but also their home. They lived above the store and provided the townspeople with a local gathering place, while selling them groceries and gasoline for their cars during the 1940s. (Photograph courtesy of Thelma Wendel Kerkman.)

St. Patrick's Catholic Church in Delmar, Brookfield Township, began as a Maquoketa mission church. The first church building was dedicated in 1882. As the congregation grew, a larger church was built and dedicated in 1928. This church houses many magnificent windows from Munich, Germany. Extensive remodeling was done in the early 1970s. (Photograph courtesy of Don Ketelsen.)

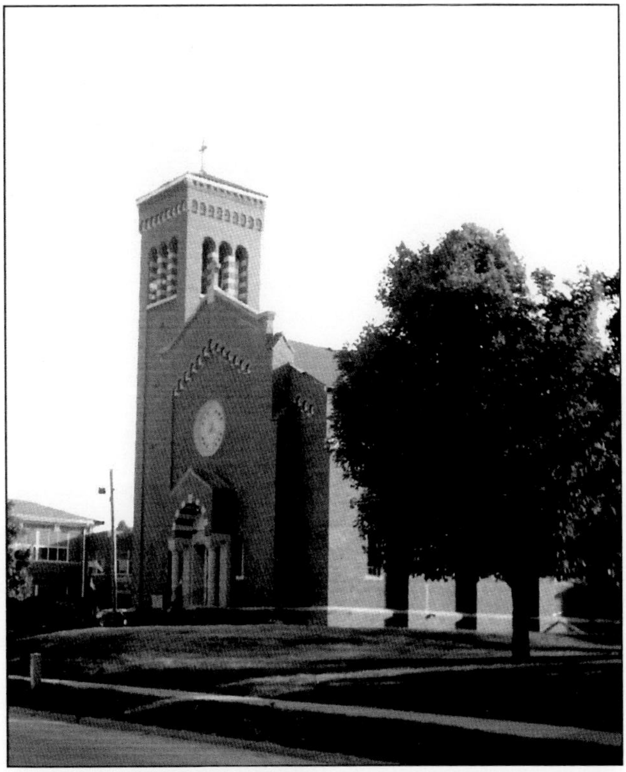

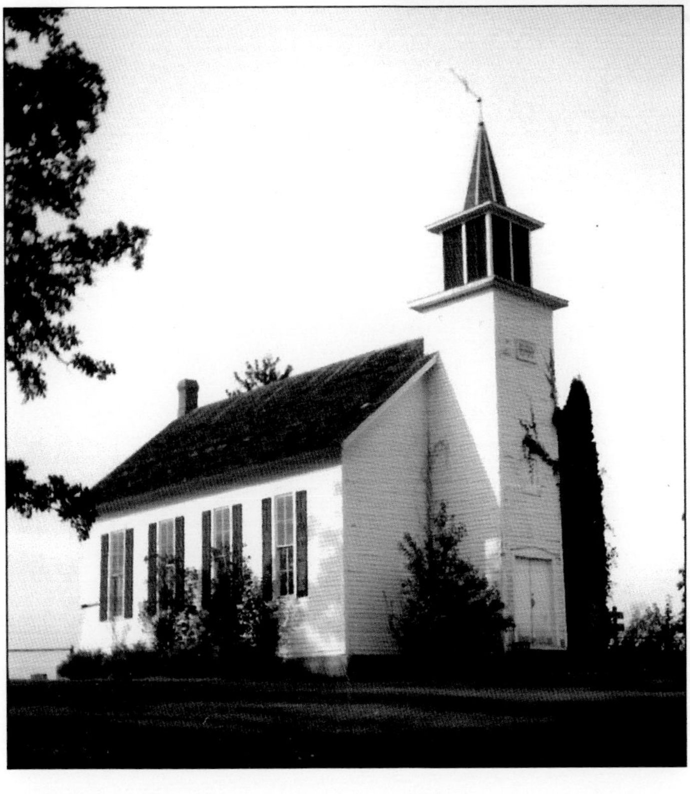

The Smithtown Church is the only surviving landmark of the village of Burgess, Sharon Township. Soon after Burgess was settled, it was given the nickname of Smithtown in recognition of David Smith, a prominent citizen. The church was not completed until 1874 and discontinued as a regular place of worship in the late 1920s. In 1929, the Smithtown Cemetery Association was established, and in 1931 it purchased the church from the Upper Iowa Methodist Conference. In 1970, the church was turned over to the Clinton County Conservation Board. (Photograph courtesy of Don Ketelsen.)

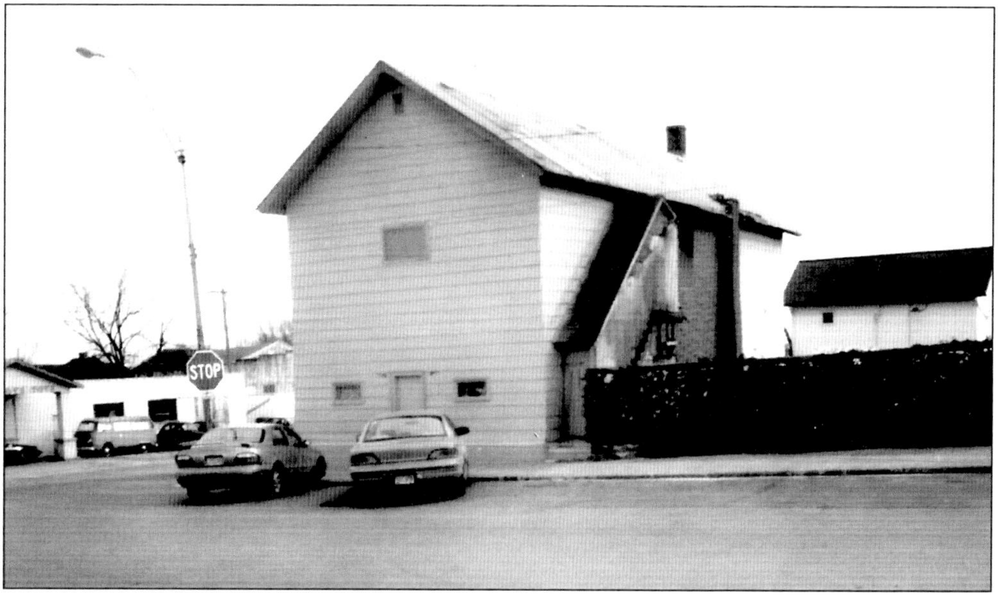

Keller's Pool Hall is one of the oldest buildings in Lost Nation, Sharon Township. It has served the community as a general store, dance hall, and school, and at one time church services were held here. (Photograph courtesy of Don Ketelsen.)

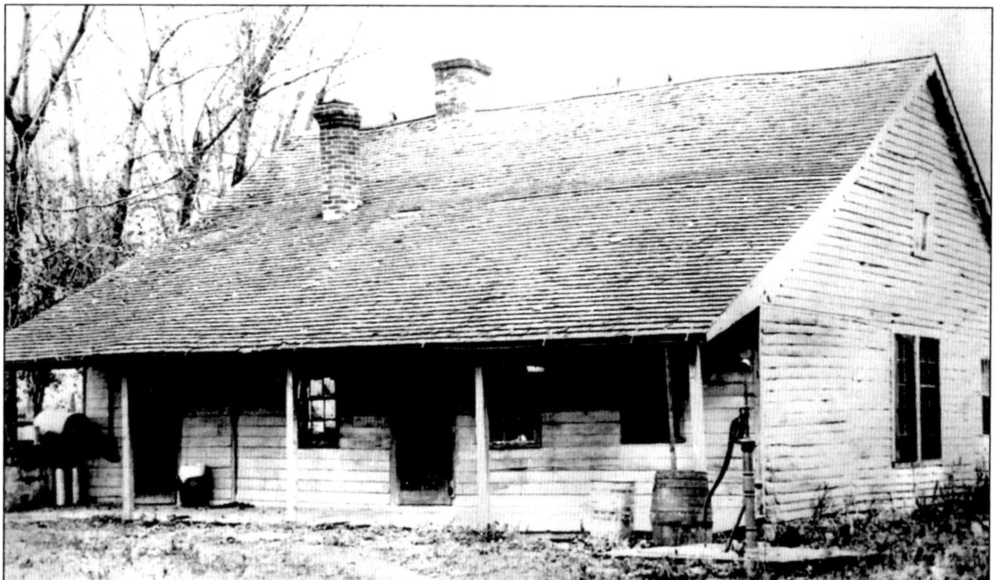

Luther Teeple, an early settler in Sharon Township, built his home, shown here, in rural Lost Nation in 1849. On February 27, 1852, a warrant was issued to Luther authorizing legal voters to hold an election at his house on April 15, 1852, for the purpose of organizing Sharon Township, electing township officers, a school fund commissioner and a judge for the second judicial district. Sharon Township, which had originally been organized in April of 1851, had been ordered that the territory "be cut off from all or any townships to which it may have been attached." This was an unnecessary order, as it had, as yet, been attached nowhere. (Photograph from the Clinton County Historical Society archives.)

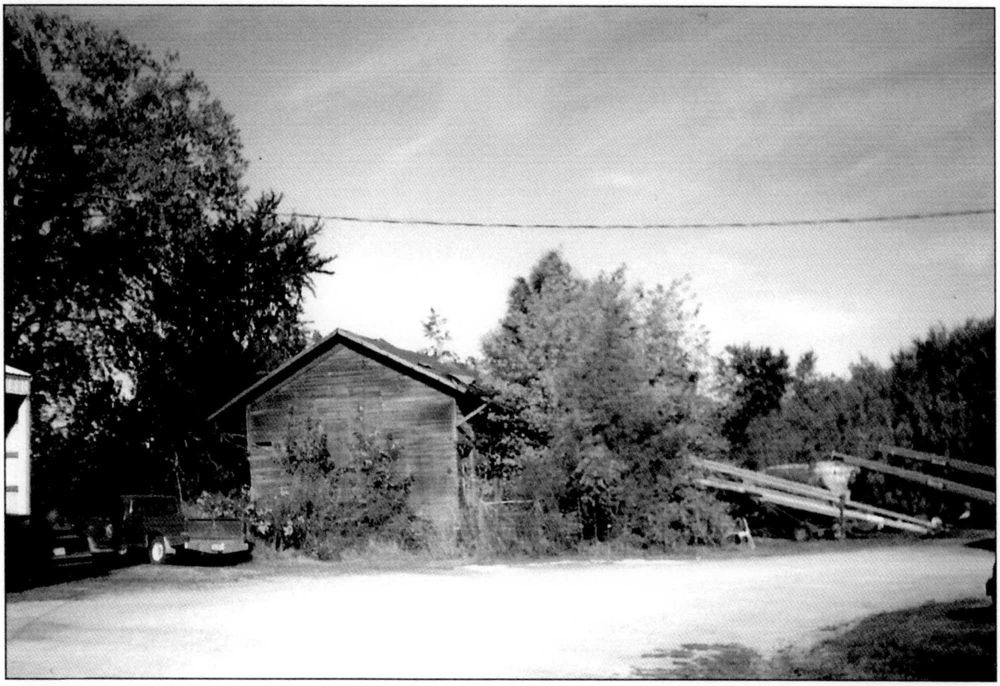

When all railroads in the area went through Delmar, Brookfield Township, this depot was a lively center of commerce. The tracks are no longer there, nor is the activity as the old depot now sits quietly. (Photograph courtesy of Don Ketelsen.)

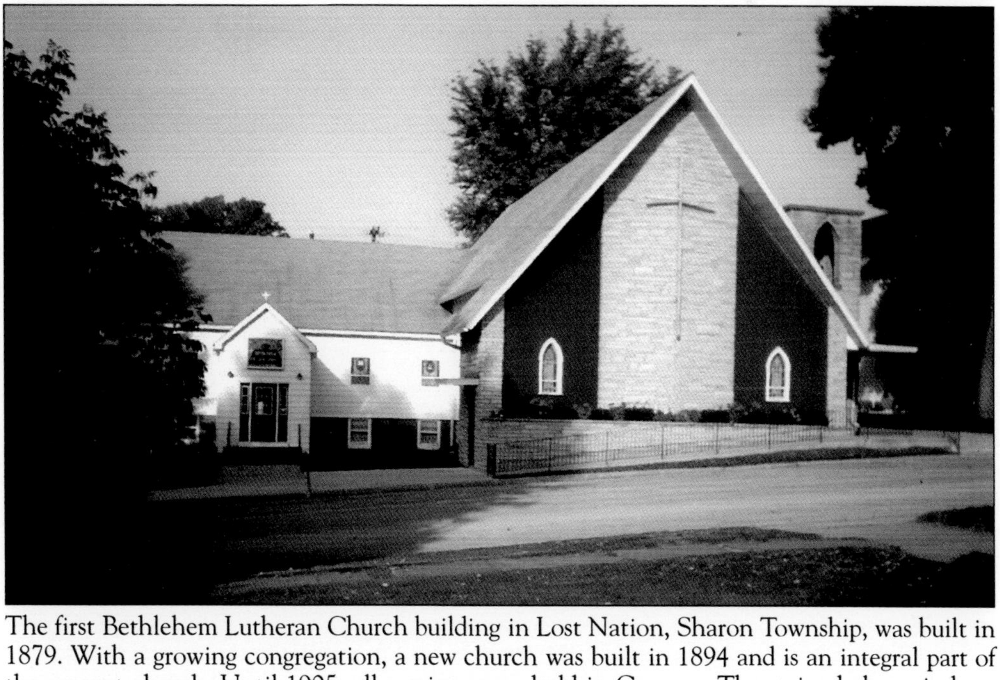

The first Bethlehem Lutheran Church building in Lost Nation, Sharon Township, was built in 1879. With a growing congregation, a new church was built in 1894 and is an integral part of the present church. Until 1905, all services were held in German. The stained glass windows and memorial offerings that have been donated over the years show the dedication of the church's members. (Photograph courtesy of Don Ketelsen.)

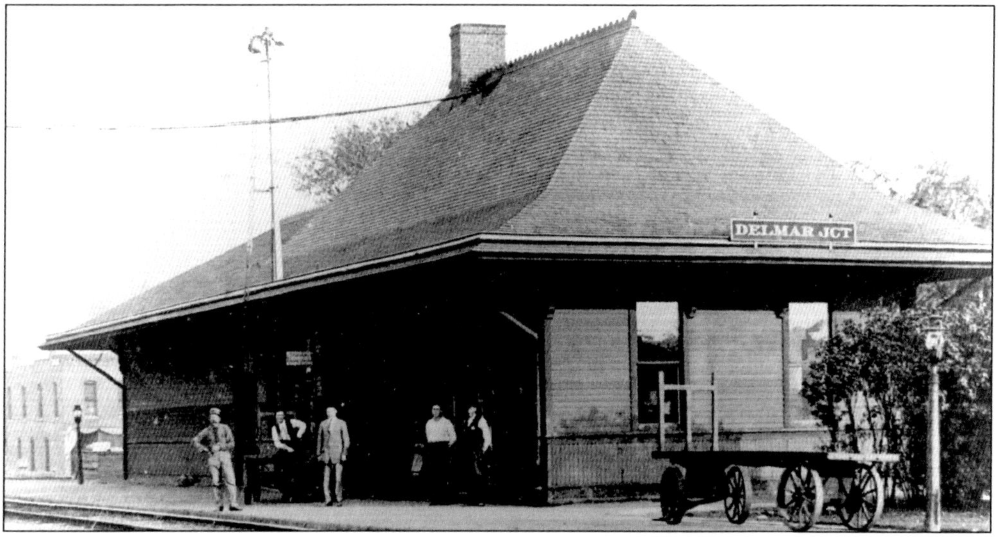

In December, 1870, when the Davenport & St. Paul railroad along with the Midland railroad finished laying their tracks within a few days of each other, train service in Delmar began that very same day. It's said the Midland railroad left an unused Northwestern rail car on a side track to use as a station and a conductor named the town after six ladies riding on his train. He took the first letter of each of their names and combined them and came up with name of Delmar. Other sources claim that Delmar was named to continue the alphabetical order of other stations on the line of Almont, Bryant, Charlotte, and then Delmar. The train station is now maintained as a museum and holds the archives of the Orphan Train which brought orphans from New York to the Midwest in the late 19th century. (Photograph from the Clinton County Historical Society archives.)

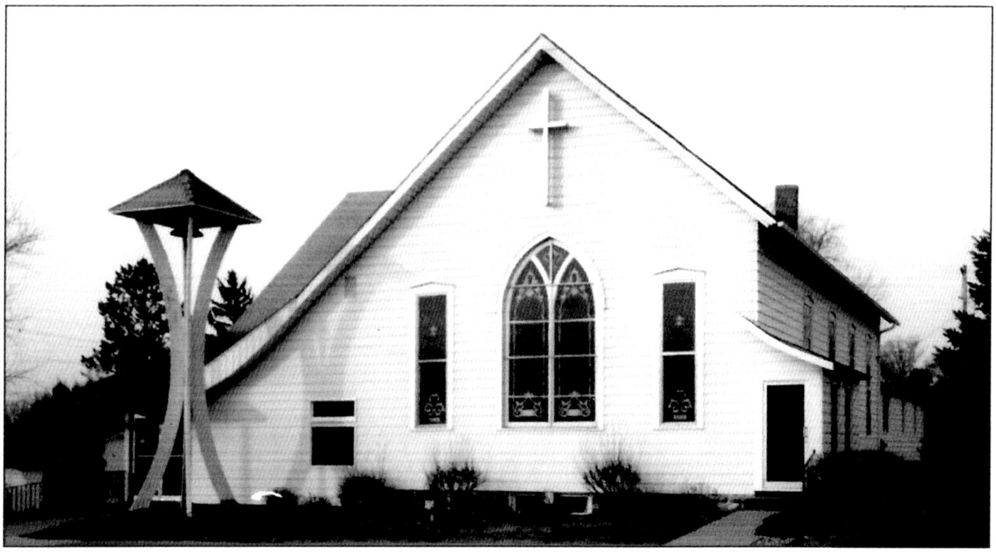

In 1874, the Union Sabbath Church in Lost Nation, Sharon Township, was built. During the years, it has been home to several protestant denominations including Congregationalists, Methodists, and Swedenborgians. In 1931, the Methodists and Reformed churches merged to become the Federated Church and held services there. On November 14, 1937, the church became the Union Presbyterian Church, as it is today. Note the unusual bell tower in front of the church. (Photograph courtesy of Don Ketelsen.)

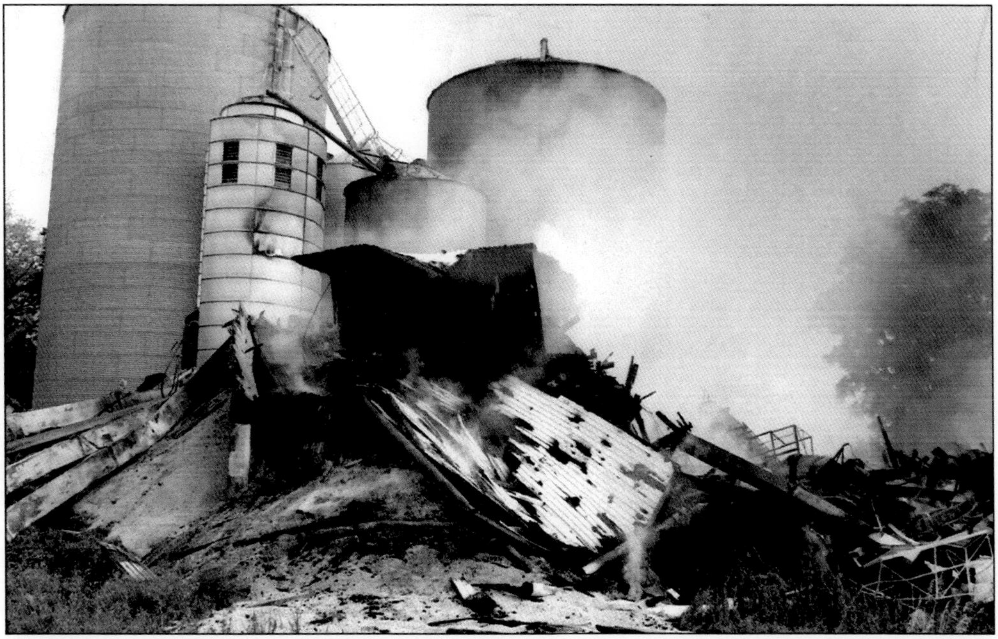

In August of 1976, a stroke of lightning set the Farmer's Supply Center, in Delmar, Brookfield Township, on fire. Though the Delmar Fire Department made valiant efforts to save the mill, it was lost. Because Delmar's farming community depended upon the mill's services, the loss was felt widely throughout the area. (Photograph from the Clinton County Historical Society archives.)

The Elwood Methodist Church was organized on New Year's Day in 1855. No church building was built until 1867, even though land had been bought for a church in 1854. The services were held in three schools until the Elwood Chapel was built. Today, the site of the Elwood Chapel is the site of the Elwood Cemetery. In 1873, a second church, known as Goddard's Church, was built. By 1904, the congregation had grown and the church shown to the right was built with a 50-foot-tall steeple encasing a 900-pound bell. The 50th anniversary of the Elwood Methodist Church would have been celebrated on August 28, 1954, but only ten days before, it was destroyed by fire. It is said that the fire departments of Delmar and Lost Nation were unable to get to the scene quickly enough due to the paving of Hwy. 136. The present church was dedicated on February 12, 1956. (Photograph courtesy of Thelma Wendel-Kerkman)

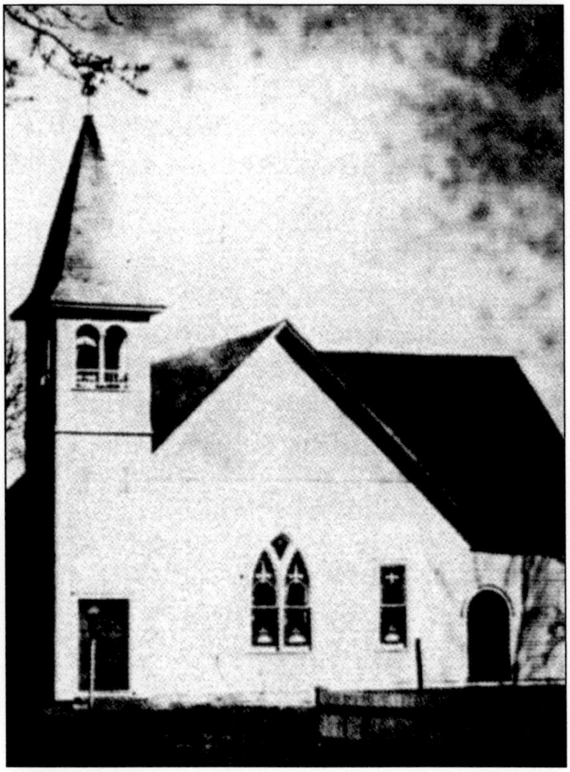

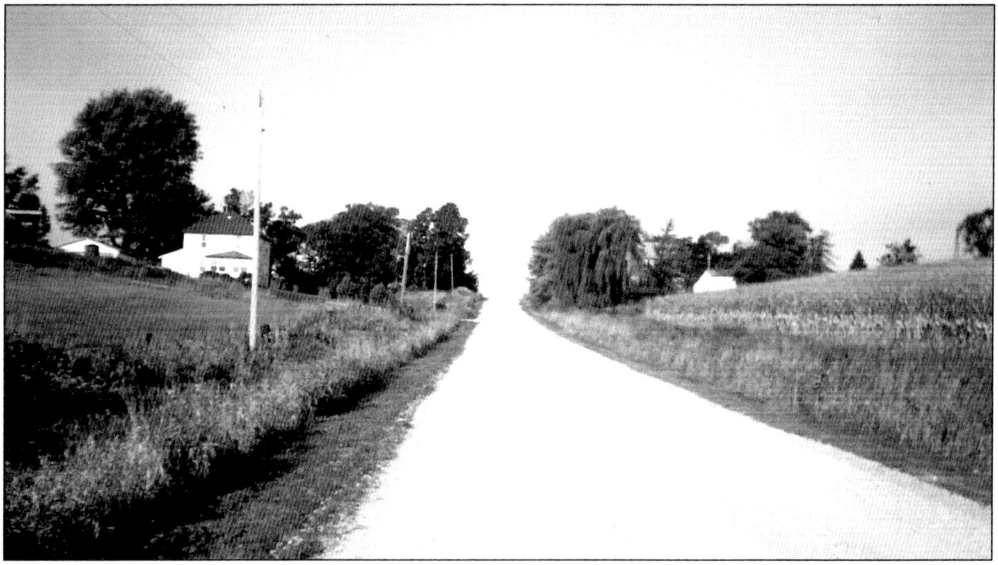

In the early part of the 1900s, the four corners of Waugh Town, Brookfield Township, were occupied by the four Waugh brothers and their families. They each owned approximately 80 acres and lived directly across from each other sharing a common water supply and farm buildings. Although never officially recognized as a town, the population was as large as many villages of the era. (Photograph courtesy of Don Ketelsen.)

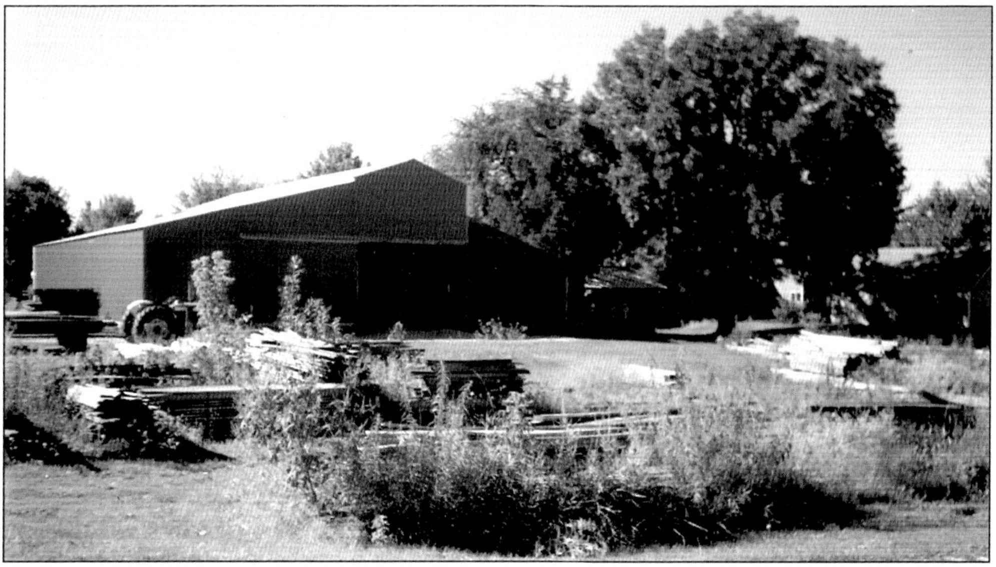

Toronto's sawmill holds many memories including the legendary tales of the "Sawdust Twins." Leon and Andrew Hansen were brothers, not twins, and were well-known for their renowned strength and tall tales. They insisted they found their plow after the cyclone of 1898 by following the furrow to Dubuque. Another brother, Oscar, in showing his strength, threw a professional wrestler out of the ring twice at a Labor Day celebration, thereby ending the attraction. During their time, they were the Saturday night entertainment in many taverns and pool halls. (Photograph courtesy of Don Ketelsen.)

Six

NORTHEAST AND CENTER

WATERFORD, WASHINGTON, DEEP CREEK, ELK RIVER, CENTER, LINCOLN, AND HAMPSHIRE TOWNSHIPS

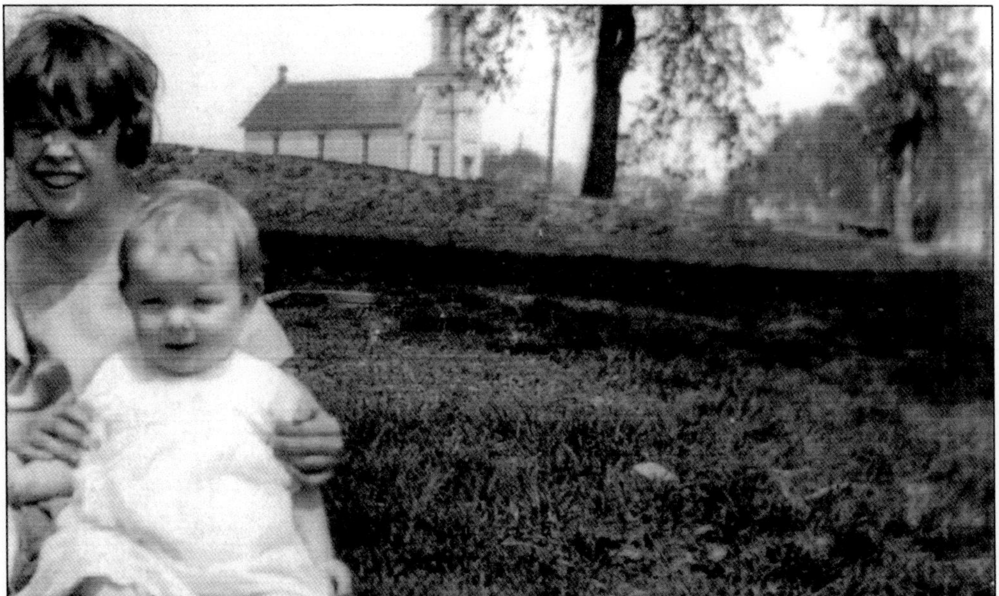

In the background of this *c.* 1924 photograph of George McClintock's daughters, Vera McClintock and Grace McClintock Pape, is the only known picture of the Union Church located south of Almont in Elk River Township. From information gathered by Elsie Eggers, the church was built by William Miller and his wife on their property in 1872. Since Mrs. Miller wanted the church services to be open to anyone who cared to worship there, she insisted it be named a Union Church before she would sign over the deed. Of the $3,000 spent building the church, $2,000 was borne by the David and Levi Shadduck families. The remaining $1,000 was donated by folks who lived in the area. By the 1930s, the church was standing empty and was razed by the end of the decade. (Photograph courtesy of Grace McClintock Pape.)

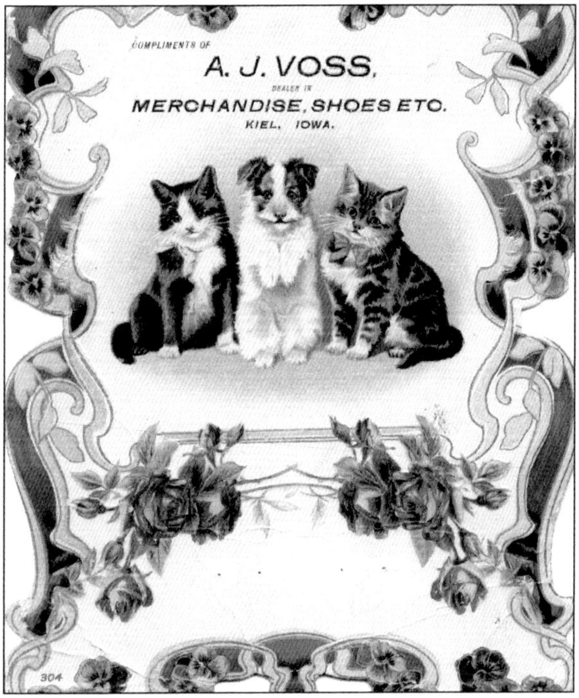

August Boock opened a general store ten miles west of Lyons in 1854 in Deep Creek Township. The road followed the curving Indian trail that ran between Lyons and Maquoketa, and Boock wished to take advantage of the stage coach business. The area settled and the stage coach stop took the name of Keil. Travelers had the advantage of a post office until 1871 when it was transferred to Bryant. A.J. Voss purchased the store from Mr. Boock in 1889 and it was maintained as a family business through three generations of the Voss family until its sale in 1993. During World War I, Keil was re-named "Ten Mile" due to the anti-German feelings which ran through the country. (Photograph from the Clinton County Historical Society archives.)

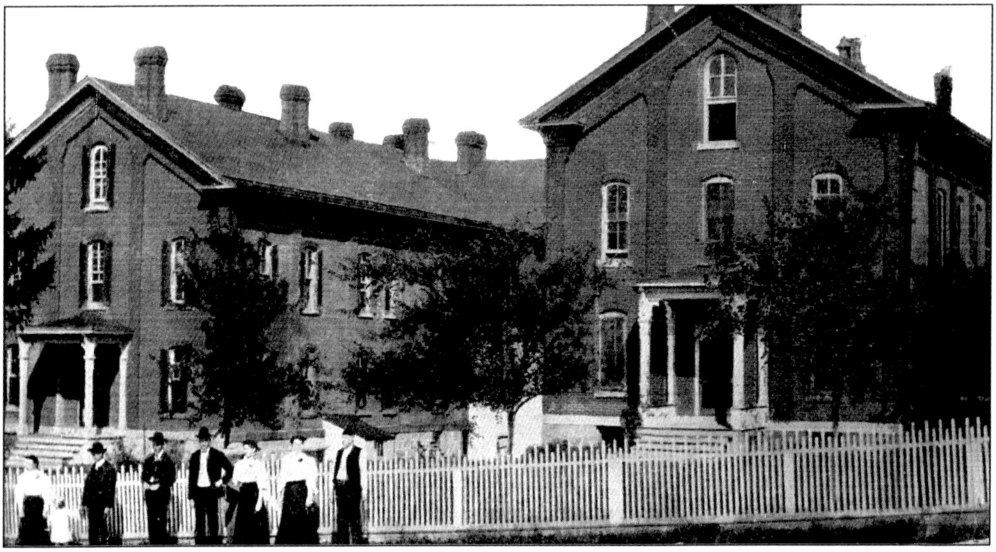

In 1857, the Clinton County Supervisors purchased 200 acres, plus 60 acres of timber, south of Charlotte in Waterford and Washington Townships. The purpose was to construct a "poor farm" to house the increasing number of indigents who were homeless due to the financial panic of that year. By 1895, the county had expanded the facility to include a hospital, dwelling, and prison for the "incurable lunatics." It became known as the Clinton County Infirmary, or the Clinton County Home. Today, the county no longer provides the care. The buildings, with the purchase pending, are leased from the county by Community Care, Inc. which provides assistance to over 120 mentally challenged or ill adults. The primary focus of care is to return these individuals to their own communities rather than providing a permanent home, as had been done in the past. (Photograph from the Clinton County Historical Society archives.)

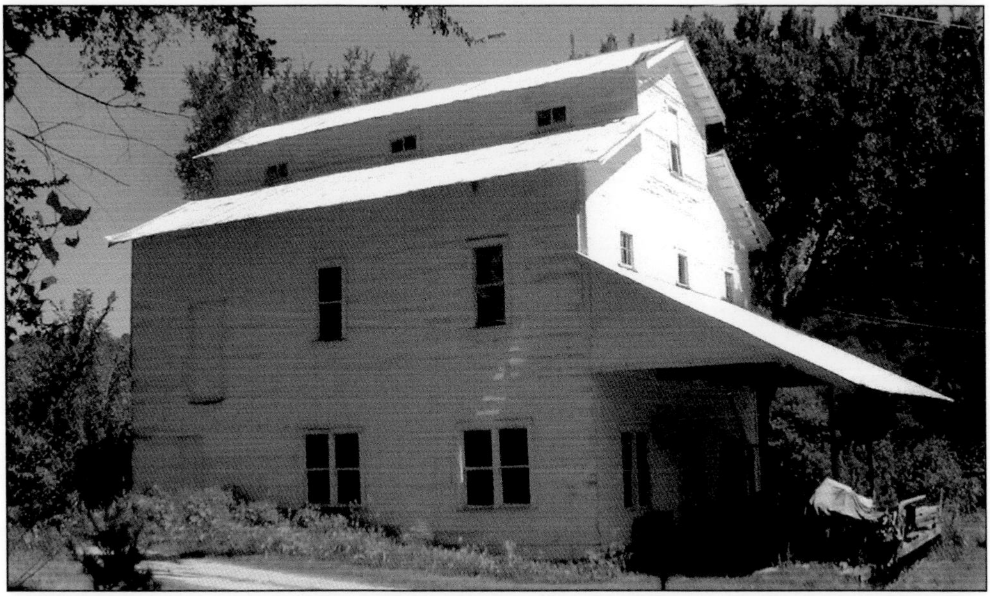

George Griswold, along with the Sloan brothers and Martin Barber, built a hemp mill in the Elk River Township. Martin Barber soon formed a partnership with William Haun and they purchased the mill. By 1846, the water-powered mill—along with a distillery, malt house, and warehouse—were in full operation in what was known as Haun's Town. The mill was a huge structure five stories high with seven elevators running from top to bottom. By 1867, it was owned by Jeremiah Wood. He then sold the mill to D. Kelso who sold it to the Ernest Struve family. In July of 1926, the mill was consumed by fire; however, was rebuilt by Ernest's son, William, and his sons. It remained a working mill until 1988 and is shown as it stands today. (Photograph courtesy of Gene and Carole Gilbert.)

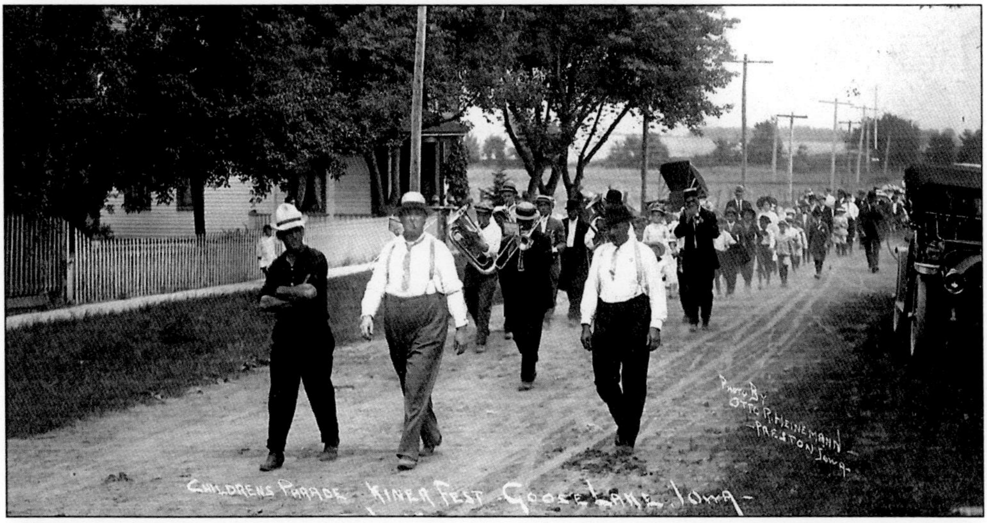

When immigrants came to America, they brought their customs with them. The heavy population of German immigrants in eastern Iowa held a Kinderfest, a festival celebrating families and children, during the summer months. A children's parade was held on June 24, 1911, during the Kinderfest held in Goose Lake, Deep Creek Township. (Photograph courtesy of Bob and Ethel Soesbe.)

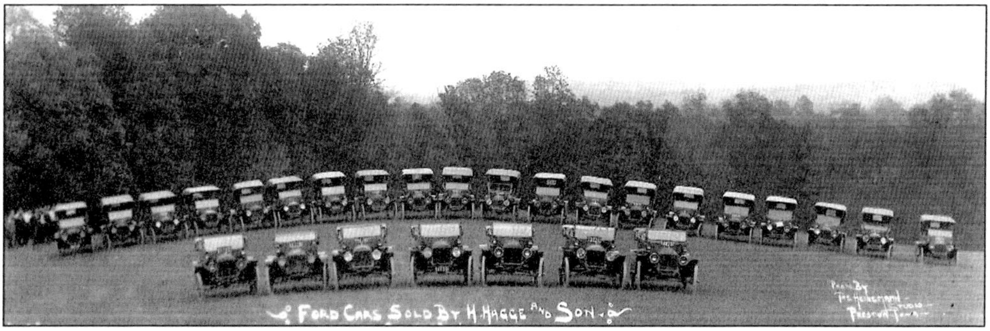

For many years, an annual Ford owners' picnic was held near Andover in Elk River Township. On May 24, 1914, the picnic was staged by Hans Hagge, the Andover blacksmith and Ford dealer, on the farm owned by Henry Eggers. (Photograph from the Clinton County Historical Society archives.)

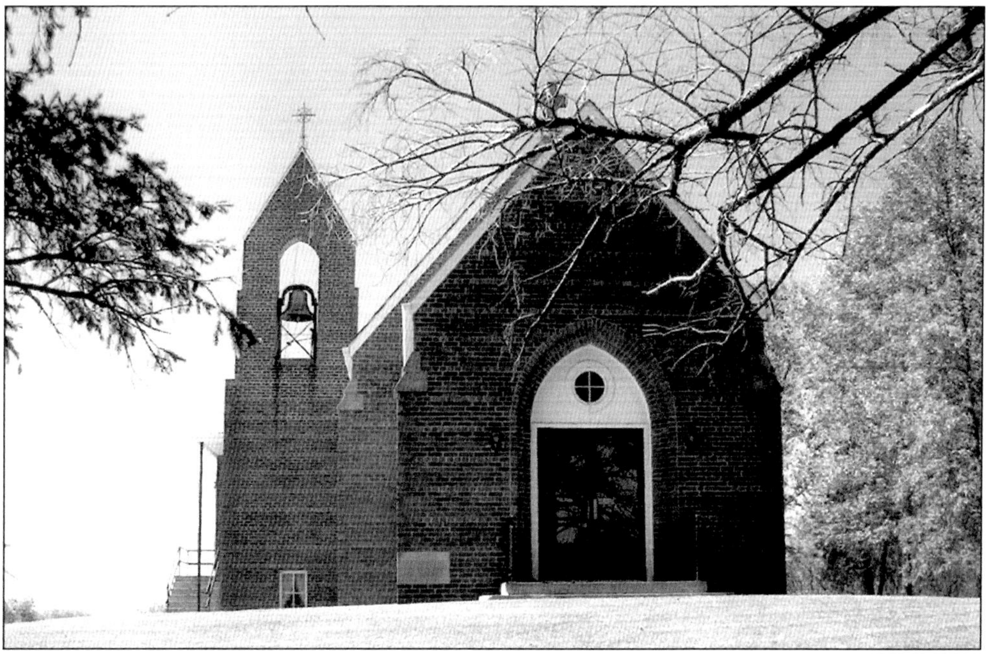

The first church at St. Patrick's Parish in Villa Nova, Washington Township, was built in 1856 for $1,000 and called Center Grove until 1883. At that time, a new church with a spire that reached 130 feet toward heaven was built for $16,000 and the name was changed. It is said there are French settlers and a Wisconsin tribal Indian buried in the church cemetery. Lightning struck the tall steeple in 1941 and the frame church was destroyed. The church was re-built of brick and the bell once again calls the faithful to worship. (Photograph courtesy of Joan Cottral Turner.)

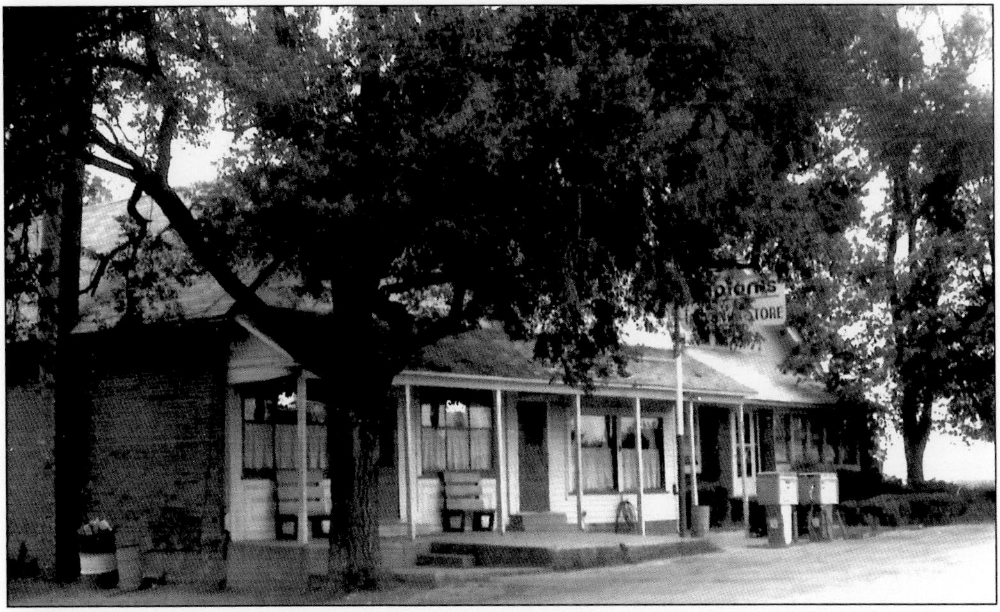

In 1840, the community of Pleasant Prairie, in Center Township, was established east of Brophy Creek. The Indians burned the town and the survivors moved a little east and settled a new village they named Suffolk. A post office was established in 1854 and the name of the village changed to Elvira after the wife of W.H. Gibbs, who platted the town. Jacob Leppers owned the first general store and saloon. He placed a sign at the crossroads stating that the best stopping place was his place. In a 1967 census of Clinton County roadways, that crossing was determined to be the busiest. (Photograph from the Clinton County Historical Society archives.)

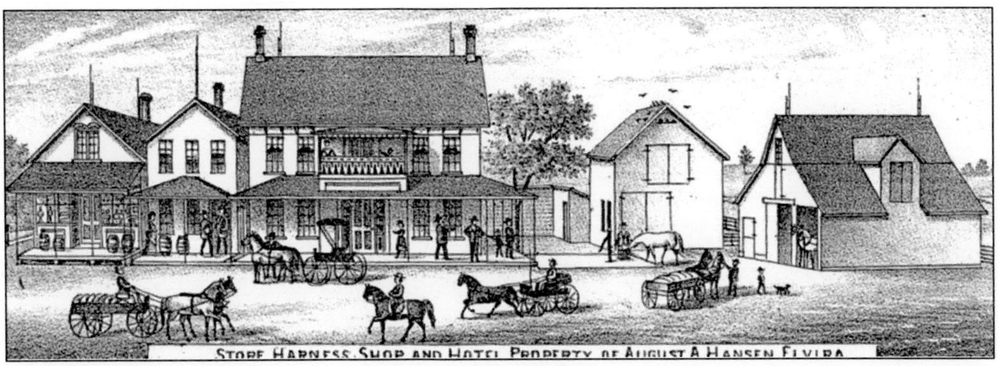

An 1886 artist's sketch shows the same Elvira view along with a hotel and harness shop belonging to August A. Hansen. He was also the postmaster, a farmer, and a realtor. Mr. Hansen moved on to settle in Verdi, Minnesota, but some of his buildings remain today. The saloon was the last to close and had been a viable business until a few years ago. (Photograph from the Clinton County Historical Society archives.)

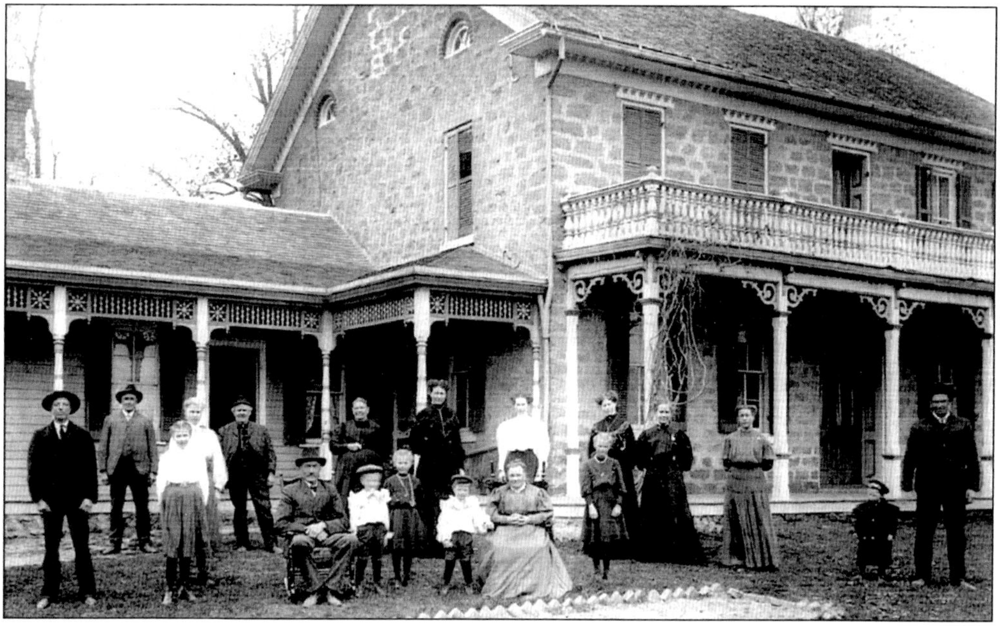

Johann Peter Dierks built this stone house in the mid-1840s to accommodate his ten children. Located in Hampshire Township on Hwy 136, it is now on the National Register of Historic Places. The original one-room frame house still stands in the kitchen area surrounded by the 1850 and 1865 additions. In 1865, the stone was quarried from the Considine Quarry in Fulton and brought across the river on boats to make it into the two-story Georgian style home it is today. The Preston Creveling family bought the home in the 1920s and lived there for almost 50 years. Bob and Arlene Rose Considine bought the home in 1996 and have accomplished a complete restoration, returning it to its original look while achieving an Iowa Best Preservation Award for their efforts. (Photograph courtesy of Bob and Arlene Rose Considine.)

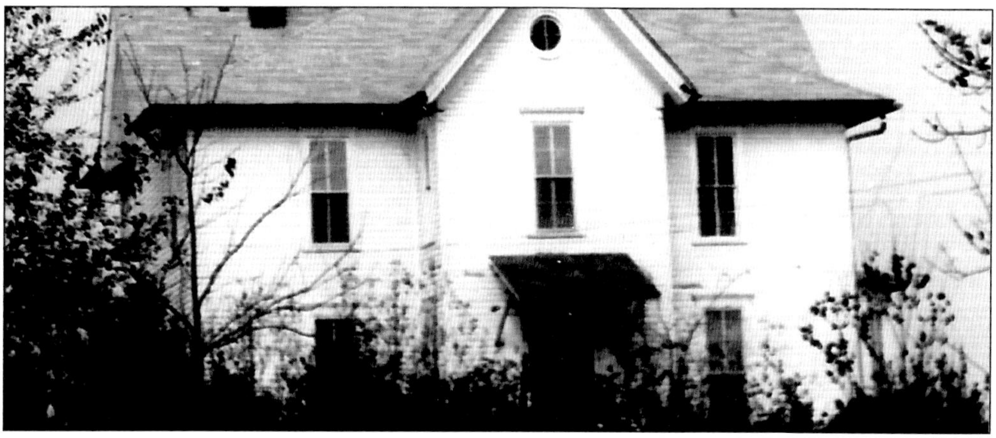

Because the railroad failed to arrive, by 1874 the town of Elvira diminished to its present size. That year, Richard A. Lyons, retired sea captain, purchased all but three of the 32 blocks of the original plat of the town. In 1882, Mr. Lyons built himself a grand home on the west edge of Elvira with six fireplaces, a winding stairway, and spacious porches. A large cupola on the roof encircled with windows can be seen for miles around. The 1968 tornado heavily damaged the home, ripping off porches and destroying the original barn on the property. (Photograph from the Clinton County Historical Society archives.)

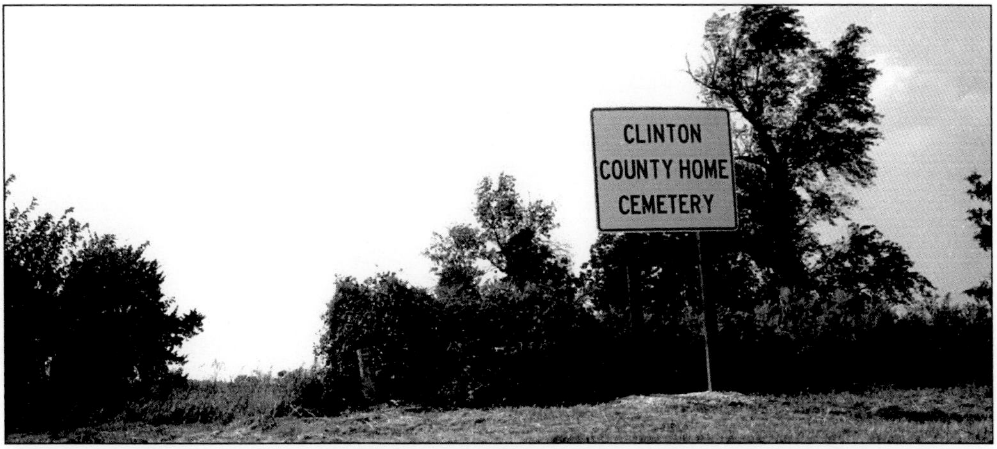

The Clinton County Home Cemetery is located south of Charlotte, in Waterford Township, on the hill west of the Community Care Facility. The confirmed burials of 212 residents are now recognized. There are no monuments or markers of any kind with the exception of the sign denoting the cemetery. (Photograph from the Clinton County Historical Society archives.)

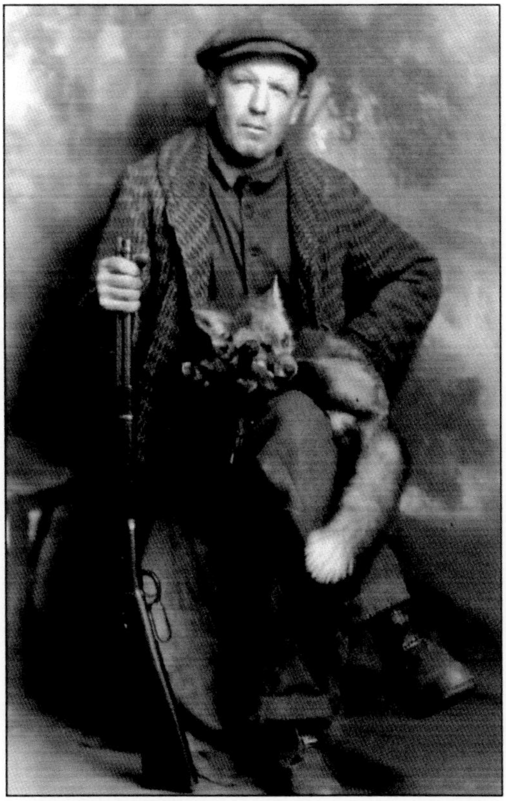

The fate of the fox was sealed in the early part of the 20th century when the local farm wives began to suffer large losses from foxes raiding their chicken houses. The farmer became a hunter to protect his chicken flocks and keep his wife happy. John Rohr, of Elk River Township, is shown pictured with the fox he shot. (Photograph courtesy of Gene and Carole Gilbert.)

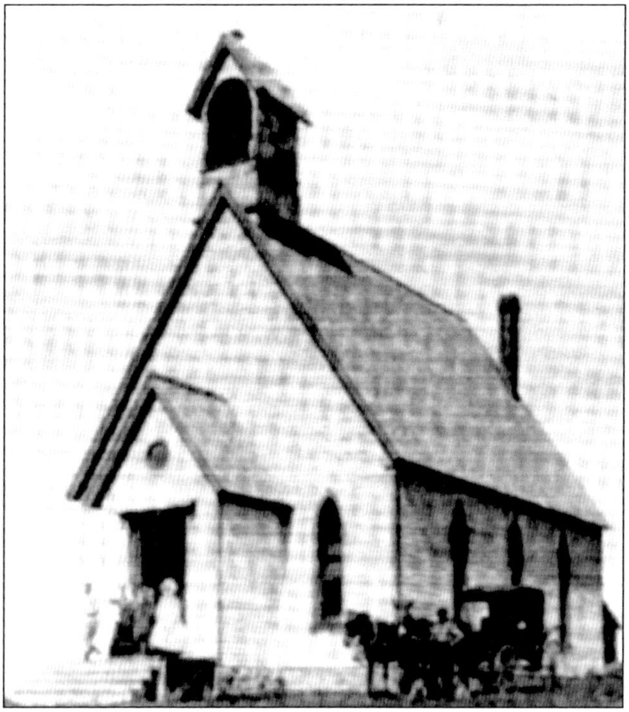

Tabernacle Church, next to Pleasant Hill Cemetery, was built in 1894 on land known as the "Seed Farm" in Lincoln Township. Anna Whitaker donated the land where the church and cemetery stood with the understanding that her family could be buried there. When the seed farm was sold, the last church service was held in 1922. The church was sold to Frank Anderson who dismantled it and used the lumber to build a barn. No one is sure how many burials remain in the cemetery, the thought is that there are five, plus John Ashpole, a veteran of the Spanish-American War. (Photograph from the Clinton County Historical Society archives.)

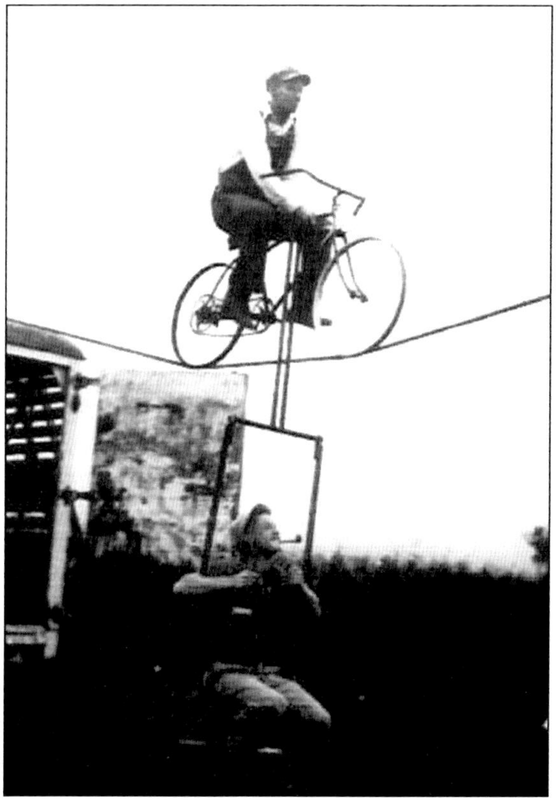

In Charlotte, Waterford Township, in 1950, Toby Jahn rode his bicycle across a rope stretched between two of Sellnau's semi trucks. They took the tires off the bicycle and built a hanging swing for his brother, Arnold Jahn, to sit in and act as a balance. Arnold was very relaxed and continued smoking his pipe as his brother made the trip across the rope safely. (Photograph courtesy of Kermit Ketelsen.)

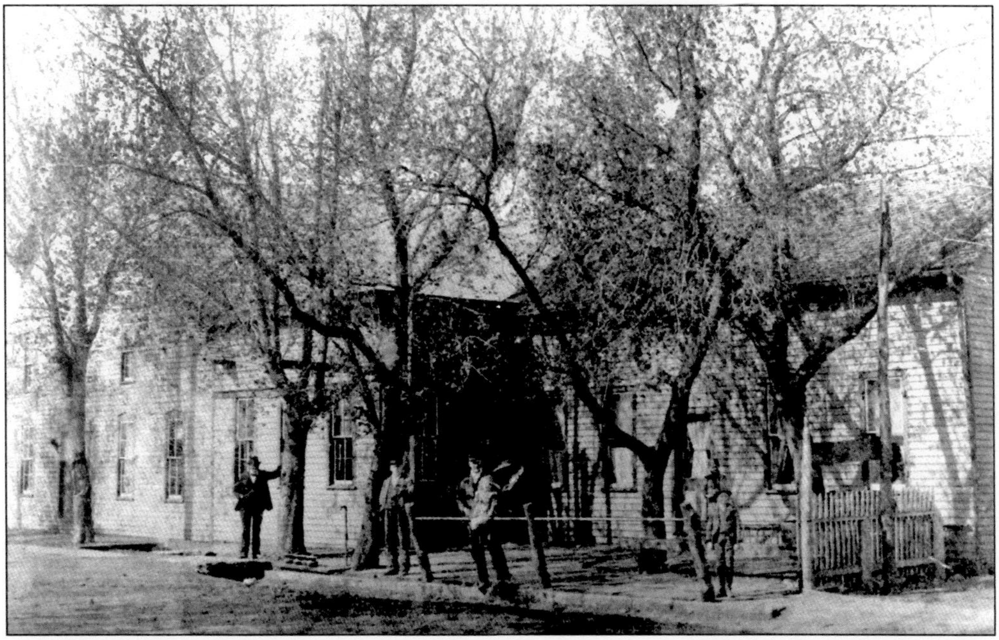

In the late 1830s, settlers began to make their way westward into Clinton County and establish homes near a large body of water that covered several square miles in what became Deep Creek Township. The settlement was named O'Brien in honor of the first resident; however, in 1873, the name was changed to Goose Lake to avoid confusion with the town of Bryant in the same township. The chosen name is thought to be due to the large number of geese and swans the water attracted. The first store in town was opened by Charles Curtis, and in 1893 it was sold to John Keiner, who also operated a tavern, restaurant, and dance hall in the same building. This photo was taken c. 1890 (Photograph from the Clinton County Historical Society archives.)

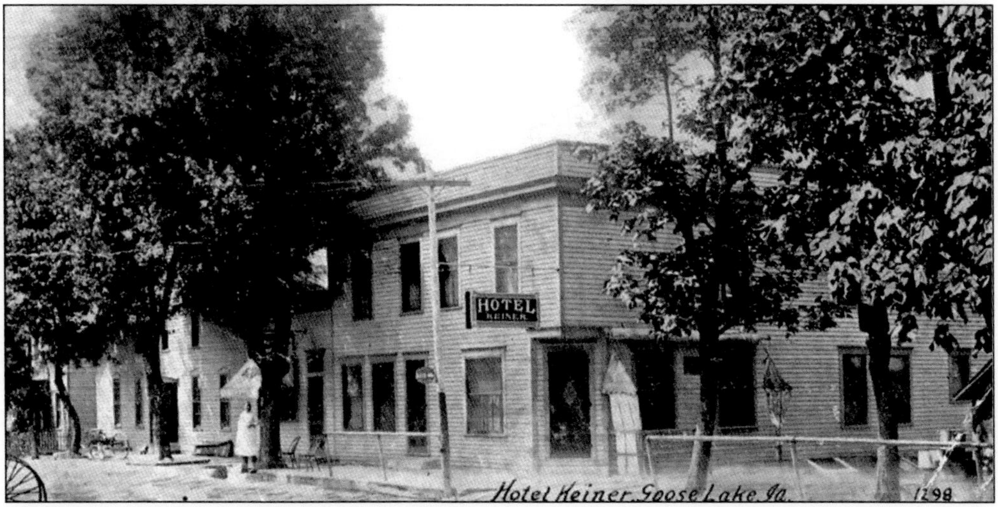

This 1915 photo shows the Hotel Keiner in Goose Lake, Deep Creek Township, which stood on Main Street just south of the post office. The hotel was a lively part of the community and is still in use today as a local tavern with room to have dances and receptions. Many modifications have taken place over the years. (Photograph from the Clinton County Historical Society archives.)

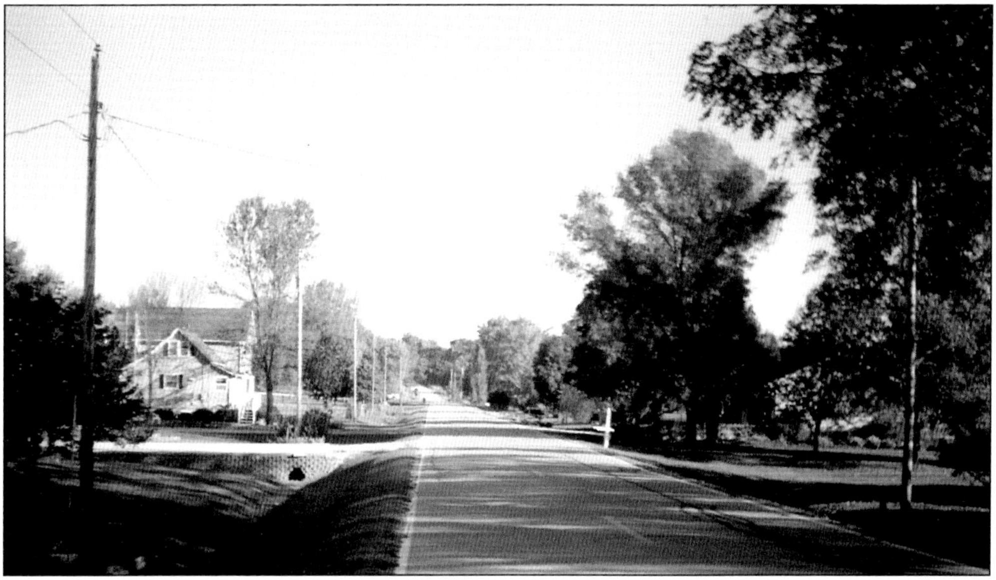

In 1846, William G. Haun was persuaded to establish a flour mill, store, and distillery in the little settlement which was named Haun's Town, Elk River Township. Mr. Haun gained a prominence as a financier. In 1851, while an elected Iowa Representative from Clinton County, he introduced an act to prohibit free Negroes and mulattoes from settling within the boundaries of the state of Iowa. It was bitterly opposed in both the house and the senate; however, it finally passed and Governor Hempstead immediately signed the bill. The measure would become law upon publication in the *Iowa City Reporter* and the *Iowa Freeman* of Mt. Pleasant, but the latter refused to publish the law. The publication clause was regarded as a trick with the desired results of killing the act. (Photograph courtesy of Don Ketelsen.)

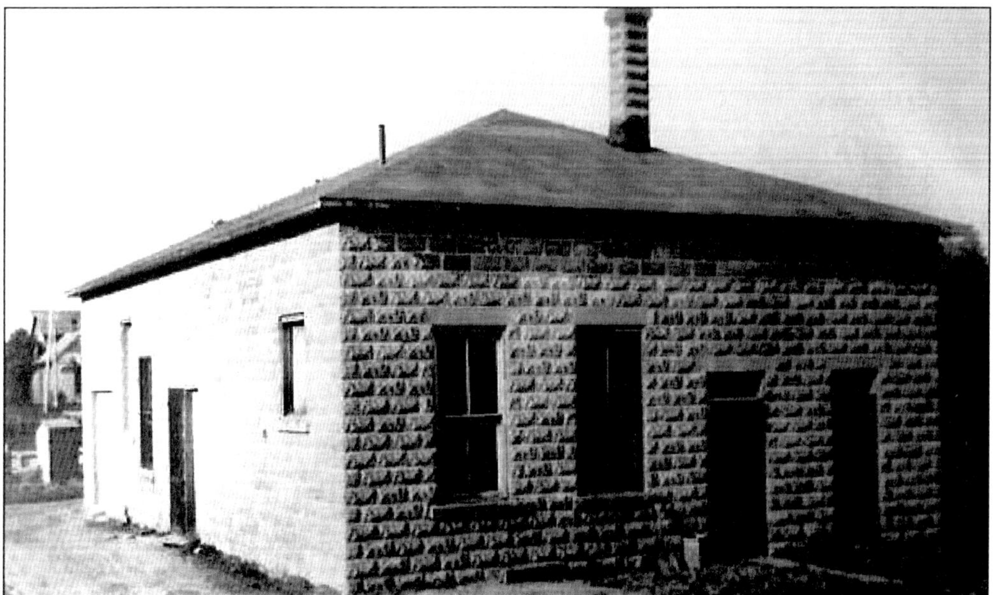

The creamery in Charlotte, Waterford Township, is shown here in November of 1914. It was located where the locker plant stands today. (Photograph courtesy of Kermit Ketelsen.)

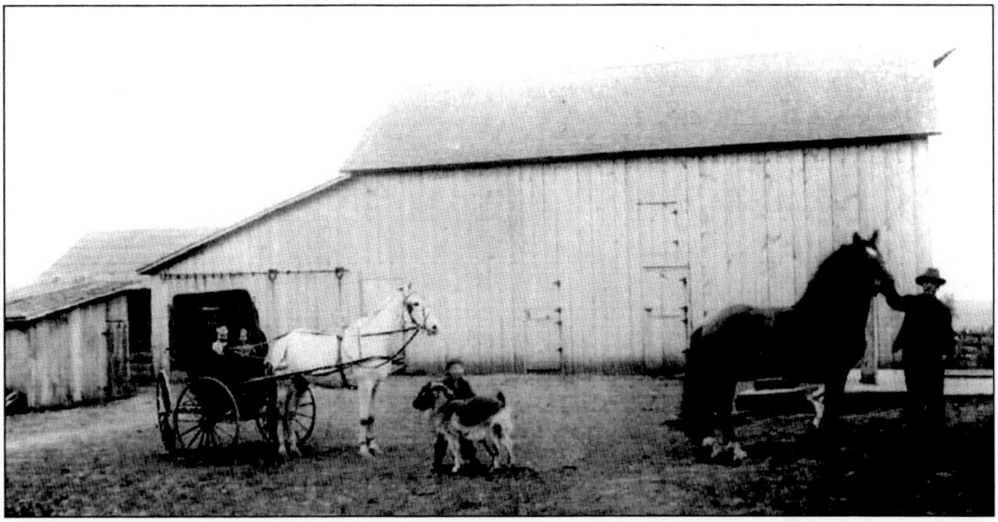

In 1854, Josiah and Mary Ann Robeson Galbraith, and seven of their 11 children, came by oxen and wagon to Lincoln Township and purchased 240 acres. By the time they had built their second home, they had also improved the land and built a solid, substantial barn. By 1905, their son Henry Galbraith, pictured with horse, lived on the farm with his family and made many modern improvements to the property. In the buggy are Henry's wife, M. Louisa, and daughters, Agnes and Wilhelmina, with son Henry holding the goat. (Photograph courtesy of Mr. and Mrs. Robert Dworschack.)

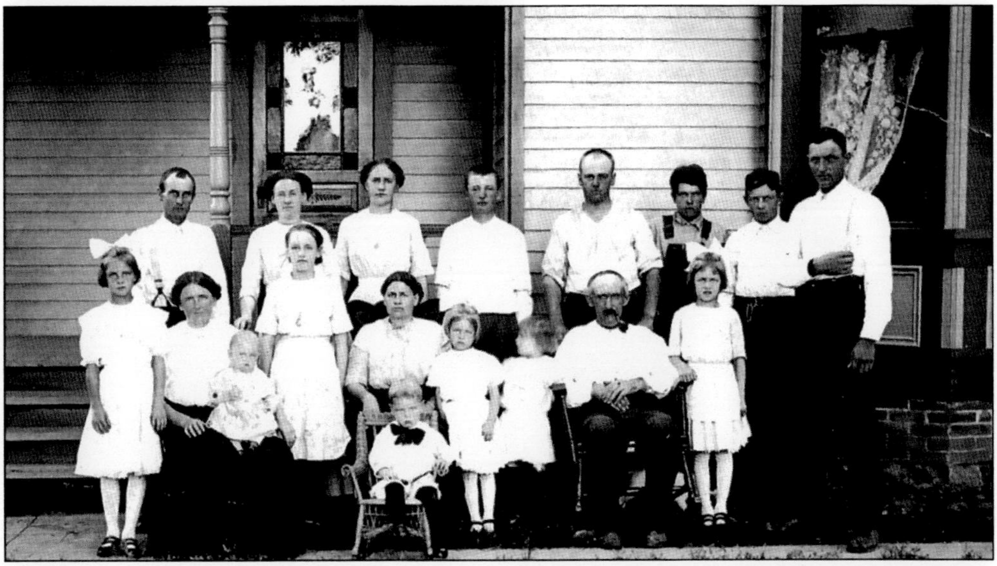

In 1912, the Henry M. Hansen family gathered at their home in Center Township, north of Elvira. Mr. Hansen immigrated to the United States with his parents in 1866 and became one of the most successful farmers in his lifetime, possessing 280 acres of finely cultivated land. Pictured are, from left to right: (back row) Chris Thomsen, Erna Hansen Jensen, Henrietta Hansen Shumake, Edward Hansen, Henry Hansen, two hired men, and William Dohrmann; (front row) Mabel Dohrmann, Agnes Hansen Thomsen, baby Berneice Thomsen, Alfrieda Hansen Cottral, Caroline Hansen Dohrmann, Wilbur Dohrmann, Evyline Dohrmann, Roberta Hansen Miller, father Henry Martin Hansen, and Hattie Dohrmann. (Photograph courtesy of Joan Cottral Turner.)

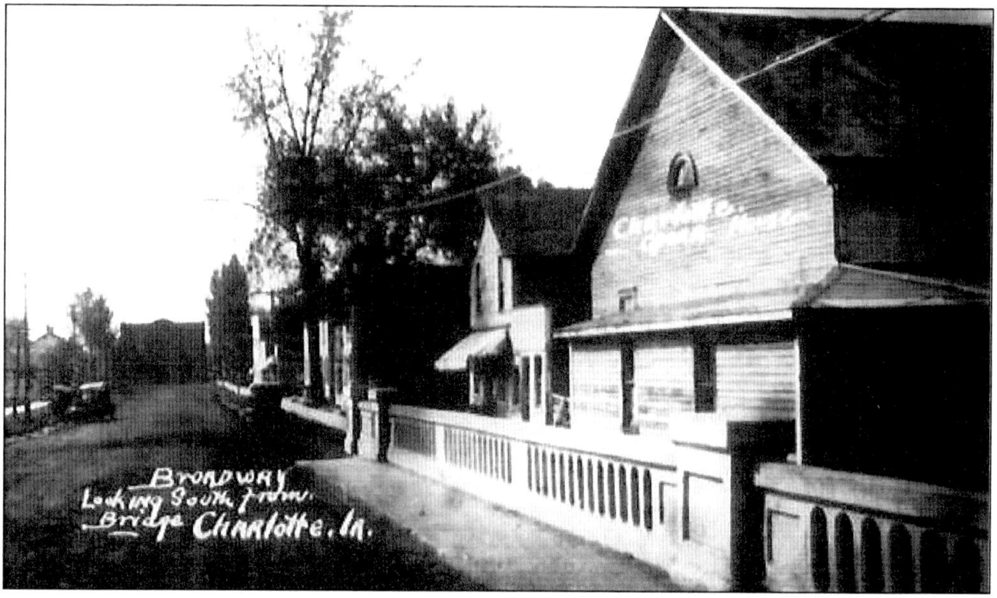

The Charlotte Opera House, located on Broadway, was almost covered by the bridge when it was built. In 1928, the Harlem Globetrotters played the local Charlotte basketball team. Since the Opera House had no locker rooms, the Globe Trotters had to run out onto the street and across the bridge to the tavern next door to change clothes. (Photograph courtesy of Kermit Ketelsen.)

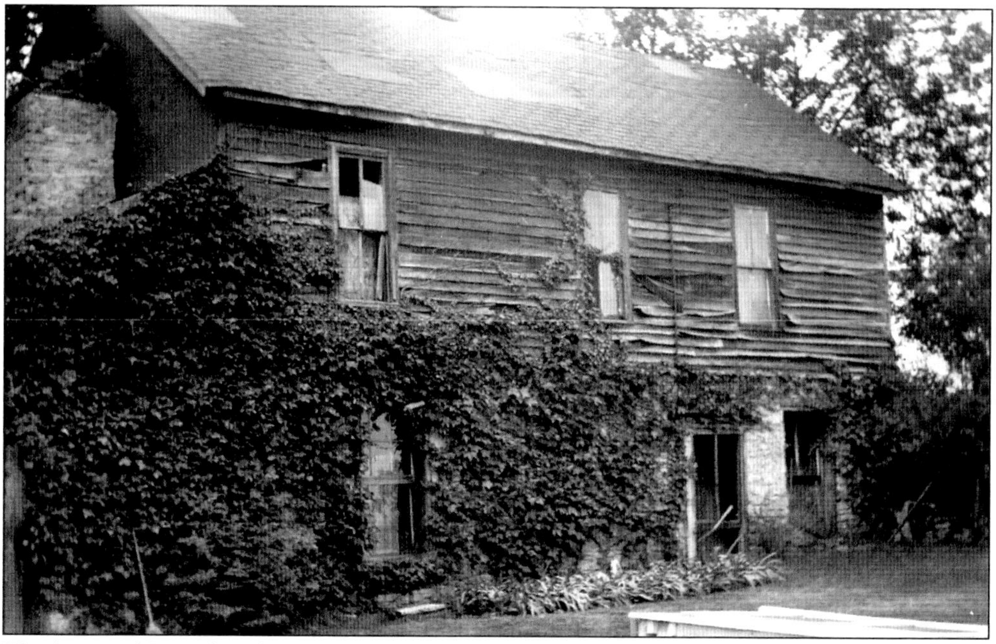

The home of Daniel and Mary Smith in Almont, Elk River Township, is shown here. Daniel was a veteran of the War of 1812 and is considered by some historical accounts to have been the first white settler in the township. Their child, Bela, died in October of 1839, and was the first recorded death in the township. The Smith at Almont Cemetery was established at that time. Mary died in 1851 and Daniel was buried beside his family in October of 1864. (Photograph from the Clinton County Historical Society archives.)

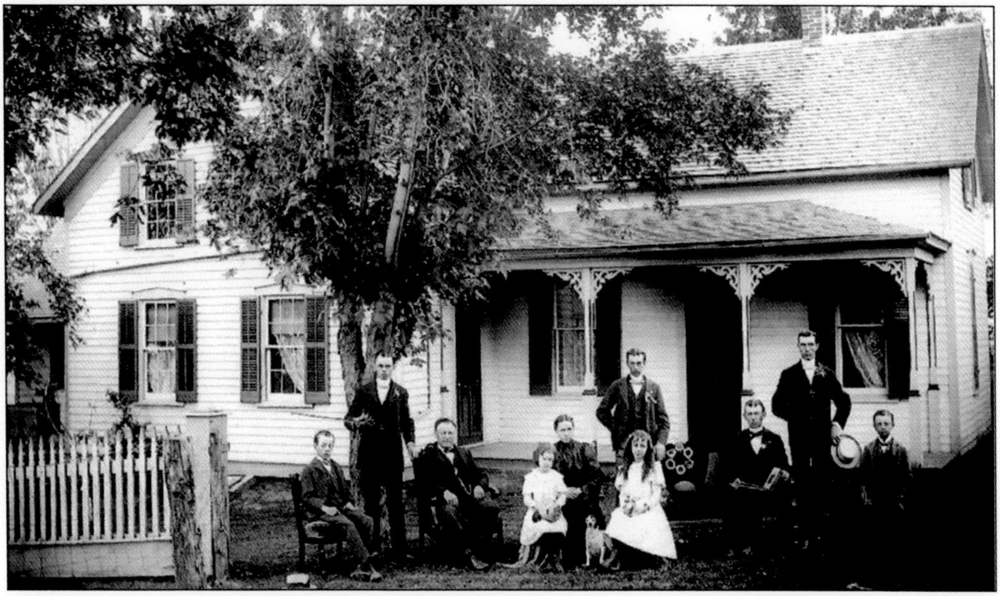

The Cornelius and Anna Hansen Petersen family is shown on the front lawn of their Washington Township family farm, c. 1890. Mr. Petersen was known for his stock-raising efforts through his improvements and successful cultivation of his many acres of land. The family's home, in the midst of its attractive surroundings, was known as a place of old-time hospitality. (Photograph courtesy of Joan Cottral Turner.)

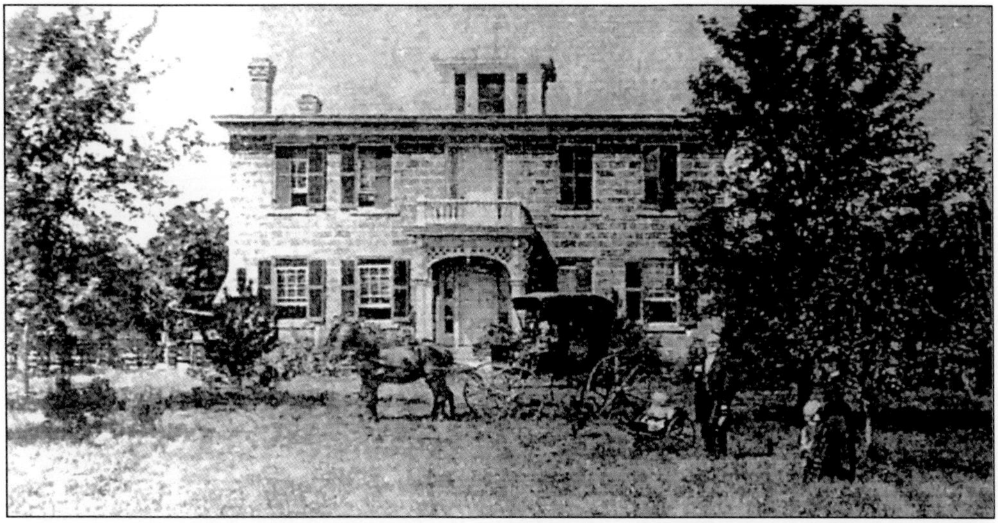

In 1865, Jacob Bohart purchased 960 acres of land from the United States government in Lincoln Township for $5 an acre. Mr. Bohart was ahead of his time when he built his large, practical barns and home. His Prairie Four Square house, shown above, had large hallways running from the front to back to allow air flow throughout the home. The outer stone was brought downriver from Galena, Illinois, and the inside stone was quarried in Camanche. The wood used in the home was cut in his own sawmill. The family lived in a log cabin while the stone house was being built. They later moved back into the cabin when the stone house was temporarily needed for a school and church. The home was sold to Albert and Mary Young Kelly and descendants of the Kelly family live in the home today. (Photograph courtesy of Fred and Doris Kube.)

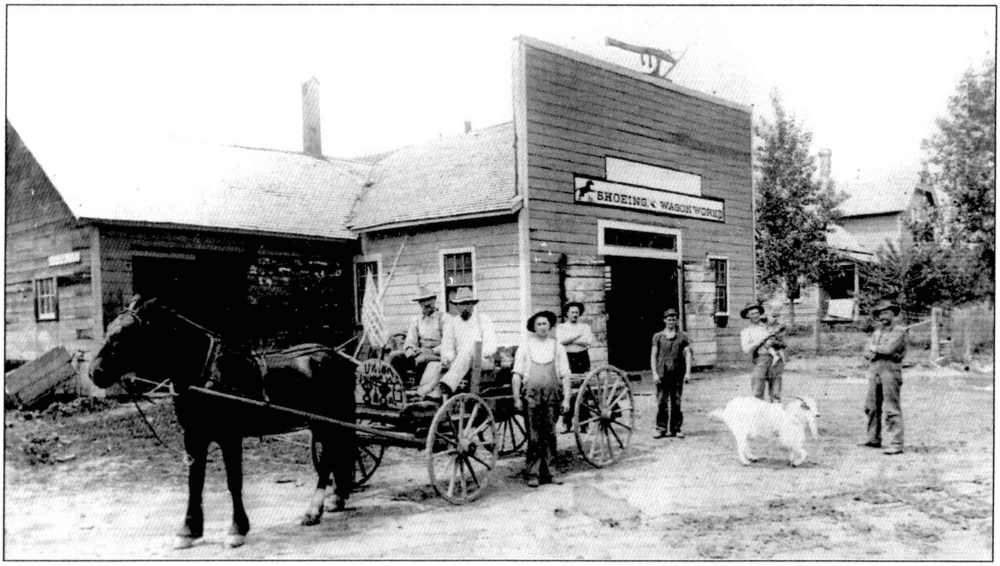

The Teeds Grove Blacksmith Shop, shown here around 1900, was built by George Huebner and owned by Claus Kross at the time of this photograph. Pictured are, from left: Pete Nissen, wagon-maker; Joe Green; Ernest Petersen; Frank Petersen; Charlie Tietjens, blacksmith; Claus R. Kross; Clarence Kross; and Stimson (Stump) Green. (Photograph from the Clinton County Historical Society archives.)

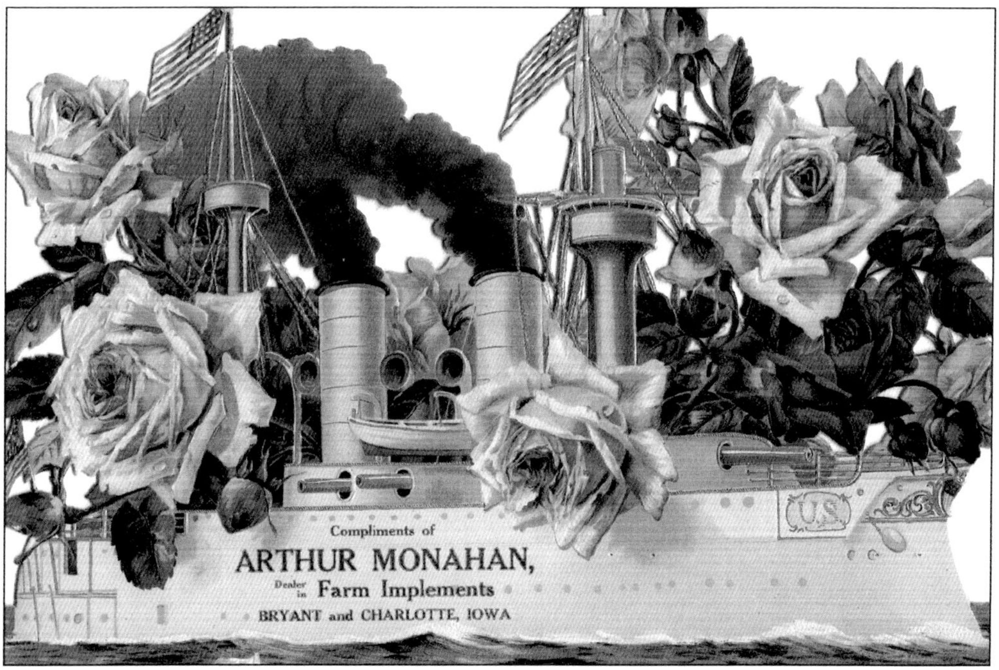

During World War II, advertising reflected the pride of the people in their Armed Forces. Arthur Monahan was a dealer in "Vehicles and Farm Implements" which included hardware, pumps, windmills, cream separators, and grass seeds. He had businesses in both Bryant, in Deep Creek Township, and Charlotte, in Waterford Township. Mr. Monahan's motto was: "Buy standard goods, I handle no others." (Photograph from the Clinton County Historical Society archives.)

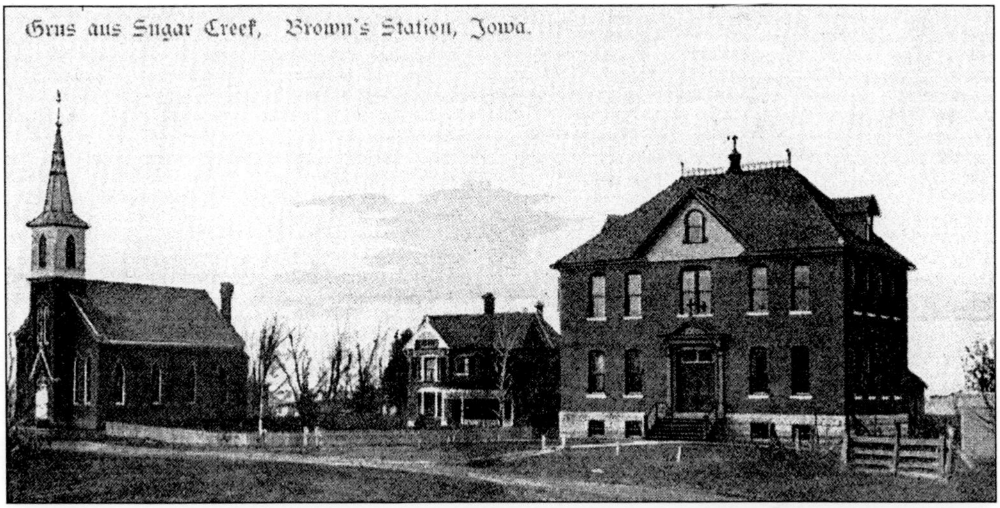

In the early 1840s, pioneer settlers cleared the hilly, wooded area in Waterford Township known as Brown's Station. In 1855, Henry Nurre, possibly the first settler in the area, donated 40 acres of land on top of a hill near his home. He donated the land in memory of his first wife to the people of the community, for a parish church, cemetery, and school. The original frame church was built for $1,500. In 1892, a rectory was built, and by 1896, the present church was built. A school was added in 1902 and closed in 1967. The church still remains the very heart of St. Joseph's congregation. (Photograph from the Clinton County Historical Society archives.)

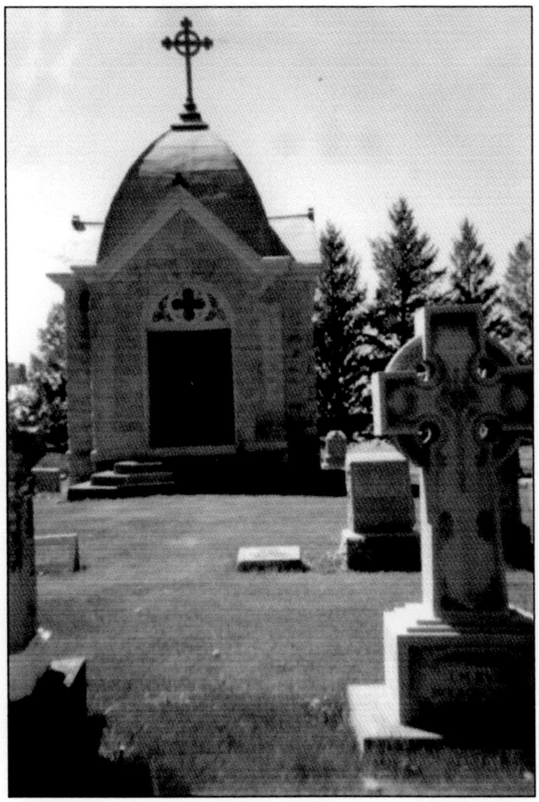

This historic mausoleum is in the cemetery located next to the Immaculate Conception Church in Petersville, Waterford Township. Catholicism spread quickly in this fertile area and church services were originally held in homes, then in a log cabin church, a frame building, and by 1903, in the splendid brick church built at a cost of $23,000. The community surrounding it was called Quigley, after a grocery merchant of that name. Later, Fr. Peter O'Dowd changed the name to Petersville in 1880. The village has disappeared; however, the church's Romanesque one-half dome towers over the countryside. (Photograph from the Clinton County Historical Society archives.)

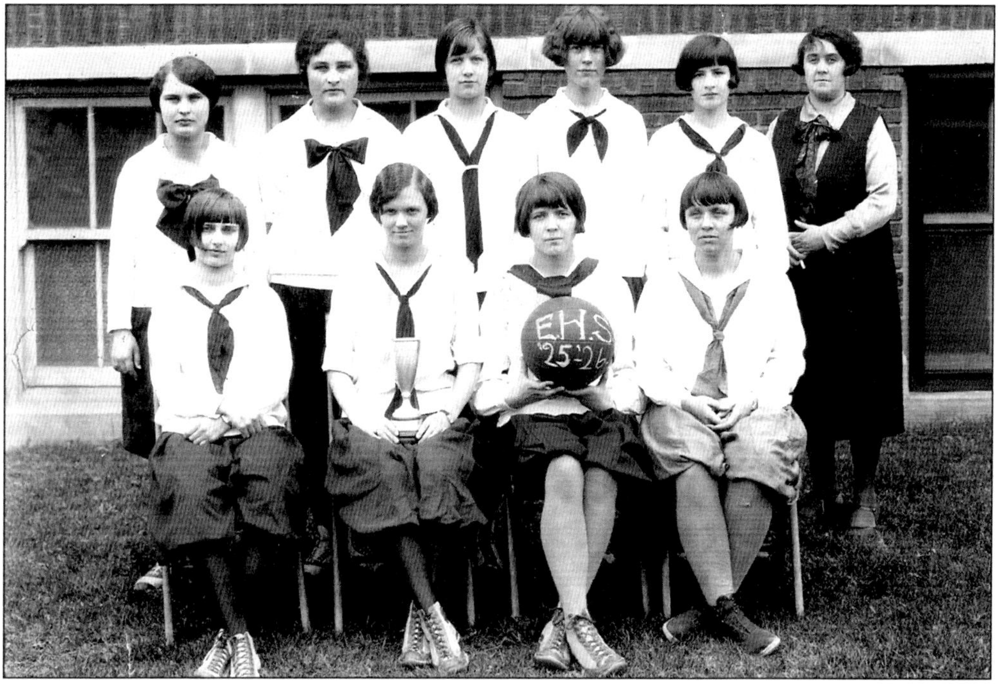

The 1925–1926 Champion Elvira Girls Basketball team posed with their coach, proudly displaying their trophy and the game ball. The regulation uniforms appear to have been cumbersome with the floppy ties on the long-sleeved blouses, knee-length bloomers, and heavy cotton stockings. Only the high-button leather shoes look comfortable. (Photograph from the Clinton County Historical Society archives.)

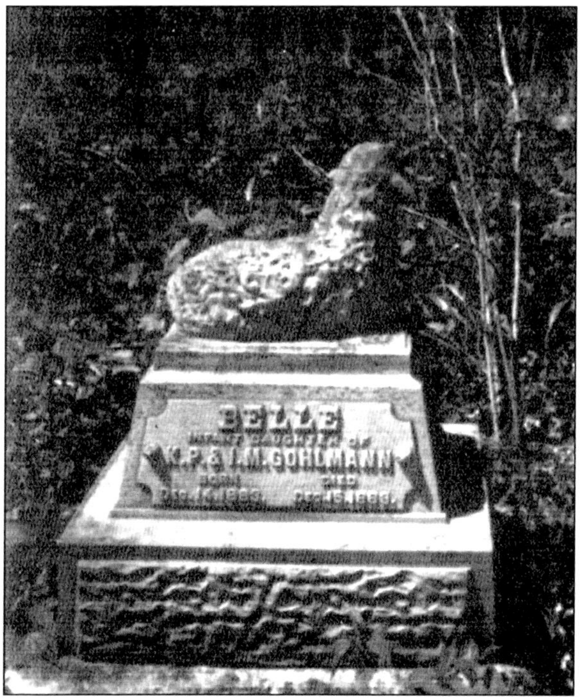

The land for Hickory Hill Cemetery, in Waterford Township, was deeded over to the Hickory Hill Graveyard Association by Maria Gohlman on December 10, 1886. It had been known as the Gohlman Cemetery until that time. The first of the 53 burials took place in 1860 and the last in 1930. This zinc marker for infant Belle Gohlman has stood the test of time remarkably well. Zinc markers were sold between 1870 and 1920 for either $2 or $4, depending on style and type of inscription. (Photograph from the Clinton County Historical Society archives.)

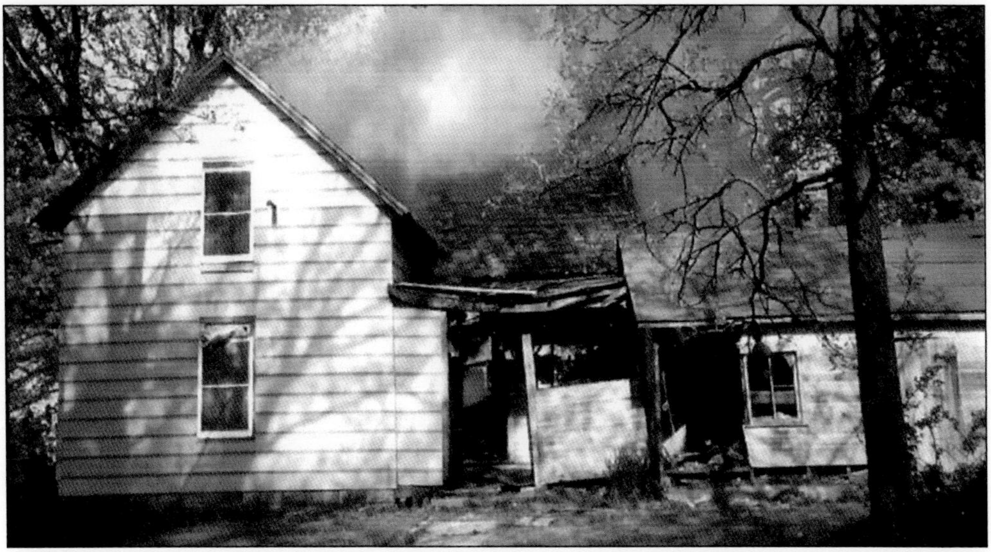

In the early years of pioneer farming, Elijah Buell's son lived in a sod house on 90 acres along the "Ridge Road," in Hampshire Township, five miles west of Lyons. Eventually, he sold his property to the William Mahmens family and they built a frame house over the sod foundation. Mr. Buell told many stories of befriending and trading with the Indians. In 1997, the Mahmens family had the Andover Fire Department burn down the old frame home, shown above, to clean up the home site. After the burn, the foundation of the old sod cabin could easily be distinguished. A few items from the Buell cabin have been reused in the restoration of the Dierks home, across the highway. (Photograph courtesy of Arlene Rose Considine.)

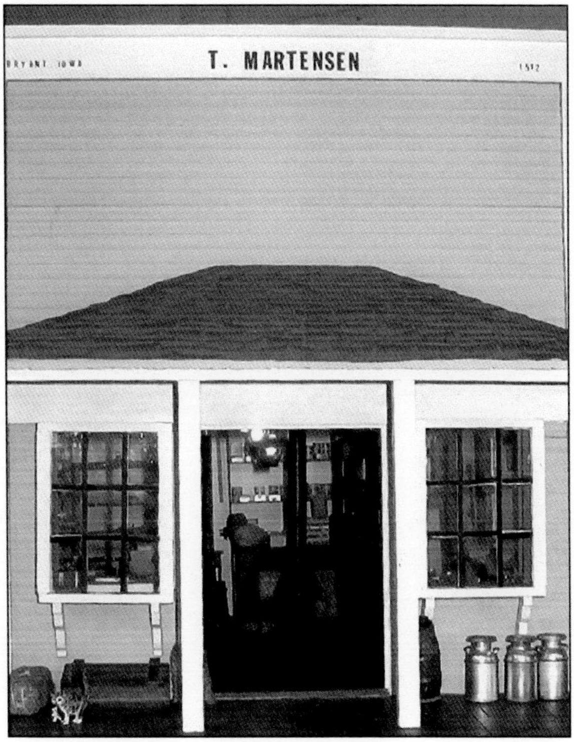

During the late 1800s, Herman Toedt and August Wessels were in the mercantile business in Bryant, Deep Creek Township. In 1912, Thomas Martensen purchased the business from Mr. Wessels. Saturdays were always a busy time at the store with farmers bringing their eggs and produce in to sell along with a list of groceries to buy. It also was the only day of the week they sold ice cream. In 1930, Mr. Martensen lost the business during the Depression and it burned down soon after it closed. In 1980, a replica of the store was given to the Martensen's daughter, Ramona Baker. It had been built over several years and includes hundreds of small scale items. The Bakers recently donated the unique model to the Clinton County Historical Society and is on display in the museum. (Photograph from the Clinton County Historical Society archives.)

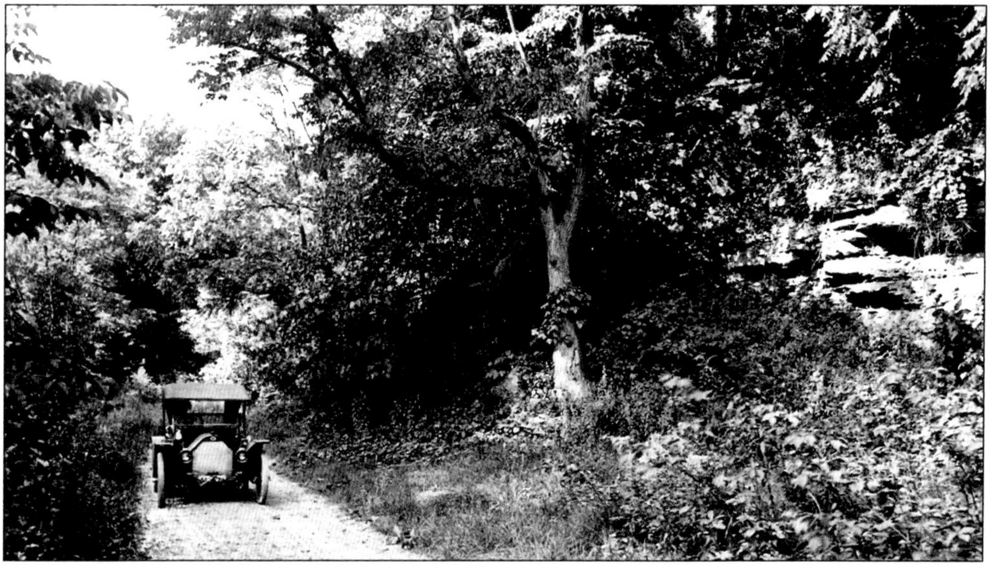

In 1870, Mr. and Mrs. James Bulger deeded land to the Chicago Clinton Dubuque Railroad for a track right-of-way in Hampshire Township along the Mississippi River. The scenery and available access road encouraged people to build homes east of the tracks. In the early '30s, the Mississippi River dam project was started and the water rose and flooded out the homes. Those that did rebuild situated their homes back from the river on the west side of the tracks. The access road was improved and at the same time, the government declared the area a federal wildlife refuge. (Photograph from the Clinton County Historical Society archives.)

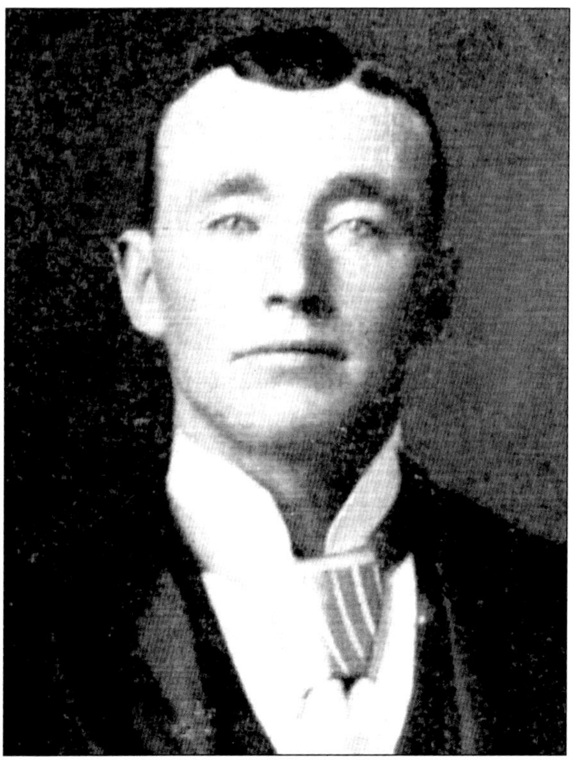

In the early part of the 1900s, Mr. R.T. Troy advertised the following: "This looks just like me and my work tells. Busy every day last winter. I'd like to work for you. I make a specialty of Live Stock and Agricultural sales and am known all over Clinton, Jackson and Scott Counties. Wire or phone me at my expense. R.T. Troy, Charlotte, Iowa." It is not known how successful Mr. Troy was with his advertisement. (Photograph from the Clinton County Historical Society archives.)

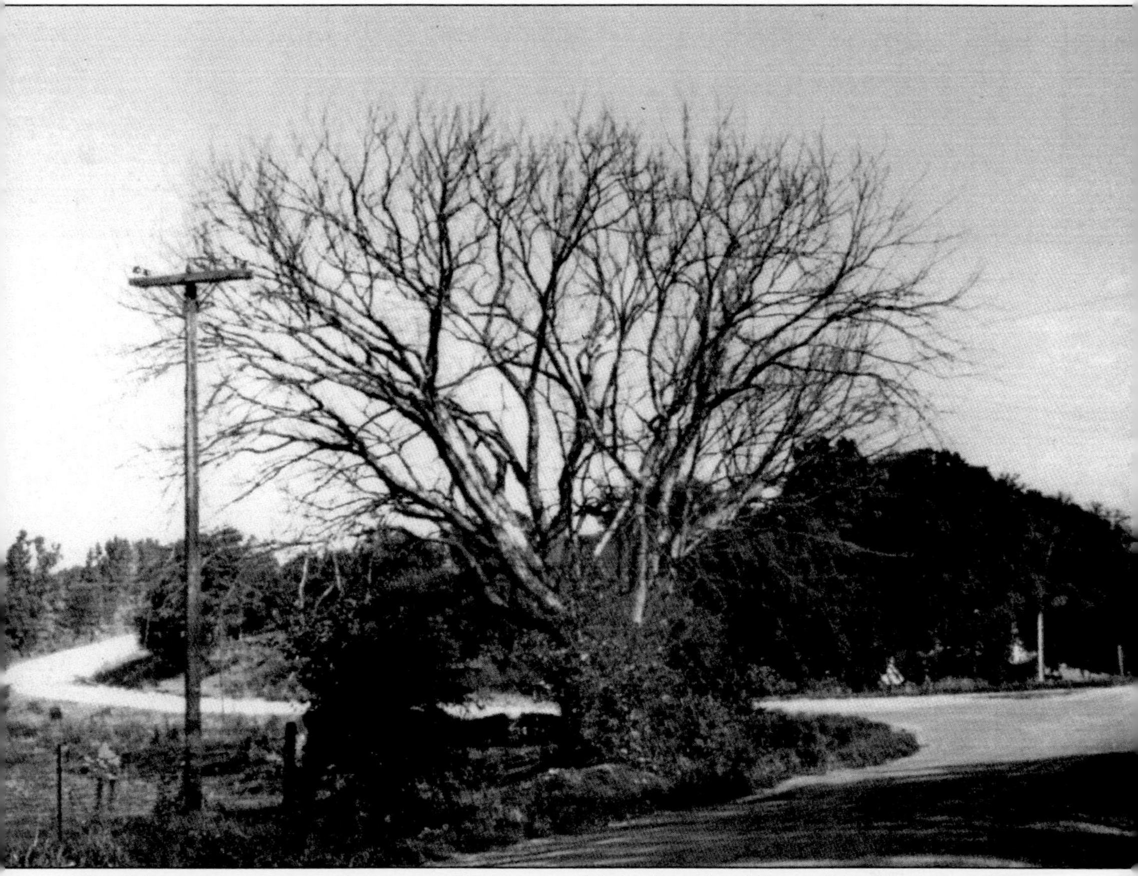

The following is a copy of an item which was published in the *Clinton Herald* on an unknown date. The signer of the article, "Defender," is thought to be S.P. Russell. From Hauntown, July 8: "The Centennial Tree—In June 1876, a Centennial Club was organized. At one of the meetings a motion was made by S.P. Russell to appoint a committee to superintend the getting and planting out of a tree on the morning of the Centennial Fourth. Accordingly, a fine young elm was selected and planted in front of the church in this place. I have no doubt that in one hundred years from now weary pilgrims may find a pleasant retreat under its leafy boughs. Defender." Unfortunately, the tree died of Elm Disease in the summer of 1967. (Photograph from the Clinton County Historical Society archives.)

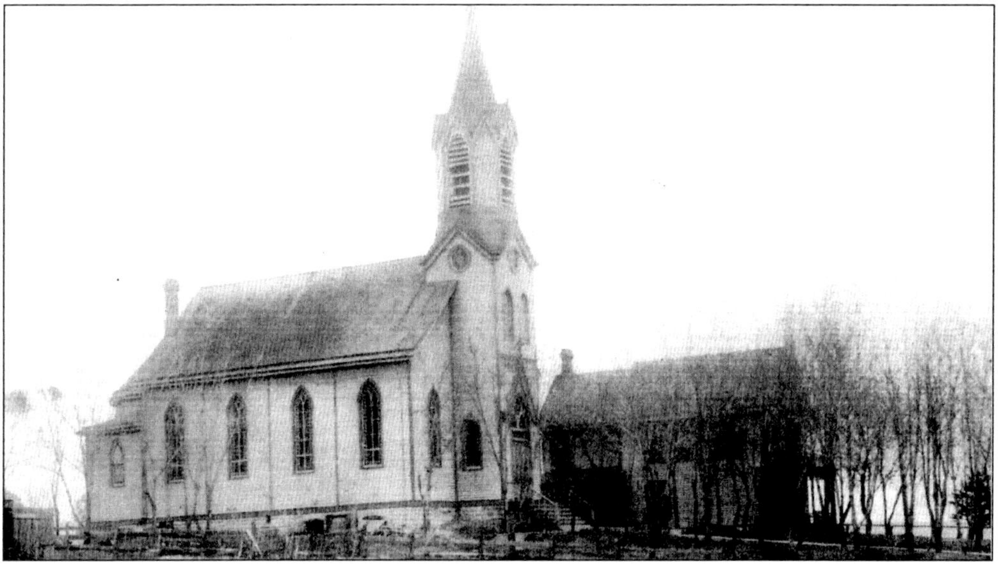

St. Mary's Parish began in 1857 when Fr. Frederick Jean purchased 40 acres at the Nine Mile area, Deep Creek Township, on Ridge Road to build a church for the county's rural residents. A legal error in the deed delayed the building of the "Old Prairie" church until 1876. In 1889, the 30 families of the parish moved to the booming town of Bryant on land purchased next to the Union Church. By 1890, the church and rectory were completed. St. Mary's lost its resident pastor in 1919 and from that time on became a mission church served by pastors in the surrounding area. A new chapter was begun in 1993 when St. Mary's Parish consolidated with St. Joseph's Parish of Sugar Creek to the advantage of both churches. (Photograph courtesy of Margaret Wagemester.)

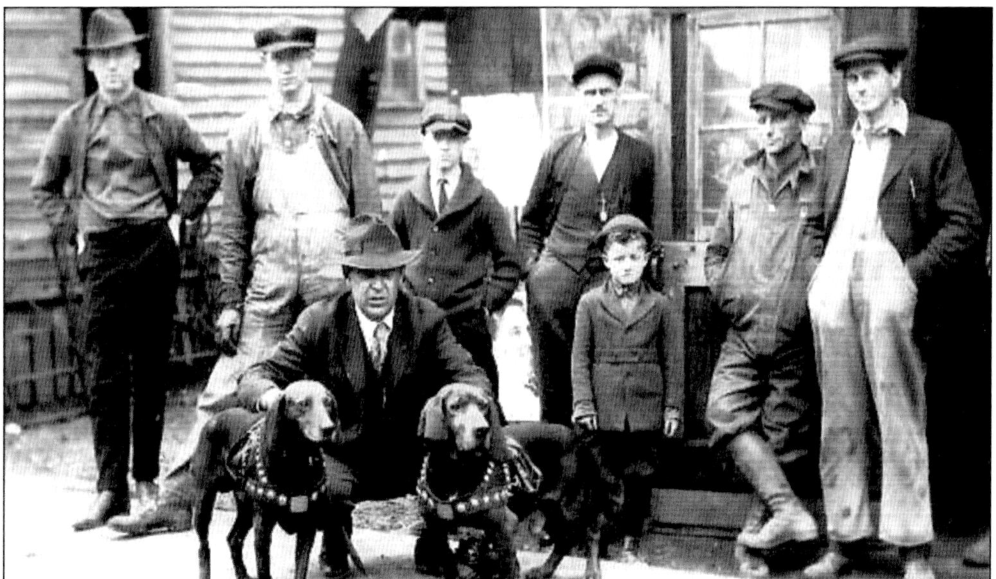

When Charlotte, Waterford Township, had an arson fire, the authorities were called in to investigate the crime with their fire dogs. It's said the dogs did their job by immediately trailing the scent right to the home of the arsonist where the authorities arrested him on the spot. (Photograph courtesy of Kermit Ketelsen.)

Seven

TRANSPORTATION

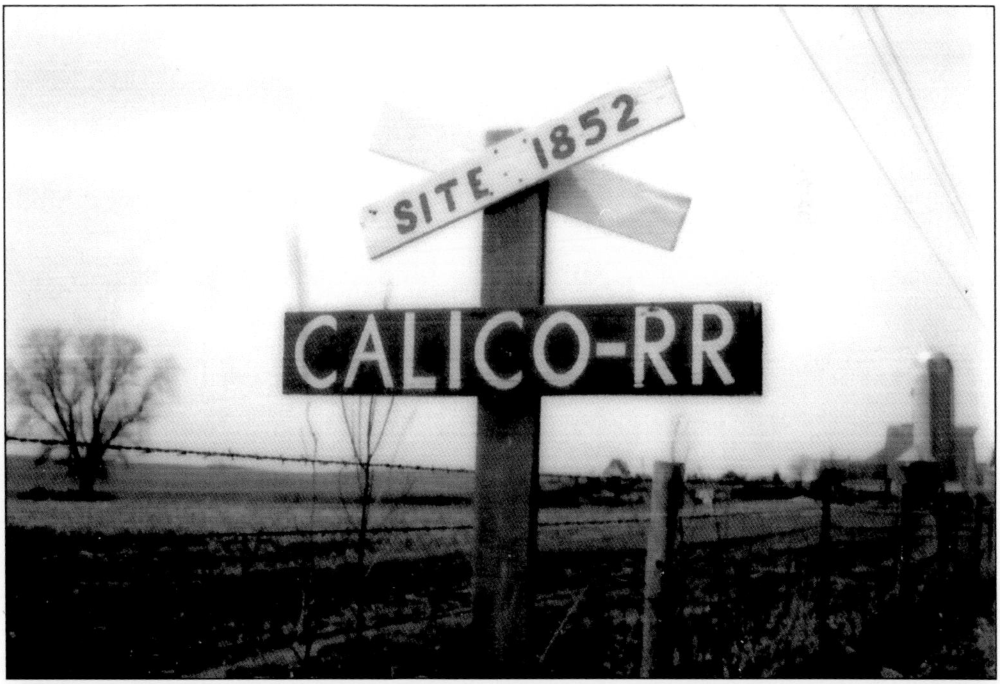

The Lyons and Iowa Central Railroad Company was organized in 1852 with the dream of building a long bridge 80 feet above the river, spanning the Mississippi from Fulton, Illinois, to Lyons, Iowa. The railroad hired several hundred men to build the road bed into Clinton County west of Lyons before the "historic bust" in 1854; however, the men went without pay other than yard goods from the company's store. The name of the L & IC RR still lives today as "The Calico Road" as evidenced by this Center Township sign. (Photograph from the Clinton County Historical Society archives.)

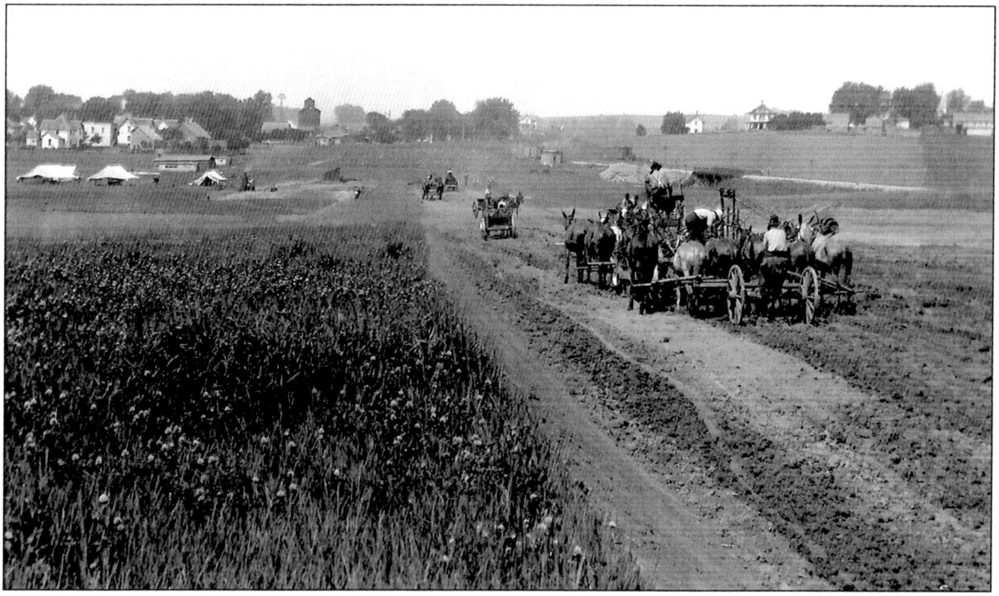

After surveying where a road was to be run, a "plow-man" would make a furrow to mark the way. Once the furrow marked the route of the proposed road, the ground was graded with horse-drawn construction equipment, as shown by the construction crew working near Lost Nation. It would be many years before travelers could count on dependable, solid roads. Needless to say, the roads were either muddy or dry and dusty for most of the year. Many early county roads followed Indian trails. This photo dates to c. 1925. (Photograph from the Clinton County Historical Society archives.)

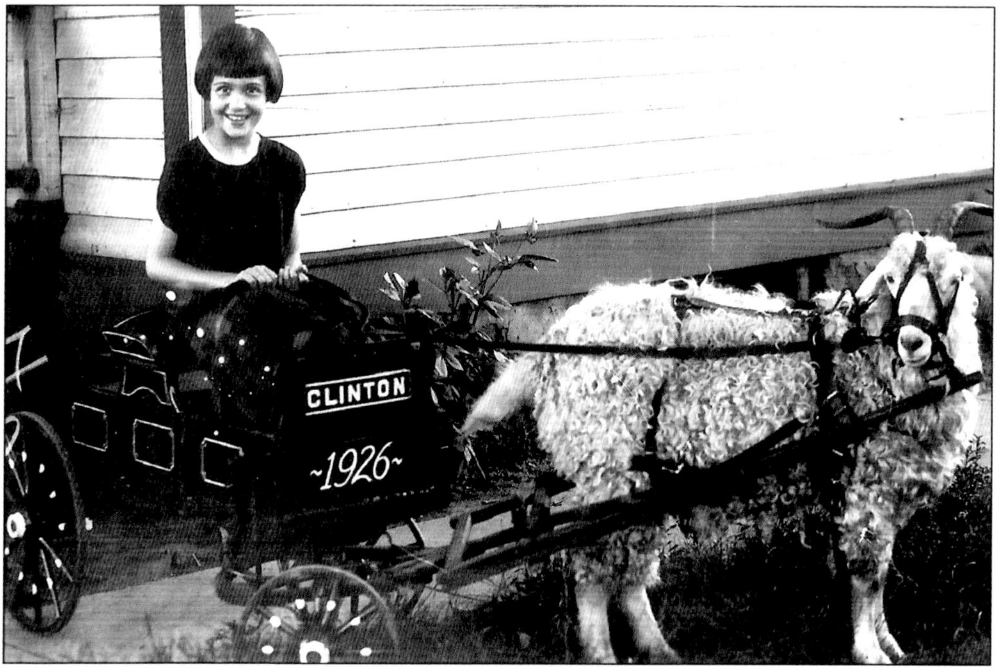

When transportation was needed, small domesticated animals were often used to pull carts and other small wagons. This young girl is shown having her picture taken in a small goat-pulled wagon. (Photograph from the Clinton County Historical Society records.)

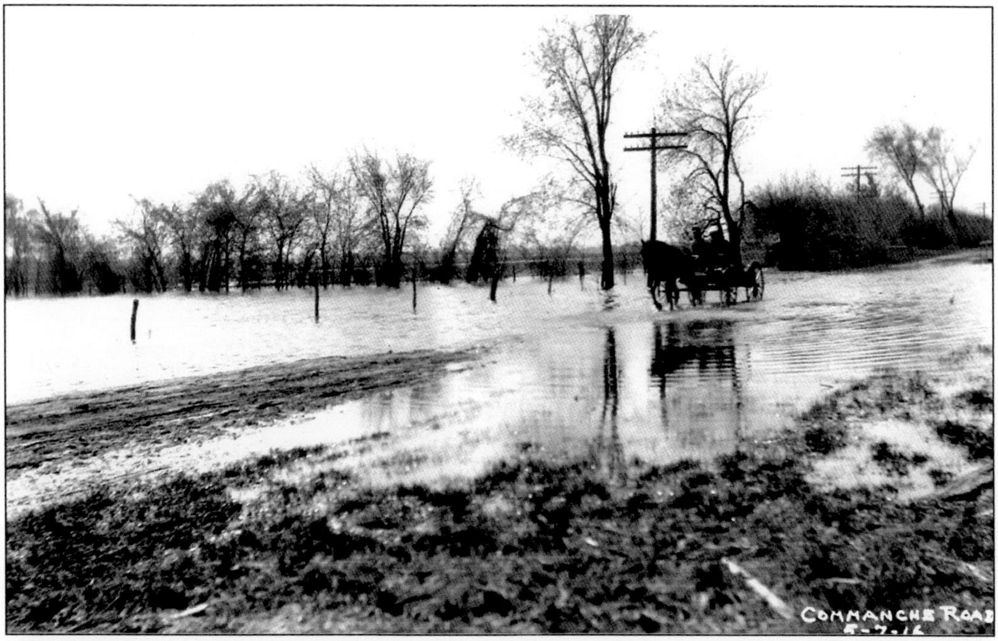

This mailman in his box-type buggy must navigate treacherous roads after the May of 1916 flood in the Camanche area. Fence posts can be seen sitting in flood waters and the water is already crossing the road. (Photograph from the Clinton County Historical Society archives.)

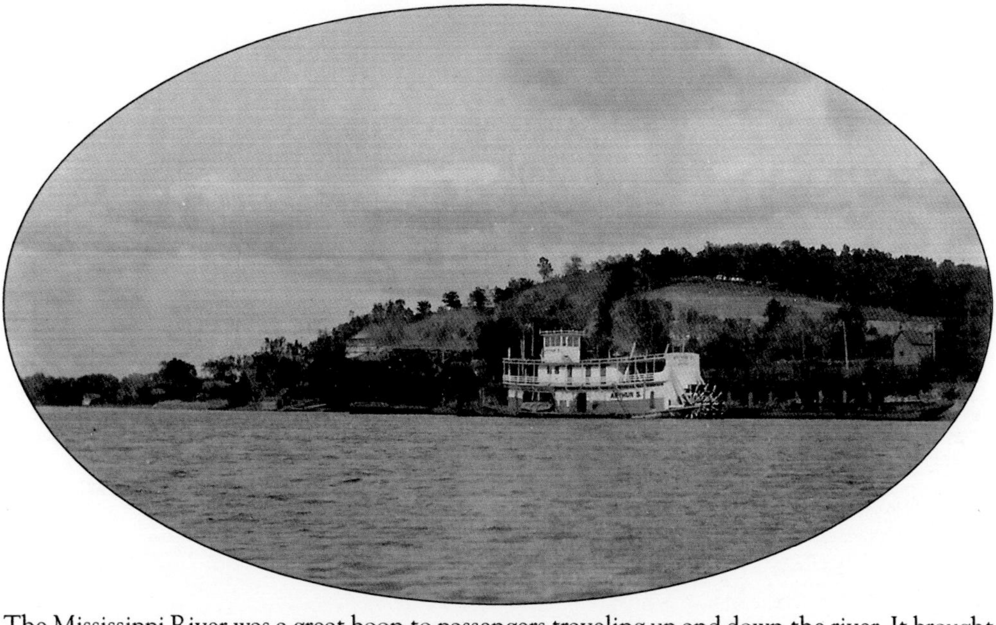

The Mississippi River was a great boon to passengers traveling up and down the river. It brought new people into the county and provided a waterway to market local products such as grain and lumber. The above photograph shows the coal dock above Lyons, Iowa. River transportation was a dangerous way to travel, as boats were destroyed by fire, by running into river objects, or through the simple changing of the channel. Experienced riverboat captains were in great demand. (Photograph from the Clinton County Historical Society archives.)

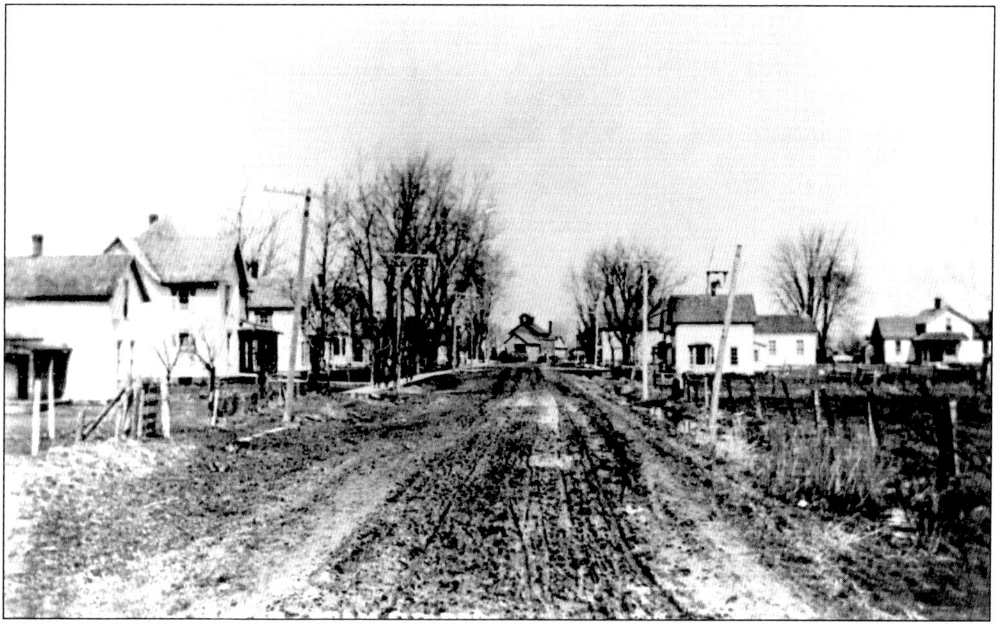

Today, most roads in the rural areas of the county are not paved and are covered with gravel, which is a huge improvement over the original dirt roads people had to contend with. Early town streets within Clinton County were also unimproved, as shown in these early photos of Welton, above, and Lost Nation, below. The mud, dust, and ruts were an everyday part of life in the spring, summer, and fall, while ice and snow were part of the scene every winter. (Photographs from the Clinton County Historical Society archives.)

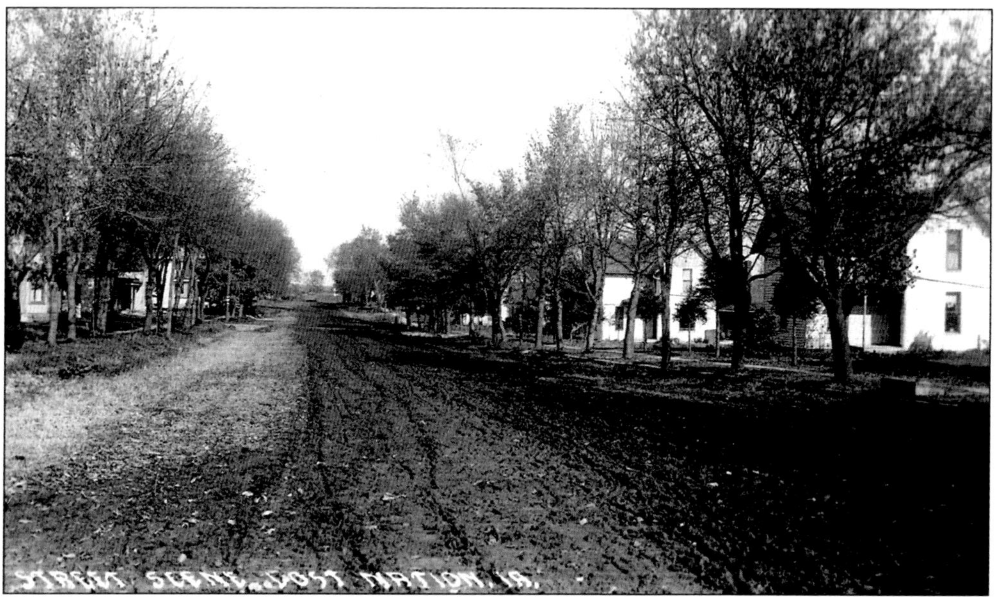

Travel by balloon has always been part of American history. The theory of using prevailing winds for travel has mesmerized the imagination of many an inventor. Mrs. Wright shows her skills with a pre-World War I balloon at an early DeWitt Fair. (Photograph from the Clinton County Historical Society archives.)

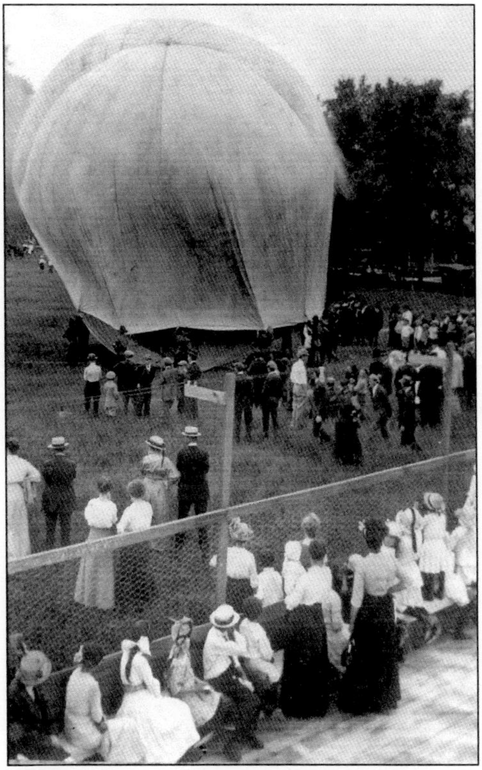

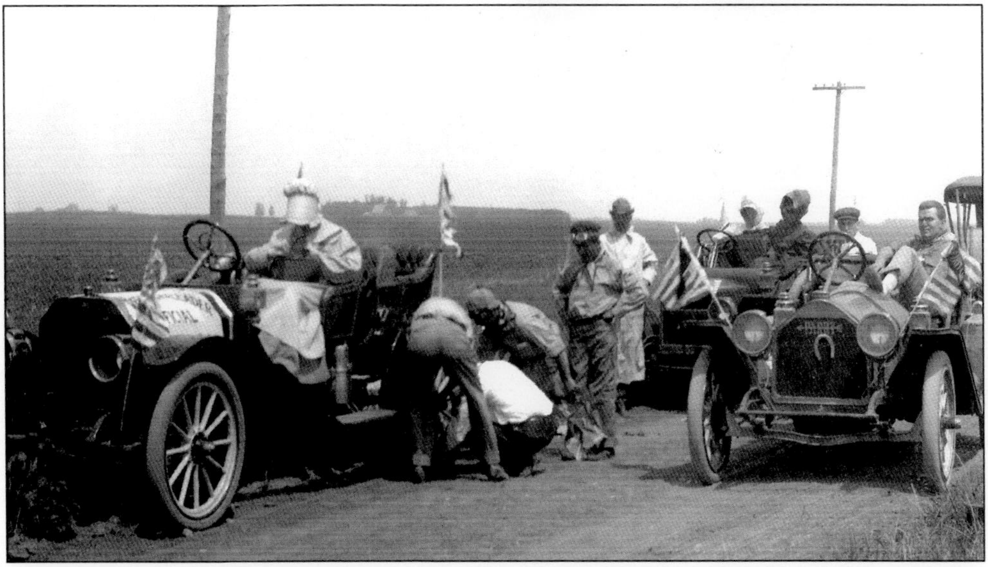

In 1908, an "Around the World" transcontinental automobile race was sponsored by the *New York Times* and the *Paris LeMatin* newspapers. The race traveled the Lincoln Highway starting in Times Square in New York and reached the west coast 170 days later. As the race progressed into Clinton County, enthusiastic crowds of people met the participants. Flat tires were a common occurrence and the local residents were more than happy to lend a hand. The winner was the American automobile, a Thomas Flyer, driven by Montague Roberts. (Photograph from the Clinton County Historical Society archives.)

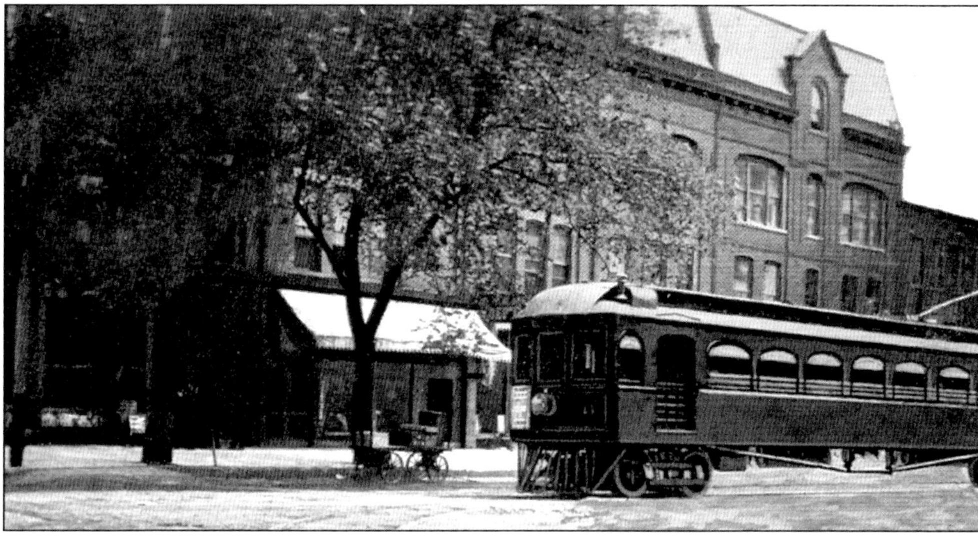

In 1904, the Illinois and Iowa Electric Railroad, known as the "I & I", began a daily run between Clinton and Scott Counties with end stops in the cities of Clinton and Davenport. While also carrying freight, the I & I did a brisk passenger business. The depot in Clinton was located at 116 Sixth Avenue South and a round trip ticket for a fairly comfortable ride in good weather was purchased for $1.20. The I & I was also the means of public transportation within Clinton County, stopping daily in Camanche, Shafton, and the Wapsie. Service on the I & I ended on March 31, 1940. (Photograph from the Clinton County Historical Society archives.)

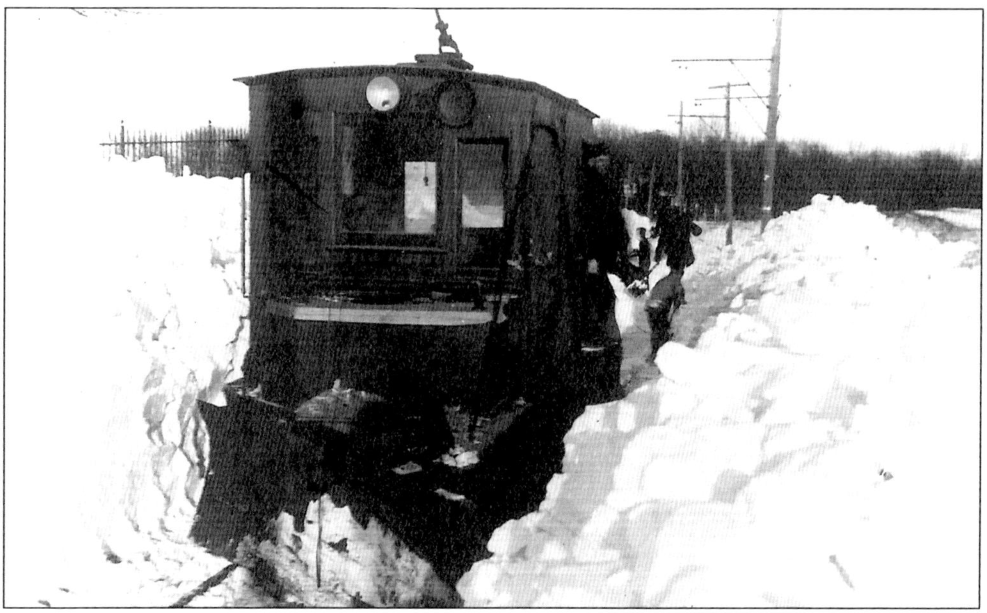

Power for the I & I was provided by a powerhouse located near Mill Creek which has since been razed. The all-electric railroad ran with their power line extended above the tracks and was fairly reliable most of the time. However, it required many man-hours during winter to keep the tracks clear of drifting and blowing snow. It was so successful that Muscatine was later added to the run. At that time, the name was changed to the CD & M Railway. (Photograph from the Clinton County Historical Society archives.)

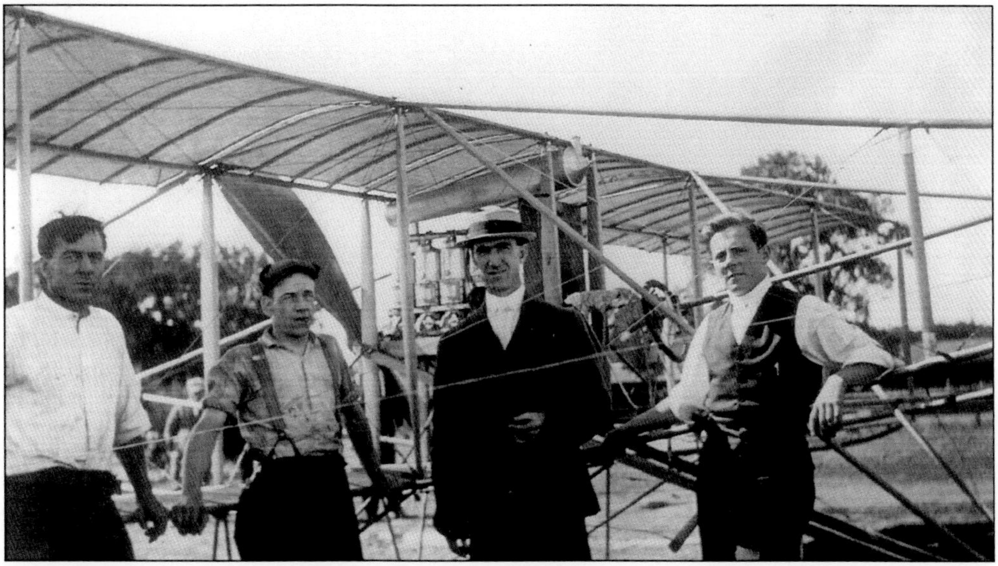

In September of 1911, the DeWitt Fair sponsored an air show of the first airplanes in Iowa. Large crowds gathered to view these modern wonders when Louis Rosenbaum, shown on the right, flew his plane from Indiana to DeWitt. Mr. Rosenbaum took off in his plane and landed and then took off again. Then, while trying to land a second time, he landed upside down and lost his life, thereby entering the history of the state as the first aviation fatality in Iowa. (Photograph from the Clinton County Historical Society archives.)

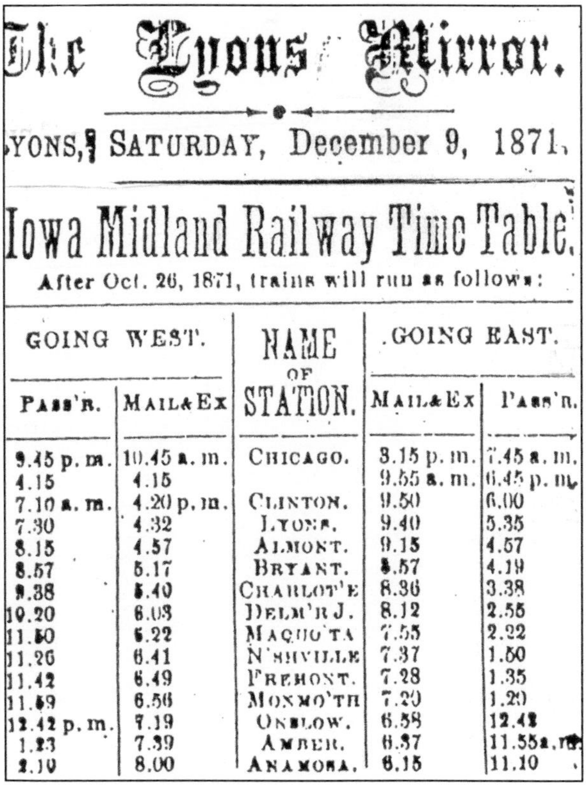

The Lyons Mirror.

LYONS, SATURDAY, December 9, 1871.

Iowa Midland Railway Time Table.

After Oct. 26, 1871, trains will run as follows:

GOING WEST.		NAME OF STATION.	GOING EAST.	
PASS'R.	MAIL&EX		MAIL&EX	PASS'R.
9.45 p. m.	10.45 a. m.	CHICAGO.	3.15 p. m.	7.45 a. m.
4.15	4.15		9.55 a. m.	6.45 p. m.
7.10 a. m.	4.20 p. m.	CLINTON.	9.50	6.00
7.30	4.32	LYONS.	9.40	5.35
8.15	4.57	ALMONT.	9.15	4.57
8.57	5.17	BRYANT.	8.57	4.19
9.38	5.40	CHARLOT'E	8.36	3.38
10.20	6.03	DELM'R J.	8.12	2.55
11.50	6.22	MAQUO'TA	7.55	2.22
11.26	6.41	N'SHVILLE	7.37	1.50
11.42	6.49	FREMONT.	7.28	1.35
11.59	6.56	MONMO'TH	7.20	1.20
12.42 p. m.	7.19	ONSLOW.	6.58	12.42
1.23	7.39	AMBER.	6.37	11.55 a. m.
2.10	8.00	ANAMOSA.	6.15	11.10

The Iowa Midland Railroad was organized in October of 1870 and was in existence until 1950. The line started in Clinton and ran north through Lyons, moving onward to Midland Junction where it turned west and traveled through Almont, Bryant, Goose Lake, Charlotte, Delmar, and then again northward to Maquoketa. A triangle was formed at Midland Junction where the Iowa Midland Railroad met the Sabula-Ackley Railroad, which had also been incorporated in 1870, and ran from Sabula through Preston, Delmar, Elwood, and Lost Nation. Clinton County residents were then able to travel more freely than ever before. (Photograph from the Clinton County Historical Society archives.)

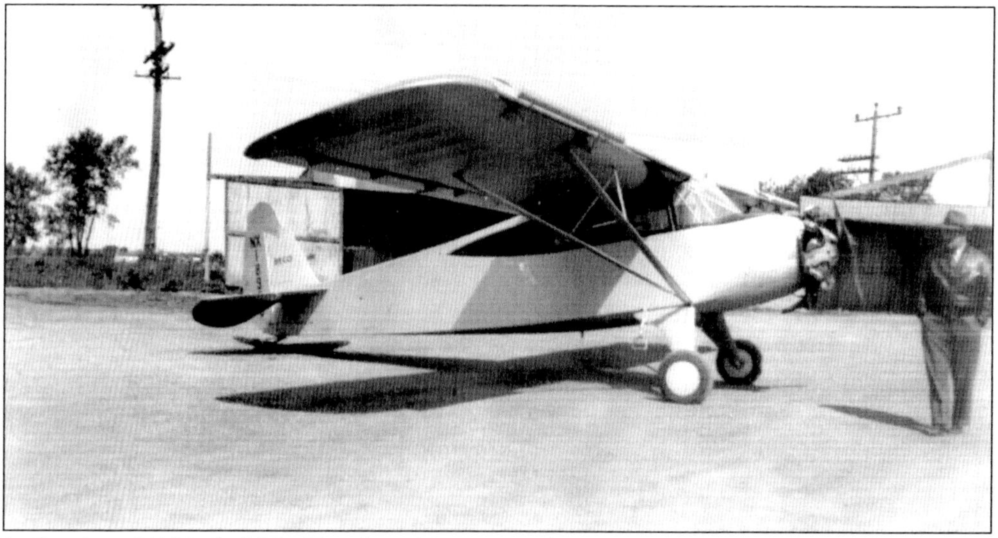

In October of 1928, the U.S. Chamber of Commerce designated this Camanche farm field—then owned by Wallace Lum, west of the roller rink—as an auxiliary airfield. This particular field was on a direct airmail route from Chicago to Omaha. A rotating beam was built and installed and the airplanes would fly in over the C & NW tracks and out over Rosehill cemetery. The airfield was decommissioned in 1934 and in 1939 was established as a private airfield. During World War II, the airfield was permanently closed. The hangars, which were two boxcars in the form of a 'T', had housed six to eight aircraft belonging local pilots. M.J. Nichols was one of the local pilots who used this airport and Lt. Stuart Towle was known to fly home in an Army biplane and use the Camanche airport. (Photograph courtesy of David Nichols.)

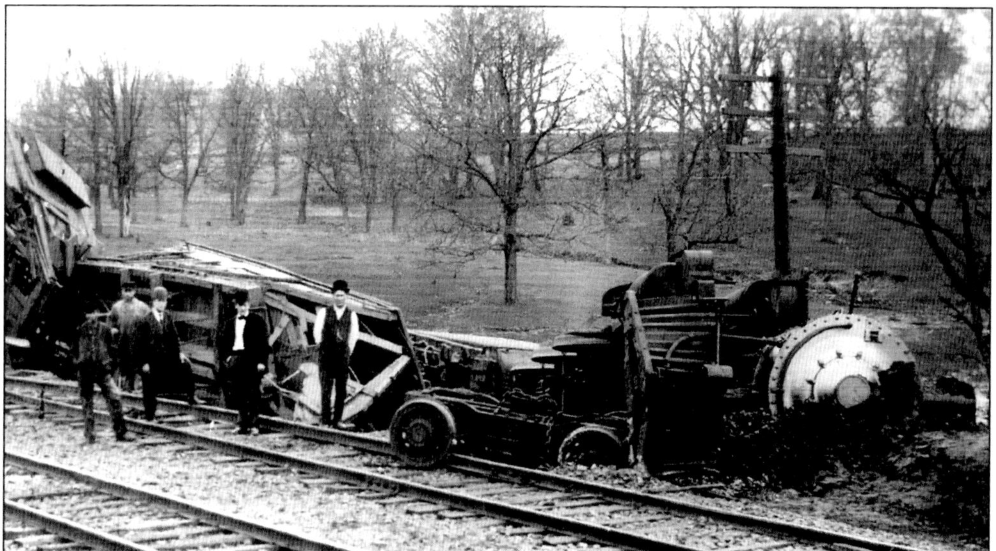

When the east wall of the railroad bridge west of DeWitt near Crystal Lake washed out on April 23, 1908, 26 loads of livestock in wooden rail cars were involved in the resulting C & NW train wreck. The engine, which weighed some 450,000 pounds, required two wreckers to set it back upright. Scores of people came to view the wreckage on that cool April day. (Photograph from the Clinton County Historical Society archives.)

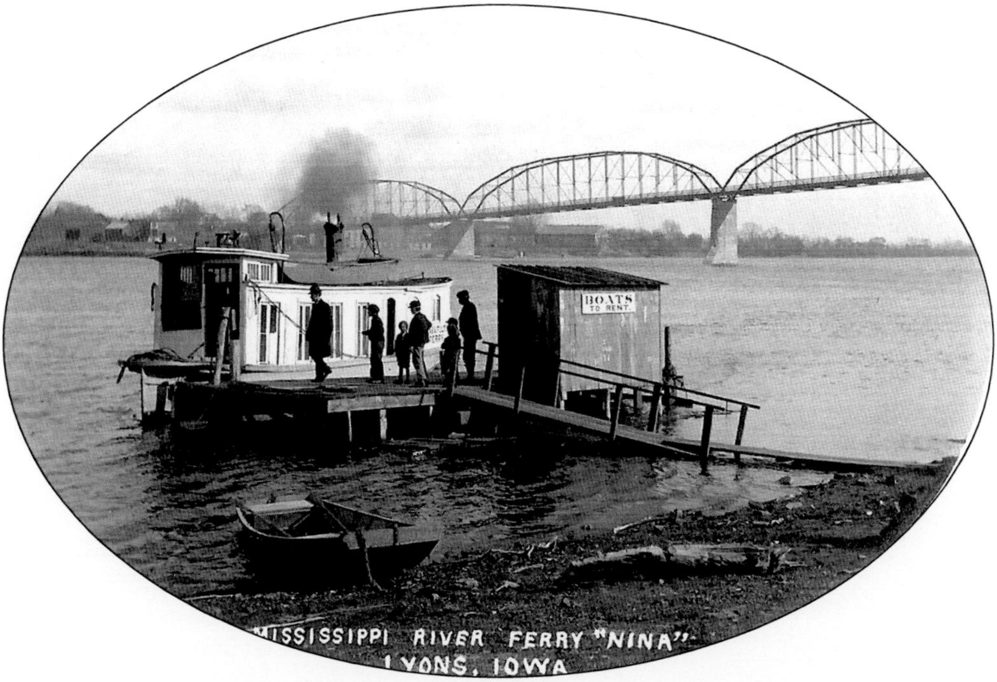

Ferry boats are still used today to cross various bodies of water. This 1890 photograph shows the Ferry *Nina* transporting people and goods across the Mississippi River between Fulton, Illinois, and Lyons, Iowa. The sign on the building offers "Boats To Rent." (Photograph from the Clinton County Historical Society archives.)

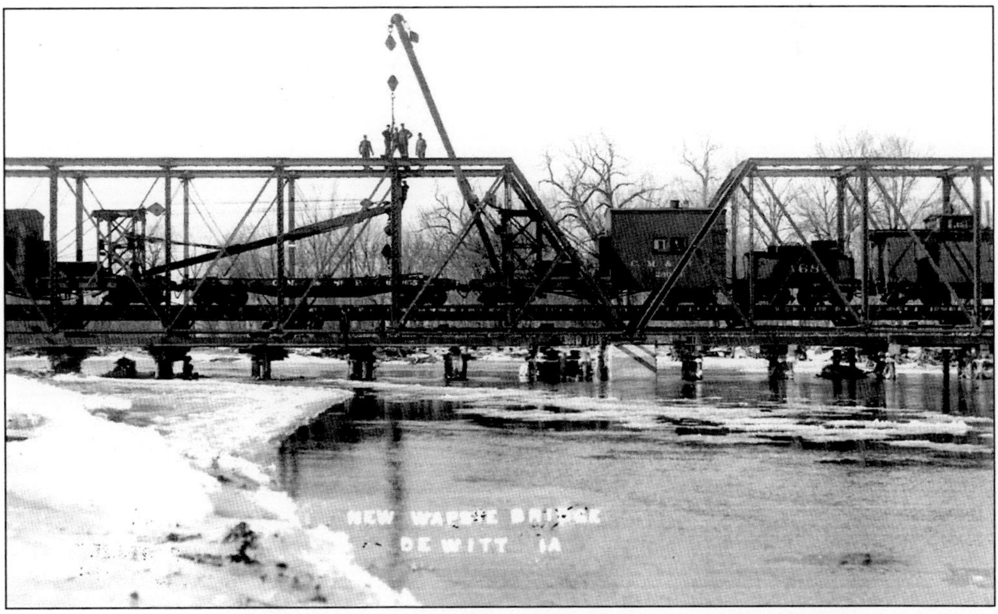

The Milwaukee Railroad Bridge across the Wapsipinicon River, south of DeWitt, was almost complete by the time this picture was taken in 1908. Cranes were lifting the spans from the flat car and putting them into place. Note the old caboose with the cupola on top on the right. (Photograph from the Clinton County Historical Society archives.)

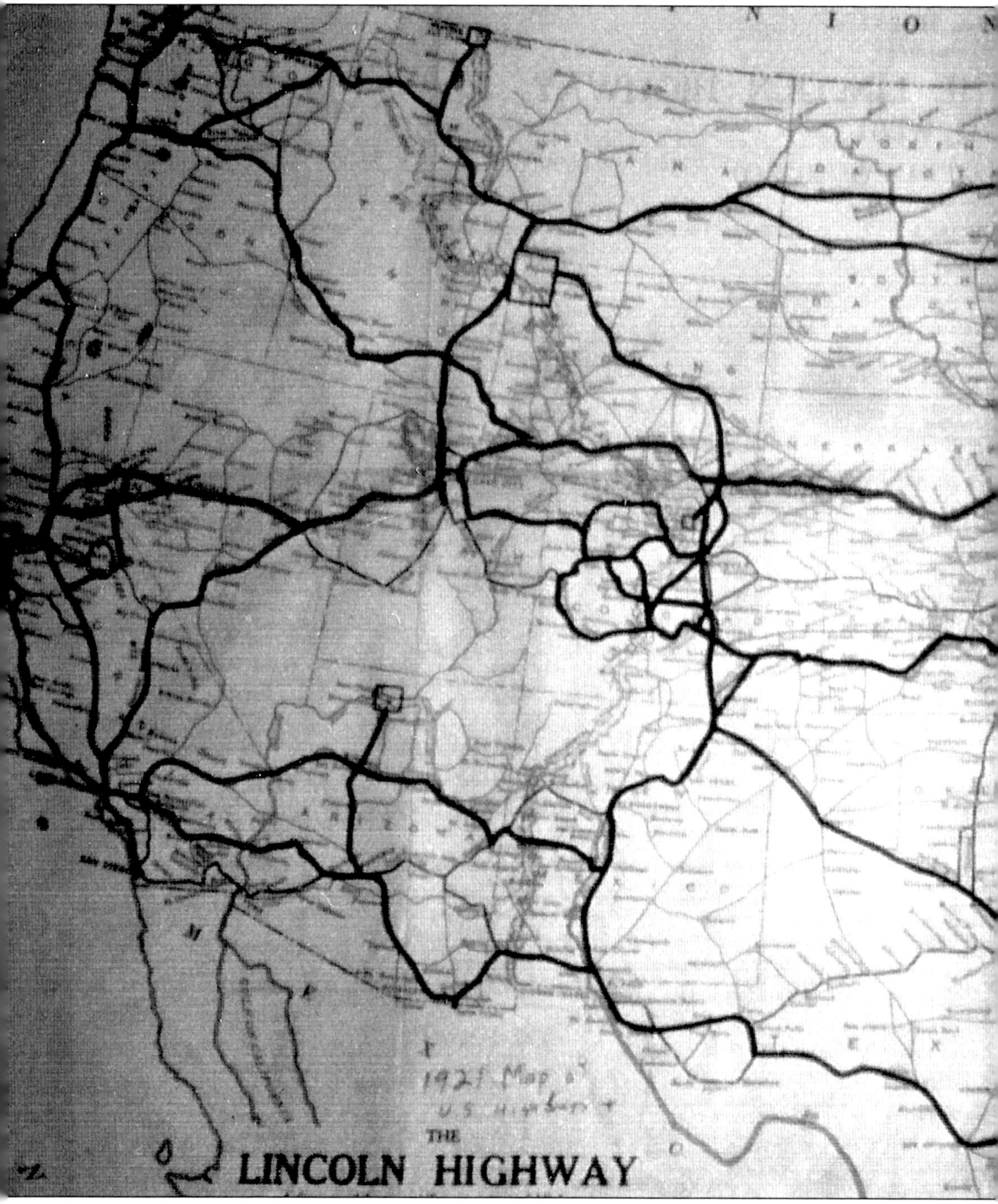

When a group of people met in New Jersey and decided that a highway should be built across America, they decided to call it the Lincoln Highway. By 1912, they began to collect pledges for construction costs. In all, $10 million was raised. However, the men involved soon discovered they needed help from different sources, and it was then decided to follow the existing Highway 30. Different cities tried to influence the direction of the road, but a path directly west prevailed. A great deal of the original road was nothing more than a good cow path; however,

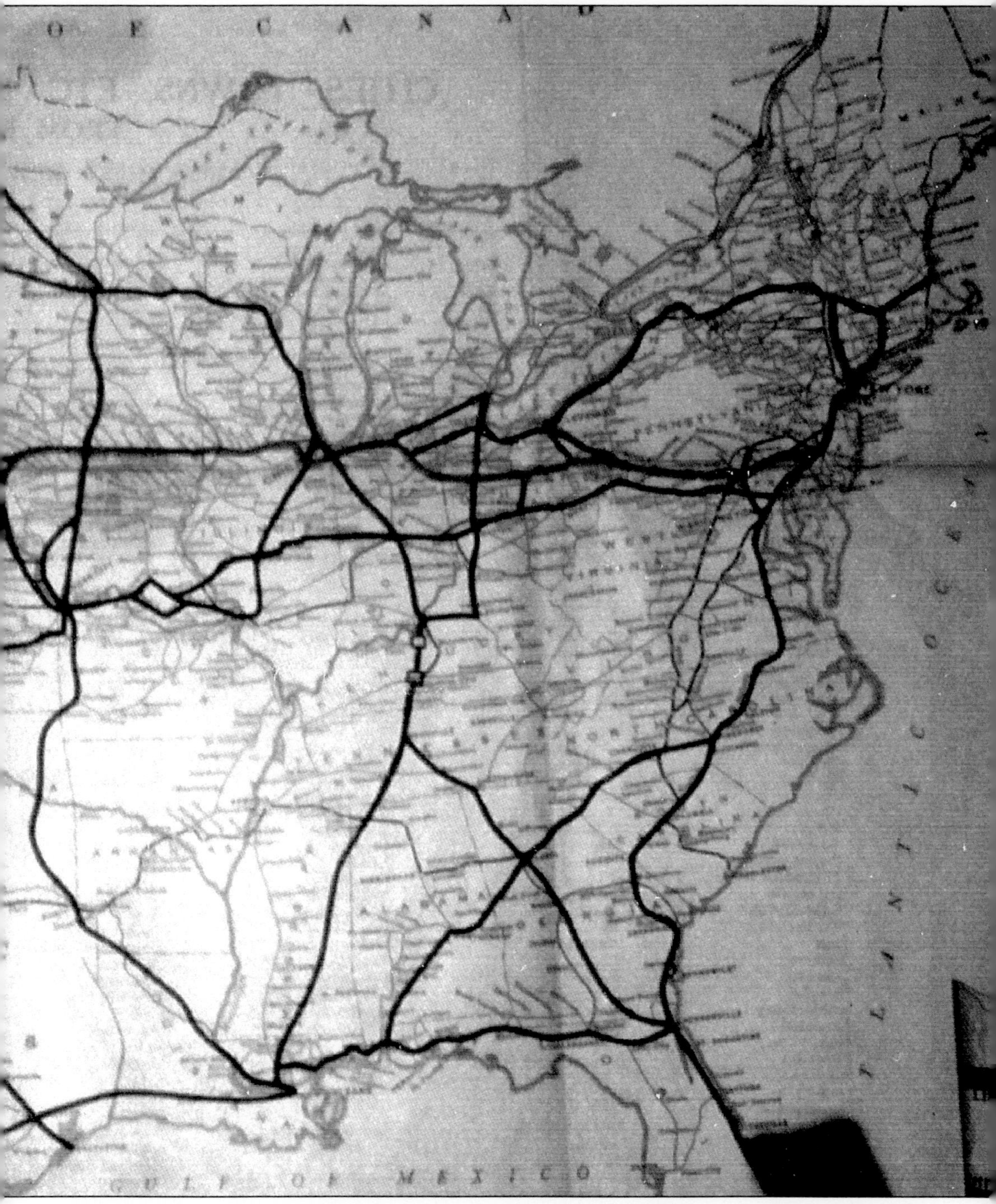

the sense of determination prevailed and the road reached San Francisco in 1915. The biggest task of all was to then upgrade the highway section by section. Clinton County was one of the first sections to be paved. The funds were donated and it was officially finished in 1928. Local Boy Scouts put up the cement mile marker posts which proclaimed the Lincoln Highway as the first trans-continental highway across the United States. (Photograph from the Clinton County Historical Society archives.)

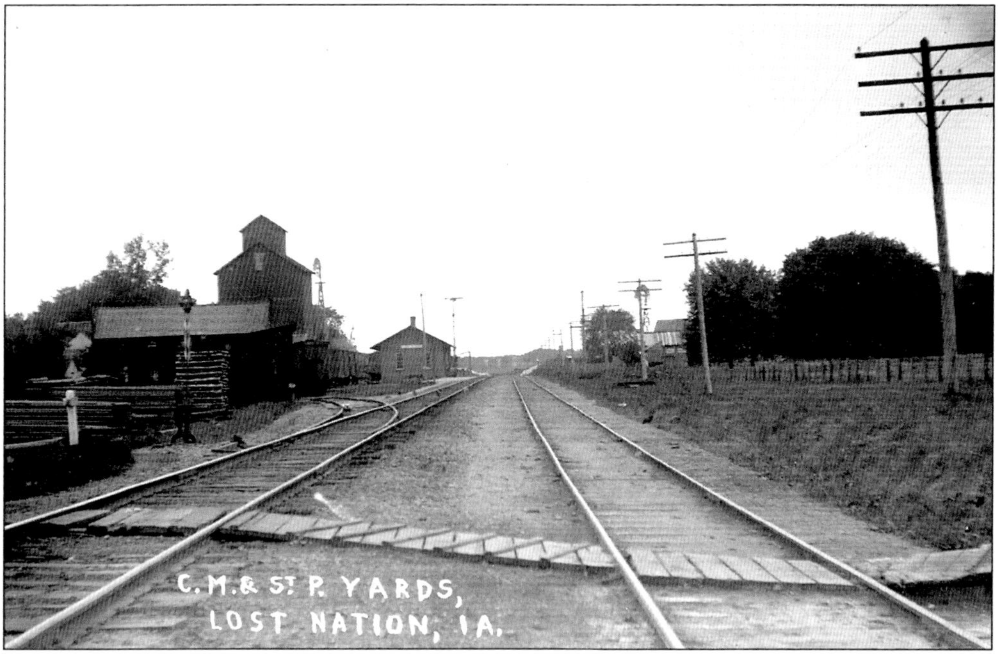

The Chicago, Milwaukee and St. Paul rail yards in Lost Nation are shown here with the depot in the background in the early 1900s. This was a double-track east–west route which allowed the farmers to move their produce away from their home market and eventually access the Mississippi River for larger markets. (Photograph from the Clinton County Historical Society archives.)

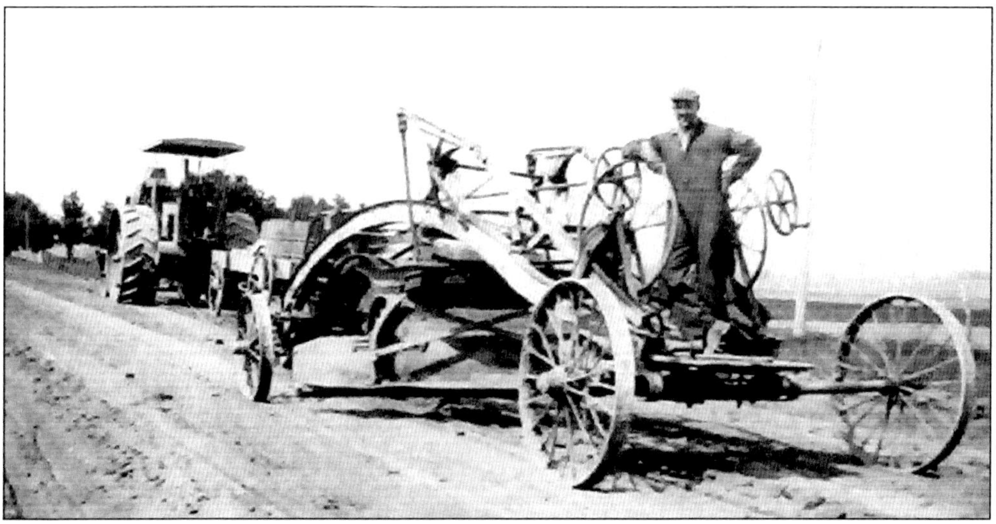

The first mechanized grading outfit in Clinton County was the 30–60 Rumley tractor and pull-type Austin Western grader shown here. Grover Drummond stands on the unit on the north-south road one mile west of Petersville. The photograph was taken by Leslie Drummond. (Photograph from the Clinton County Historical Society archives.)

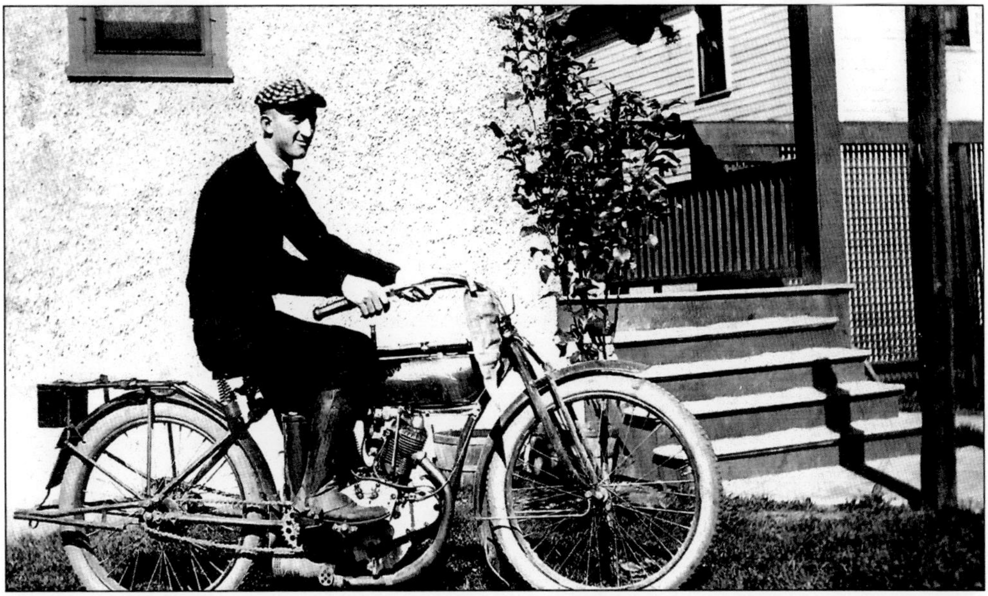

The "Indian" model motorcycle was a popular mode of transportation in the 1910s and 1920s. The use of the motorcycle became almost a necessity during World War I, and the "Indian" motorcycle was one of the main models used. In some towns, police patrolled the streets on "Indians." From the information available in our archives, we believe this "Indian" is being ridden by Louis Bassler. (Photograph from the Clinton County Historical Society archives.)

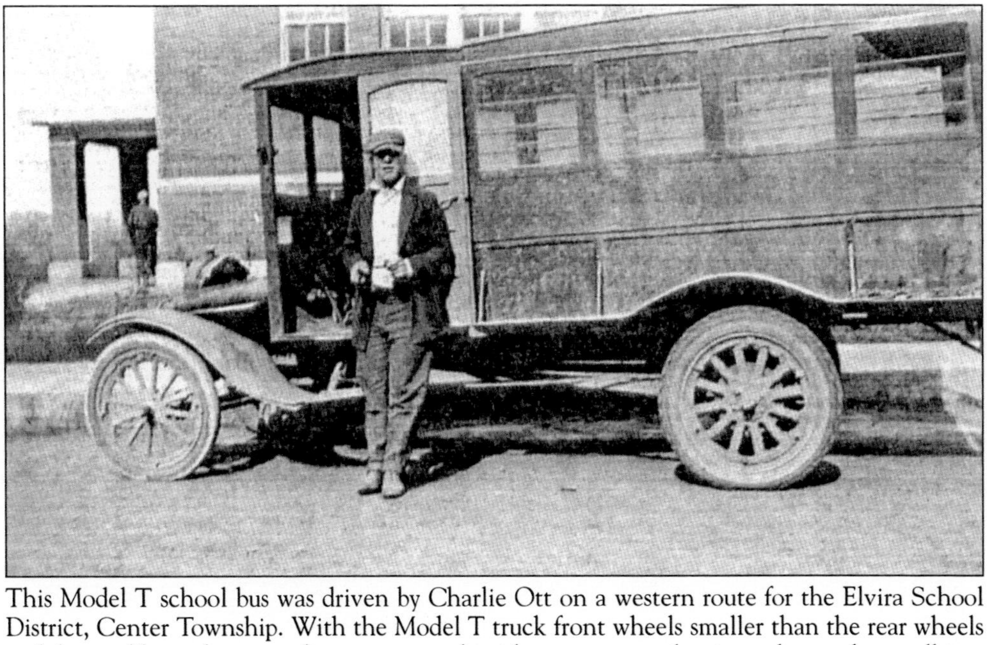

This Model T school bus was driven by Charlie Ott on a western route for the Elvira School District, Center Township. With the Model T truck front wheels smaller than the rear wheels and the muddy roads to travel, one assumes the ride was not easy, but it was better than walking. (Photograph courtesy of Marian Paasch.)

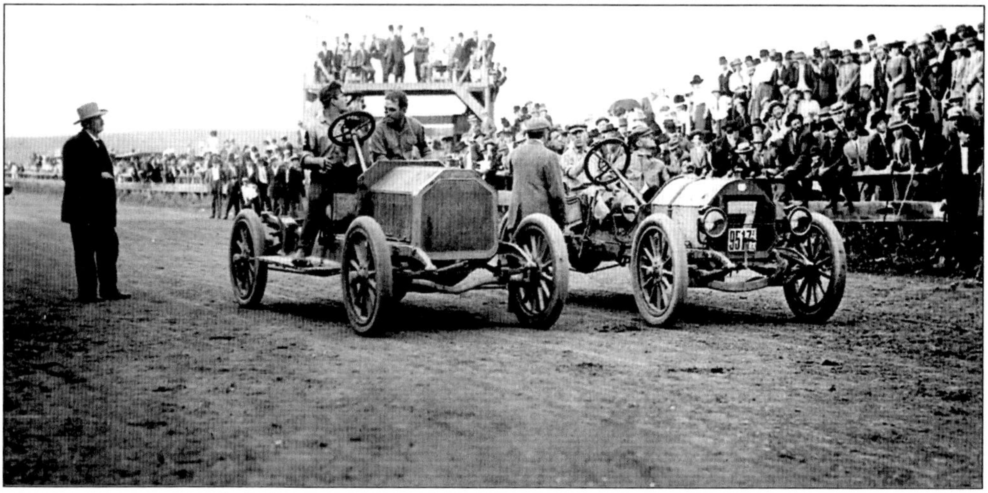

The DeWitt Fair included auto races in their 1911 calendar of events. F.W. Kent of Iowa City captures the intense excitement, as it is obvious the spectators are anxiously waiting to see the results of the race. (Photograph from the Clinton County Historical Society archives.)

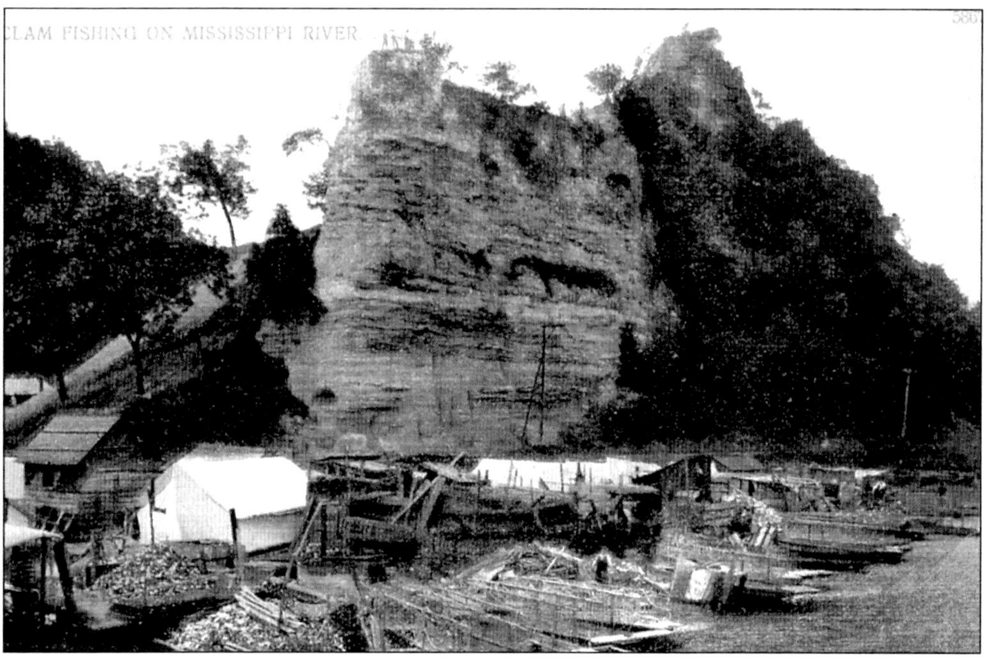

The Mississippi River clamming industry was of vital importance to early Clinton County settlers. The clamming grounds ran from the Jackson County border to the Scott County border and provided employment for many people. This photograph shows piles of clams waiting for the packet boats to transport them to the factories where buttons and jewelry were made of the shells and the meat was used for livestock feed. (Photograph from the Clinton County Historical Society archives.)

Eight
Schools

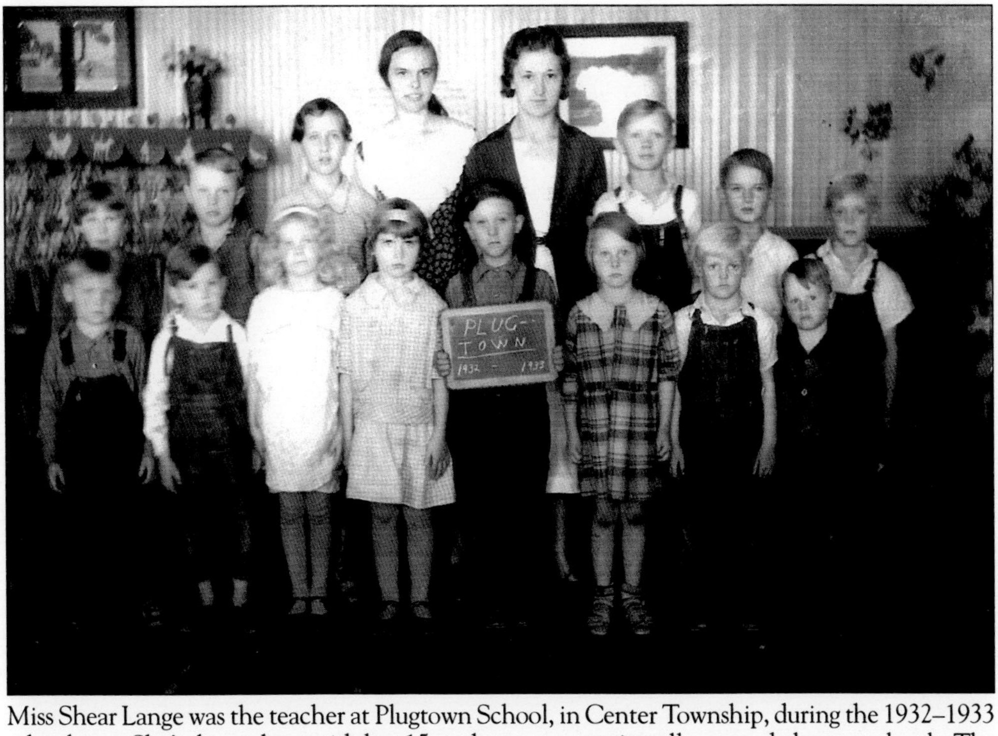

Miss Shear Lange was the teacher at Plugtown School, in Center Township, during the 1932–1933 school year. She's shown here with her 15 students representing all ages and classroom levels. The school is long gone and the little village of Plugtown no longer exists. The town got its name from the practice of the local farmers who came to the grocery store once a week to purchase a plug of tobacco. (Photograph from the Clinton County Historical Society archives.)

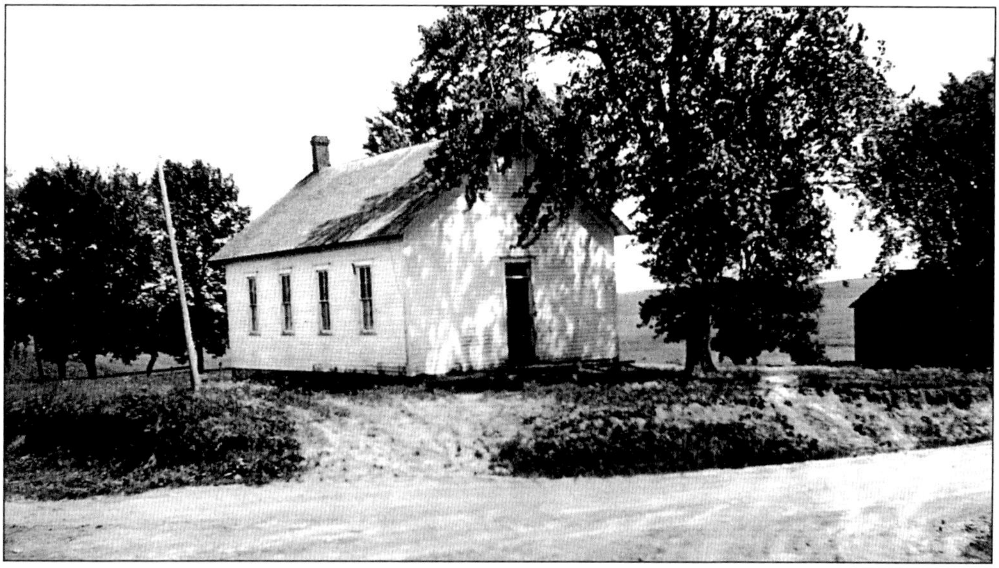

The German Valley School, located three miles east of Lost Nation in Brookfield Township, was established around 1865. This clapboard building is actually the second school built on the site, and was constructed around 1900 when the original structure was outgrown by an expanding population in the area. Some of the German families who sent their children to the school were Behrens, Teskeys, Schepers, Ruggebergs, Kramers, Dalchows, Adrains, Hohns, and Schoenthalers. (Photograph from the Clinton County Historical Society archives.)

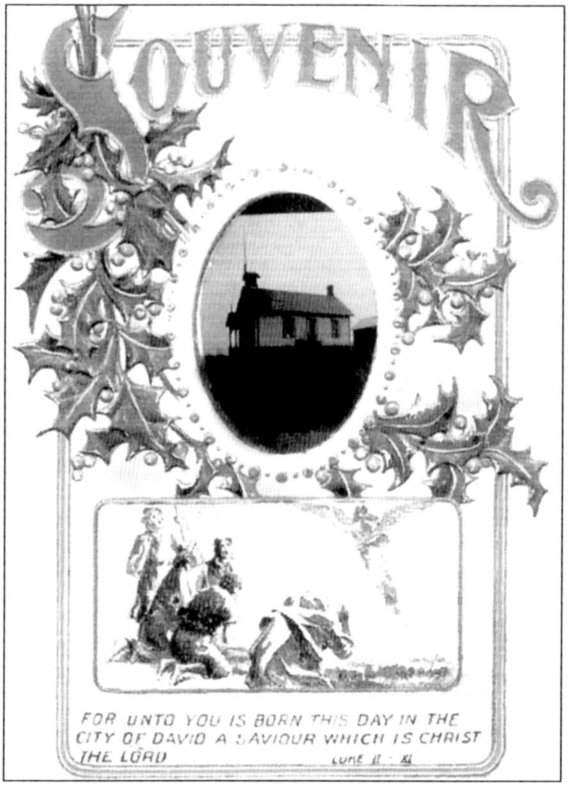

The District #4 Galbraith School, located in Lincoln Township, hosted a Christmas celebration in 1904. The cover of the program displays the only known picture of the school. Inside, the program lists the teacher as Pearl E. Lambertson, Henry Galbraith as school district president, Elmer Traver as secretary and 25 students are listed as pupils. (Photograph courtesy of Mike and Deanna Galbraith.)

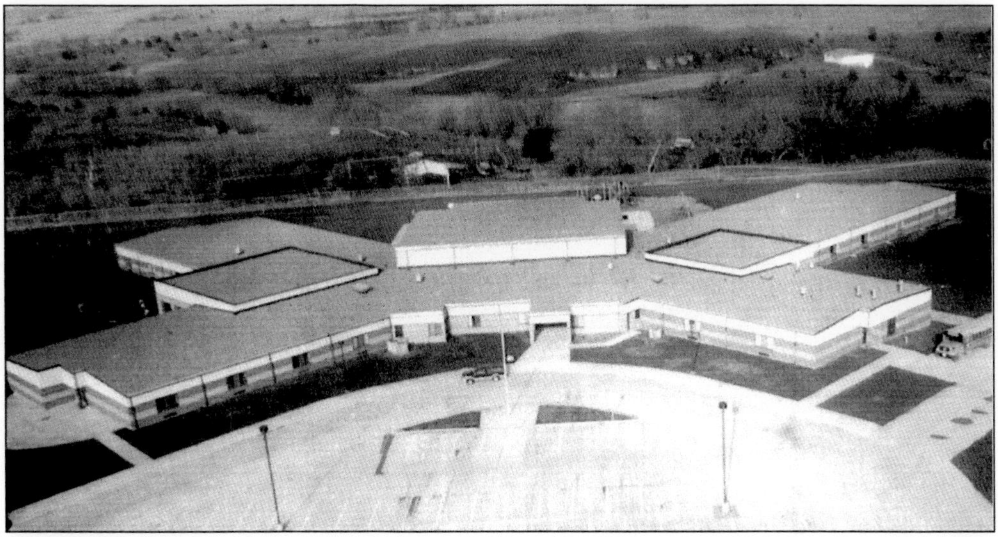

The Northeast Community School District was formed July 1, 1961. It is comprised of five small communities and covers an area of 178 square miles. The communities include Charlotte, Goose Lake, Andover, Bryant, and Elvira. The elementary school, shown above, was built from 1995 to 1997 and its dedication was held on August 10, 1997. (Photograph courtesy of Patsy Farrell.)

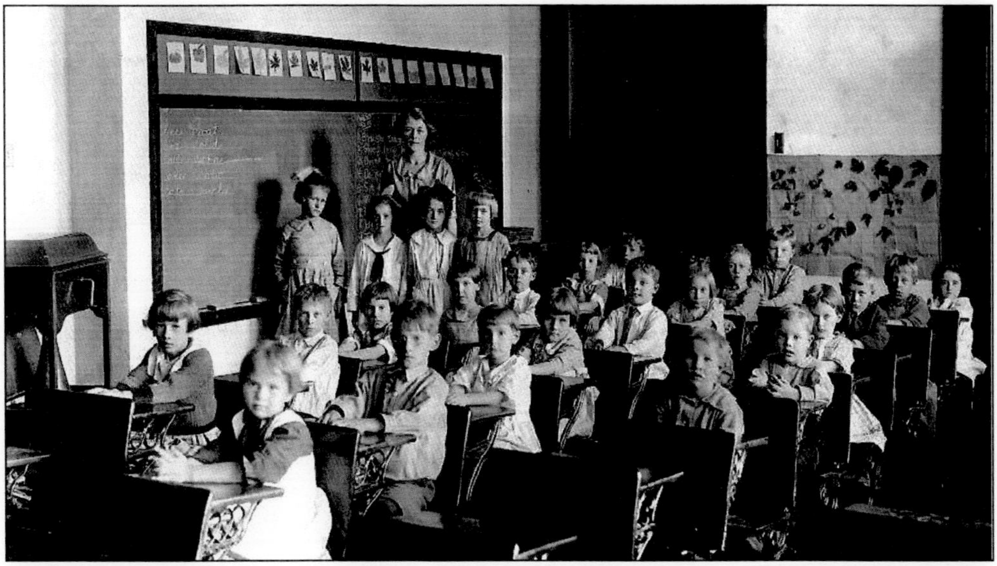

When the rural schools of Elvira, Cener Township, consolidated, a new brick schoolhouse was built in 1920 and opened in 1921. It was closed for a time during the 1922 school year due to a diphtheria epidemic. The school building still stands today; however, it is not used as a school and is owned privately. The 1922–1923 first and second grades are pictured from left to right: (first row) Herbert Steen, Unknown, Helen Ingwersen, Clarence Cousins, Maurice Camp, and Blanche McDevitt; (second row) Adaline Benson, LeRoy Wilden, Frieda Schroeder, Lucille Dannatt, Unknown, Jeanette Thompson, Harold Goddard, and Herman Meyer; (third row) Dorothy Schroeder, George Fatchett, Leona Wilden, Lois Seamer, Paul McDevitt, Hazel Wilden, and Wilmer Mess; (standing) Margaret Mickelbust Lange, Teacher; with Vera Mommsen, unknown, unknown, and Lucille Goers. (Photograph courtesy of Marian Paasch.)

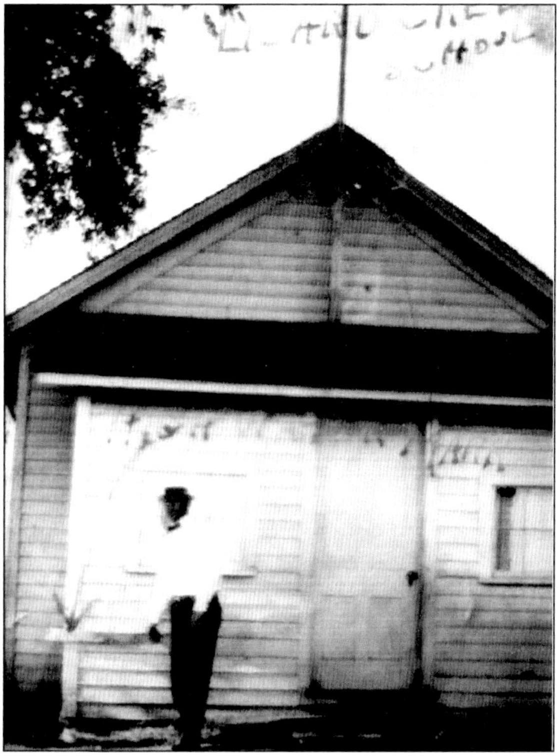

Lizard Creek School in Spring Rock Township, located on the Homrighausen farm, was built in the 1890s. The Davisson School was located about three miles away and Don Hamdorf, museum volunteer, remembers students holding basketball games between the two schools. Of course, all games were played outdoors and the schools were about even in the number of games won. The pupils took turns carrying water from the neighbors to the school while hauling coal and wood from the shed out back. After the area flooded and the school floated down Lizard Creek during one particular rainy season, it was decided that a furnace would be installed when the school was re-set of its foundation. The school closed in the 1940s and the abandoned building was soon leveled. (Photograph courtesy of Kermit Ketelsen.)

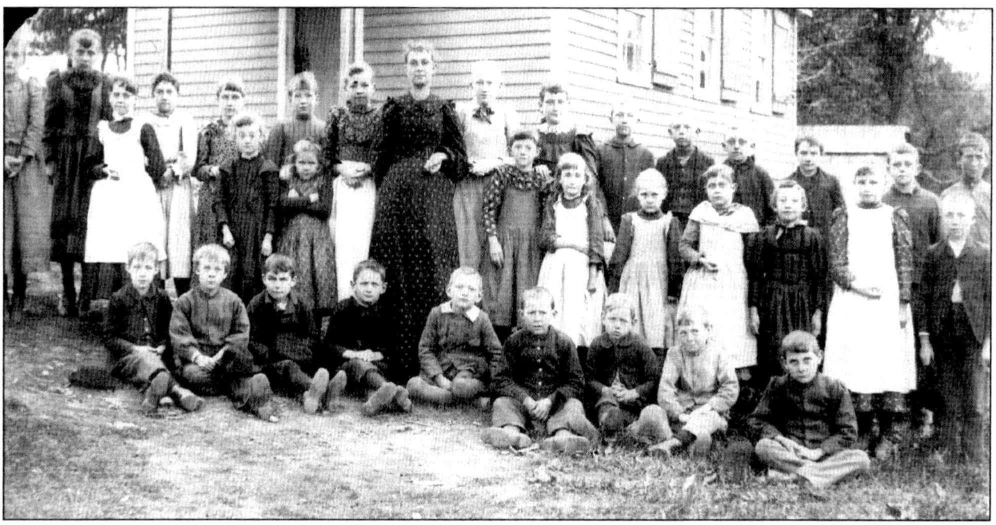

There were so many Determans in Hampshire Township that one entire area of the township became known as "The Determan Settlement." Clemens Determan donated an acre of land for a school, which would be a Catholic German school, and would be known as The Determan Settlement School. It was to be a branch of the St. Boniface Catholic Church in Lyons, Iowa, and German language and religion classes were required. The first teacher was a man; however, female teachers who could read and speak German were later hired. Josie Krogman taught at the school from 1914 through 1918. Shortly after that, the school was closed and the acre of land went back to the farm. Today, there is no trace of the settlement or the school. (Photograph courtesy of Nadine Claseman Krogman.)

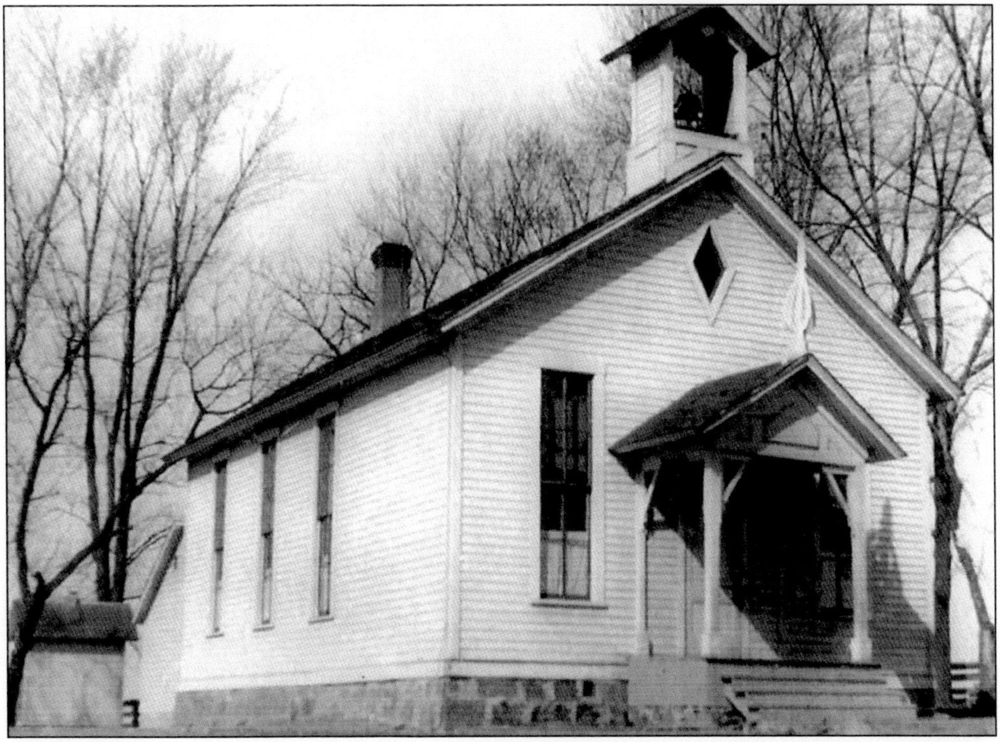

The little settlement of Bryant in Deep Creek Township had its own school from 1878 until 1958. When the school closed in 1958, the students went to Northeast Community School in Goose Lake, Iowa. The shed behind the school, shown in the photograph above, was used to store the firewood to provide heat during winter months. In 1927, a basement was built under the school. On July 30, 1964, the abandoned school building was sold to Mike and Deanna Galbraith who remodeled it into a two-story home, pictured below. (Photographs courtesy of Mike and Deanna Galbraith.)

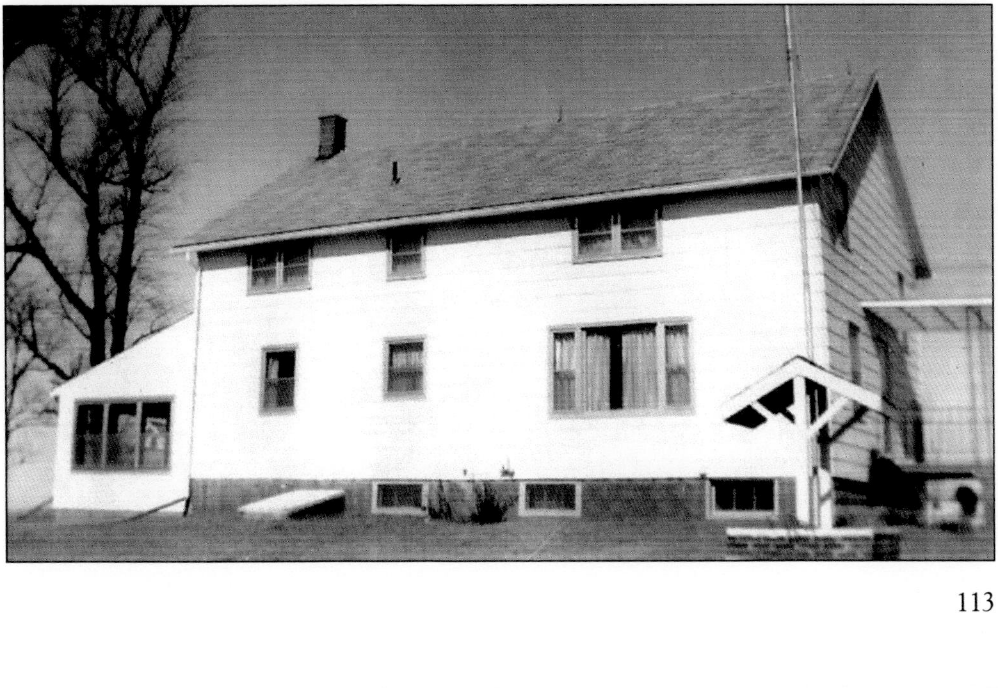

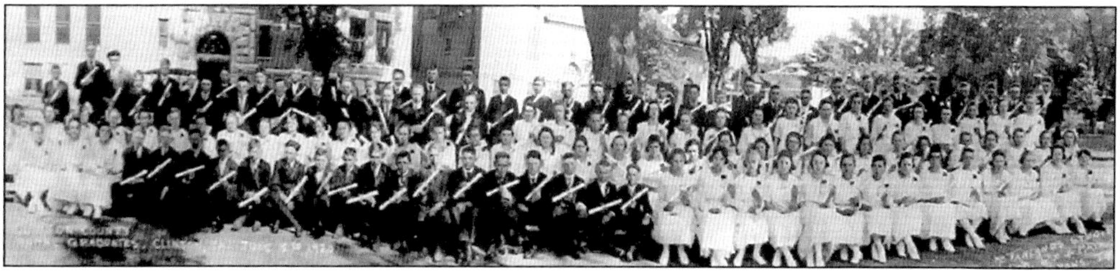

Until the 1930s, all eighth grade pupils of Clinton County rural schools were brought into the Clinton County Courthouse in Clinton each year in early May to take their final examinations. The grades were then sent back to their various teachers who then determined which students would graduate. At the end of May or early June, the graduating students would return to the courthouse to receive their diplomas before having a group picture taken. The young ladies dressed in starched white dresses and the young men wore suits and ties for the ceremony. (Photograph from the Clinton County Historical Society archives.)

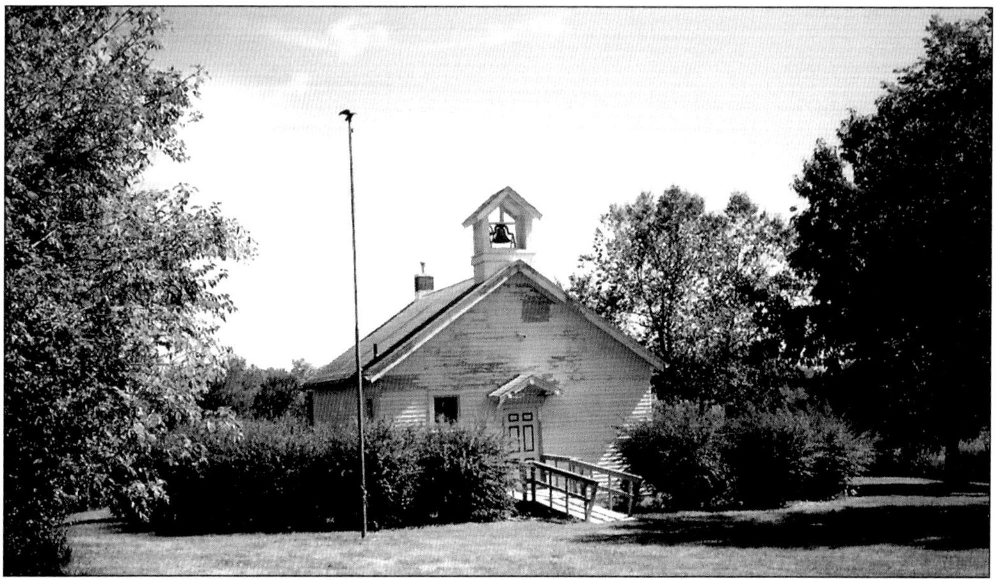

Flannery School was built in 1935 north of DeWitt. It was the last rural school in Clinton County in repairable condition when it was relocated to the Soaring Eagles Nature Center on the edge of Eagle Point Park in Clinton in 1975. Today, the school is being restored and is open to the public. School children visit the school for classes to show them "how it used to be." (Photograph from the Clinton County Historical Society archives.)

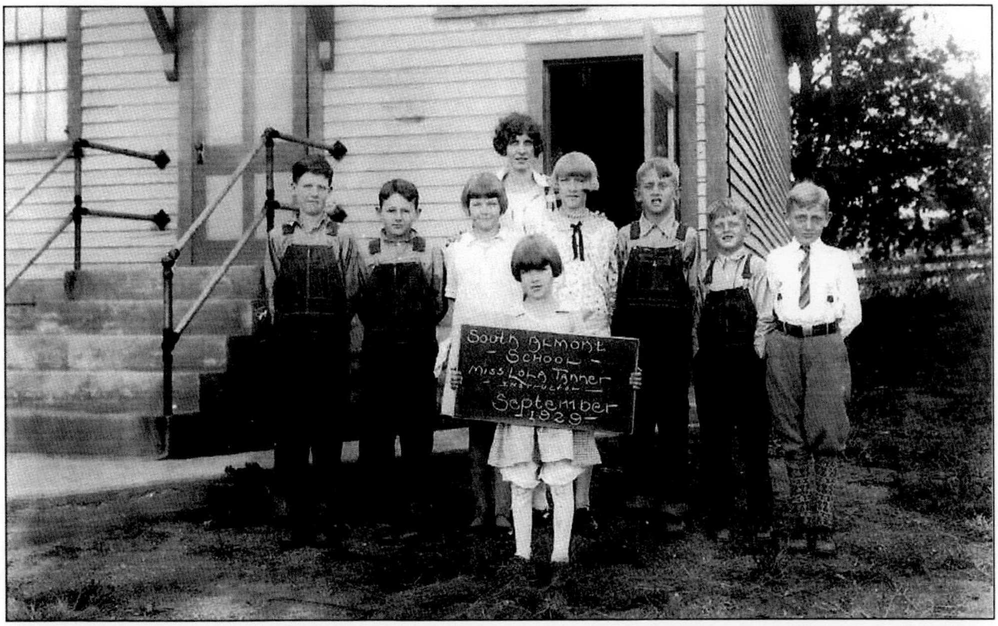

The South Almont School #9 was located one mile south of Almont in Elk River Township. This photograph shows the students attending that school in 1929. John L. Wilson, a well-respected farmer who served in both the State of Iowa General Assembly and Senate from the 25th to the 33rd sessions, attended the school as a child. Four generations of the Wilson family attended the South Almont School—John's son, Charles Mathew Wilson, John's granddaughter, Ione Wilson Rickoff, and John's great-granddaughter, Jane Anne Rickoff Koons. (Photograph courtesy of Ione Wilson Rickoff.)

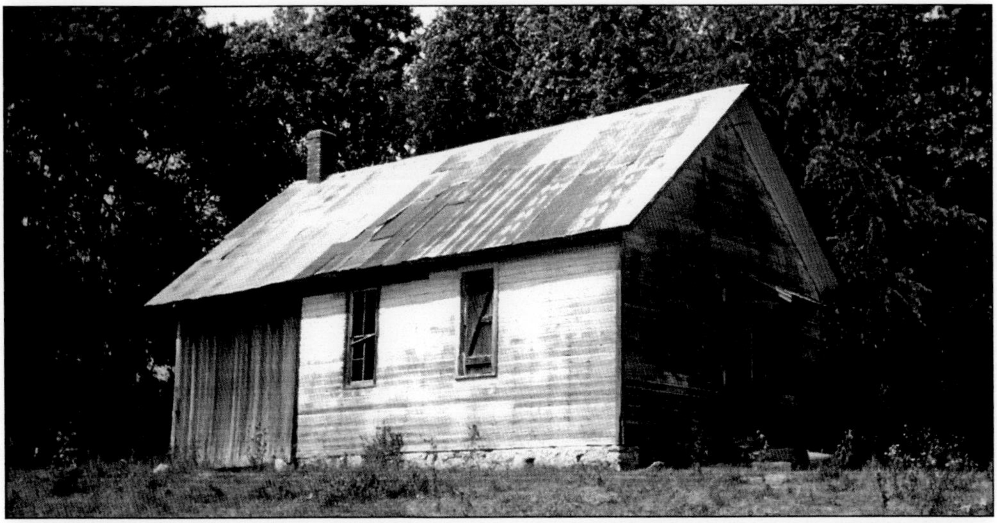

The old Waterford Township #5 school, built in the 1870s and closed in 1962–1963, is located on John Camp's farm in rural Charlotte. Along with the right of way to the train lines, this is all that remains of the village of Riggs Station. The village grew as a result of the Chicago, Milwaukee and St. Paul railroad laying tracks through the area. At one time, Riggs Station bustled with a depot, school, post office, and stock yards. Today, the school alone stands to remind the world of the memories there. (Photograph courtesy of the John Camp family.)

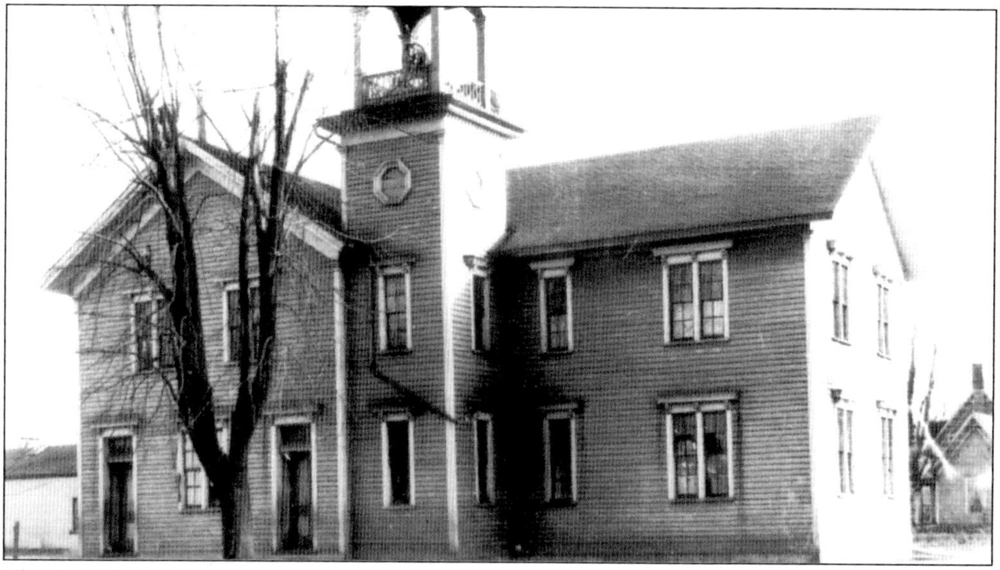

The first school in Camanche was started in 1838 as a subscription school. Teachers' salaries and school expenses were raised through the fees charged for many years. The first public school, built of logs, was followed by an imposing brick building in 1851, which was also used as a public meeting place until it was destroyed by the 1860 tornado. The school was then replaced by a frame building that remained in use until September of 1928, when a new school was opened. In 1927, bonds had been issued to raise the needed $23,000 for a new building. The old frame school was bought by Mr. Wolfe and remodeled into a residence. (Photograph courtesy of David Nichols.)

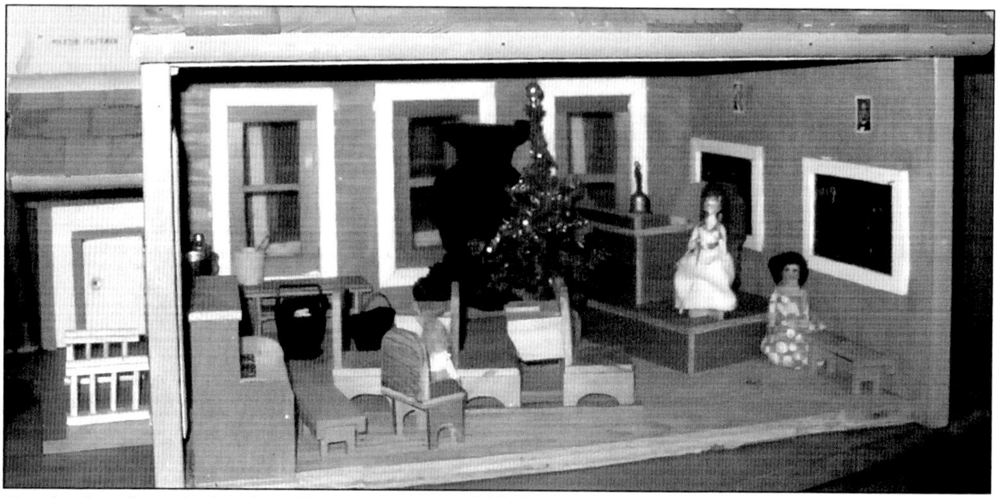

On the last day of school in 1911, a 10-year-old lad, Martin Hoffman, with 32 of his classmates, left Washington School #7 of Hampshire Township. In his hand, he clutched a memory book containing the picture of his teacher. As the years flew by, Martin grew to adulthood and farmed for many years. The memories of his little school and his favorite teacher never left him. During his retirement, Martin recreated a replica of the school in his basement. The photograph above shows the model of his school which includes student desks, a cloak room, pot-bellied stove, teacher's desk platform, and the water bucket which all the children drank from. The replica of Washington School is on display in the school room at the Clinton County Historical Society. (Photograph from the Clinton County Historical Society archives.)

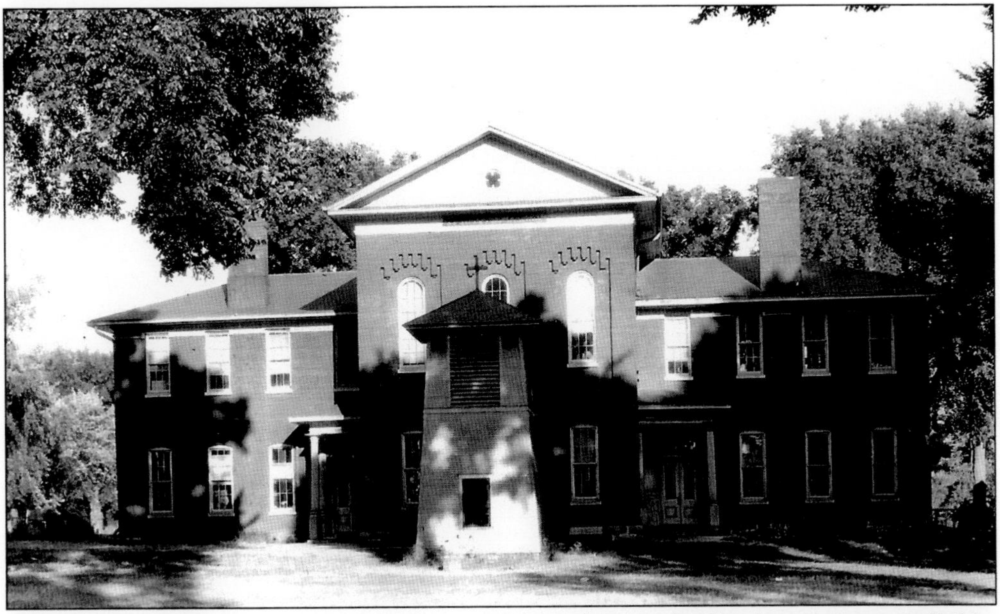

On January 10, 1890, the first St. Joseph's Catholic School in DeWitt began classes staffed by the Sisters of Mercy. A major fire destroyed the building in 1920 and St. Joseph's purchased this building in 1925 from the public school system. It served as the parish school until a new building was built in 1956. (Photograph from the Clinton County Historical Society archives.)

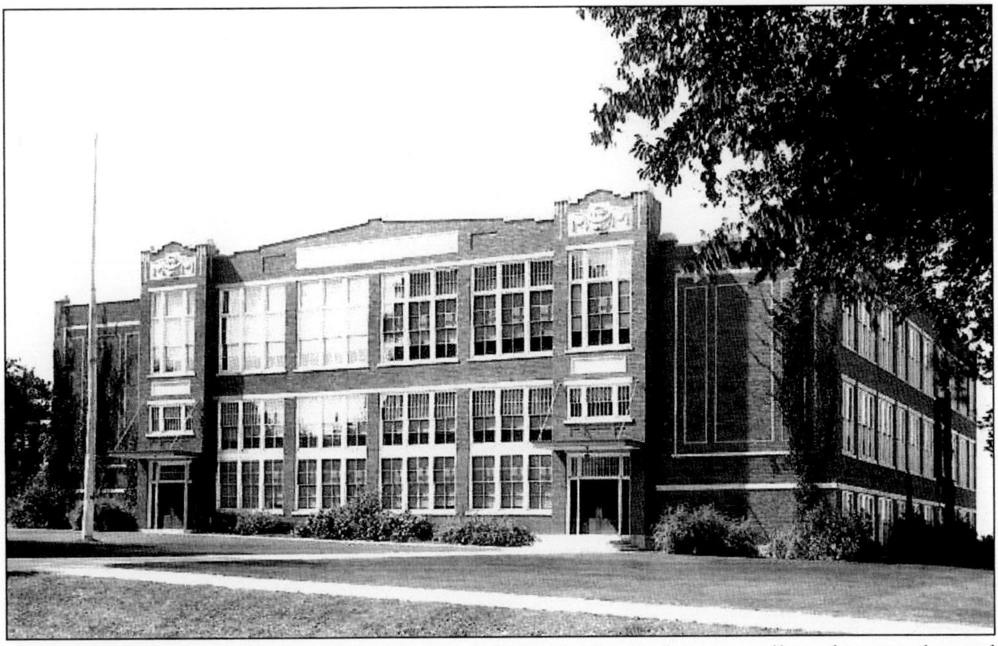

The DeWitt Public School is shown here in 1923. In the early years, all grades were housed in the same building, with kindergarten and lower elementary grades in the basement, upper elementary grades on the first floor, and the high school on the top floor. Later, when separate schools were built, this building was used as the junior high school. (Photograph from the Central Community Historical Society archives.)

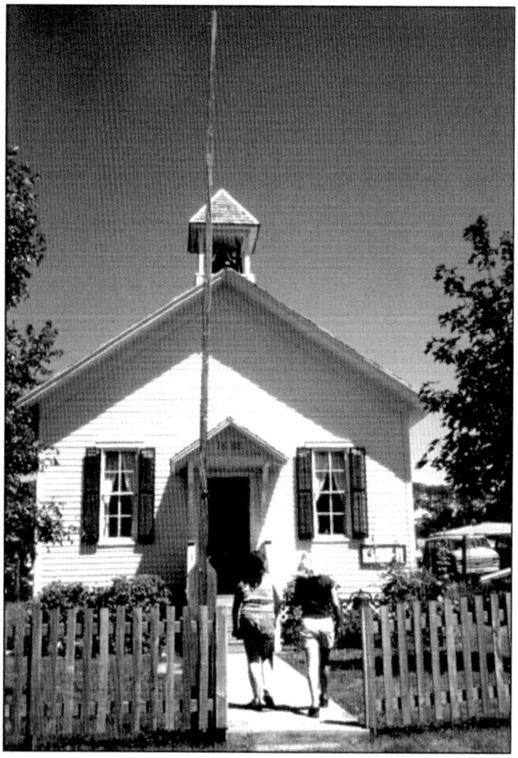

Teeds Grove School, located in Elk River Township, was built in 1888 and closed in 1947. In 1948, the building was moved onto the grounds of Miles High School in Jackson County, Iowa, where it was used for many years as a music room. Later, it was bought by the John L. Franks Lumber Company and used for lumber storage. Finally, the building has found a home on the "Old Threshers" grounds in Miles where it has been restored into the school it once was for all ages to explore and enjoy. (Photograph courtesy of Jan Hansen.)

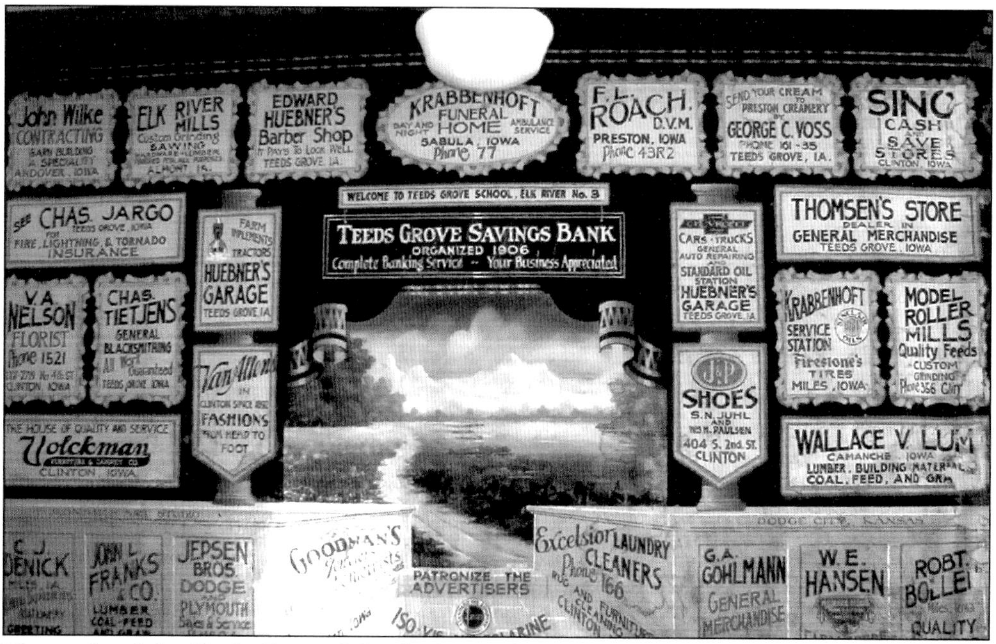

The pride of the Teeds Grove School #3 was this unusual painted advertising curtain. The advertising, painted on the velvet curtain, was bought by businesses far and wide in the 1930s. To be the student who handled the curtain was an honor indeed. The revered curtain was bought by a group of interested men at a Teeds Grove auction and restored. Once again, it hangs in its original school where it truly belongs. (Photograph courtesy of Jan Hansen.)

Six

POTPOURRI

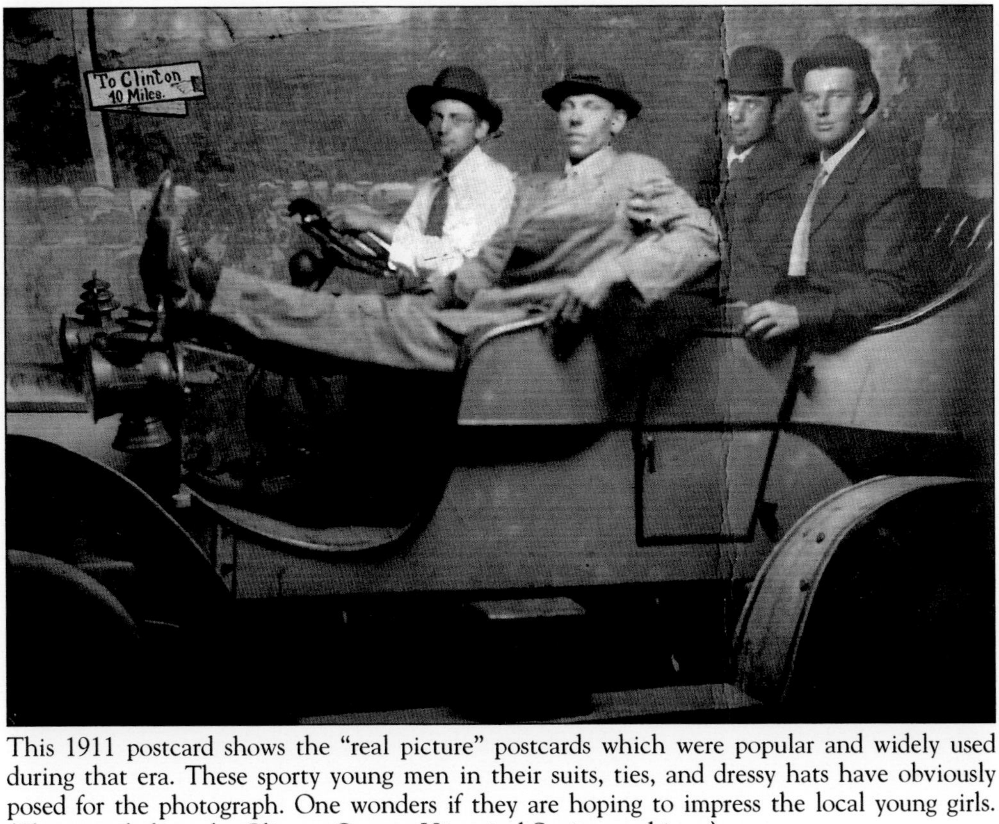

This 1911 postcard shows the "real picture" postcards which were popular and widely used during that era. These sporty young men in their suits, ties, and dressy hats have obviously posed for the photograph. One wonders if they are hoping to impress the local young girls. (Photograph from the Clinton County Historical Society archives.)

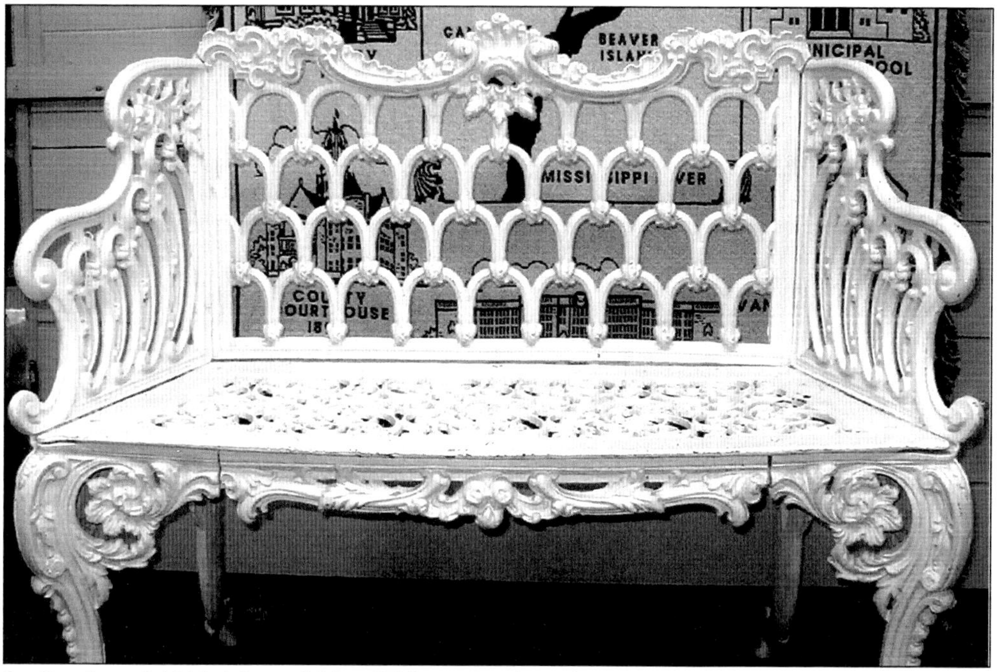

In October of 1913, Mr. and Mrs. William Sperling, living on eight acres near Teeds Grove in Elk River Township, lost their 16-year-old daughter. The death of their only child was devastating to the Sperlings and Mrs. Sperling walked nearly every day through the farm fields to the Teeds Grove cemetery where the child was buried. The family placed this cast iron bench at the grave so that Mrs. Sperling would have a place to rest after her two-mile journey. The bench is now on display at the Clinton County Historical Society Museum as a memorial to the Sperling family. (Photograph from the Clinton County Historical Society archives.)

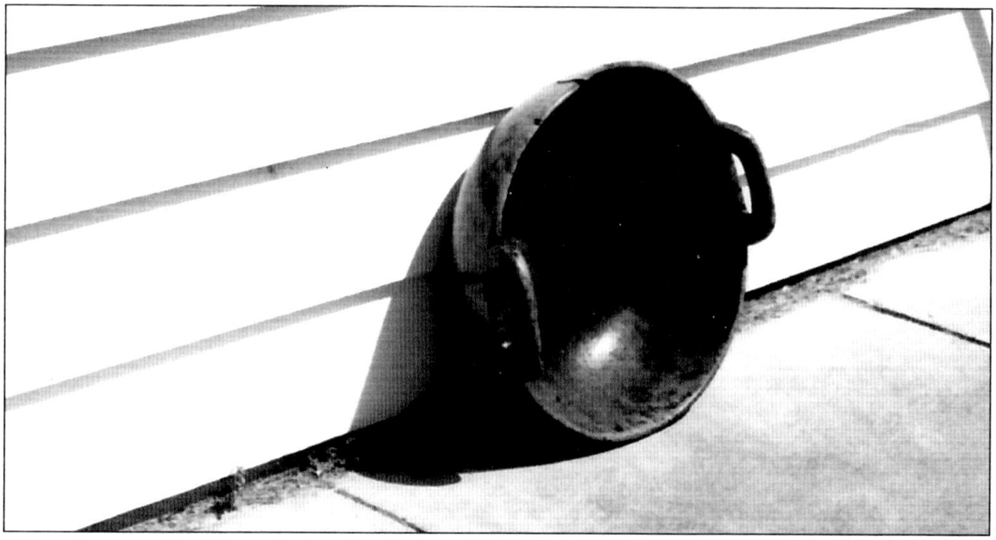

When Heman Shaff brought his family by covered wagon to Clinton County from Sodus, New York, in 1837, they brought along this wooden bowl which had been carved in one piece from the knot of a tree. It remains in the family yet today. (Photograph from the Clinton County Historical Society archives.)

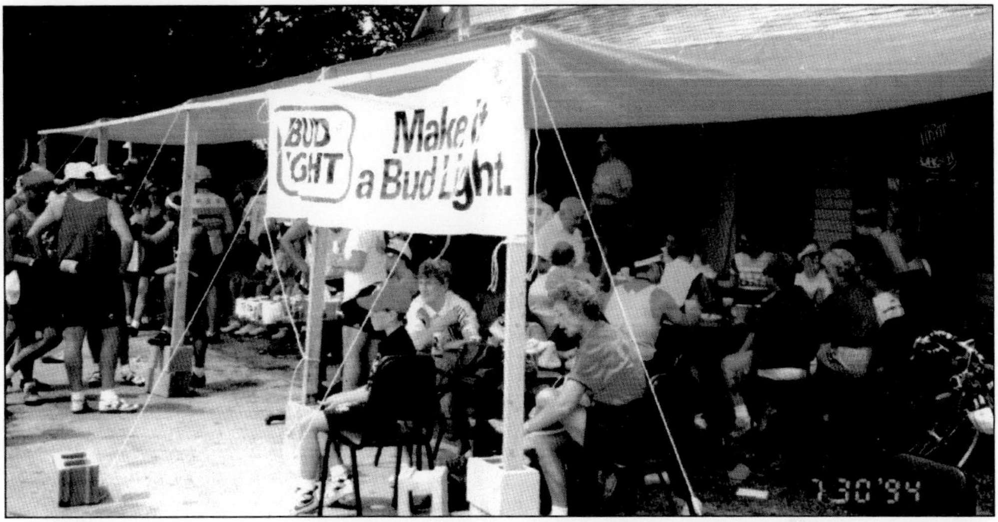

In 1973, RAGBRAI, the Register's Annual Great Bike Ride across Iowa, began when a few friends got together for a causal ride across the State of Iowa. No one could have imagined at the time that it would become the longest, largest, and oldest bicycle touring event in the world. Going from the west to the east, riders dip their rear wheels in the Missouri River when they leave for their week's tour and their front wheels in the Mississippi River when they arrive. RAGBRAI XXII began in Council Bluffs on July 24, 1994 and ended in Clinton on July 30. The riders enjoyed beautiful weather and the stops along the way. Elvira, in Center Township, was the last stop for rest, food, and drink before Clinton. A horse tank, filled with river water and a catfish, had been set up and many riders dipped their tires in the tank and ended their ride there. (Photograph courtesy Dave and Billie Hull.)

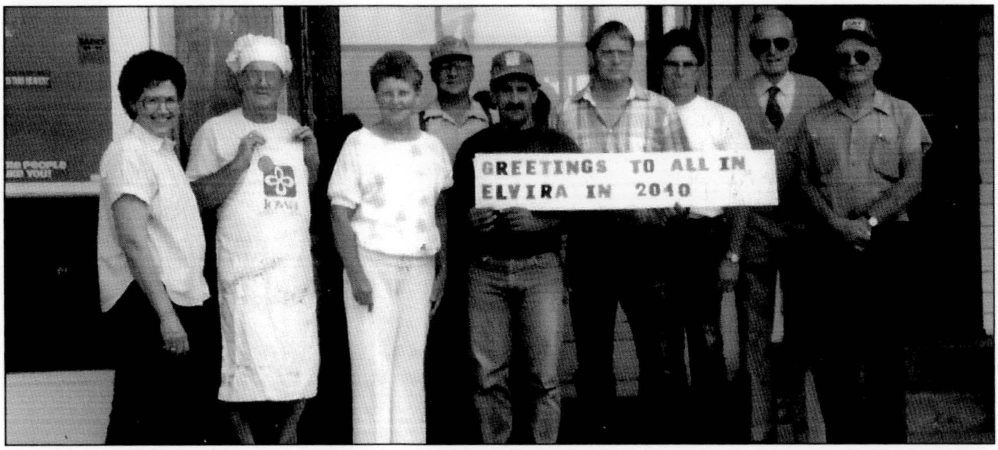

When the citizens of Elvira, Center Township, decided to donate items of interest to the two time capsules that were being filled during the 1990 Clinton County Sesquicentennial, they included their photograph and a message to those that would open the capsules, *Greetings to All in Elvira in 2040*. The two time capsules are identical wooden boxes made by Waclow Pieczynski, of Clinton, and stored at the Clinton County Courthouse. Duplicate items, i.e. papers, toys, photos, business cards, movie films, etc., are stored in both boxes, one to be opened at 50 years in 2040 and the other to be opened in 2090 at 100 years. Elvira citizens are pictured from left: Janice Burken, David Hull, Lucille Meyer, Jerry Rickertsen, Barry Hull, Scott Hansen, Paul Ocker, Lloyd Harmsen, and Don Stolk. (Photograph courtesy of David and Billie Hull.)

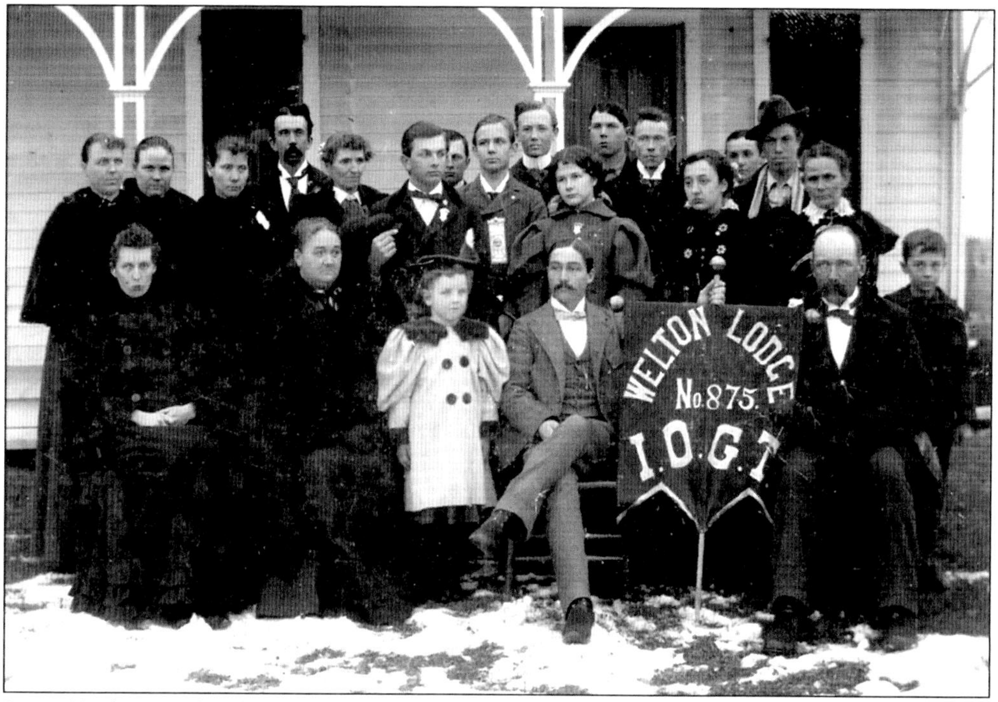

In 1855, the people of the state of Iowa approved a law prohibiting the sale of intoxicating liquors except for medicinal purposes. Due to an outcry from some segments of the population, the law was modified to allow for the sale of beer and wine. Temperance societies sprang up throughout the state and Clinton County was no exception. This posed photograph shows the Independent Order of Good Templars, Lodge #875, of Welton, *c.* 1880. (Photograph from the Clinton County Historical Society archives.)

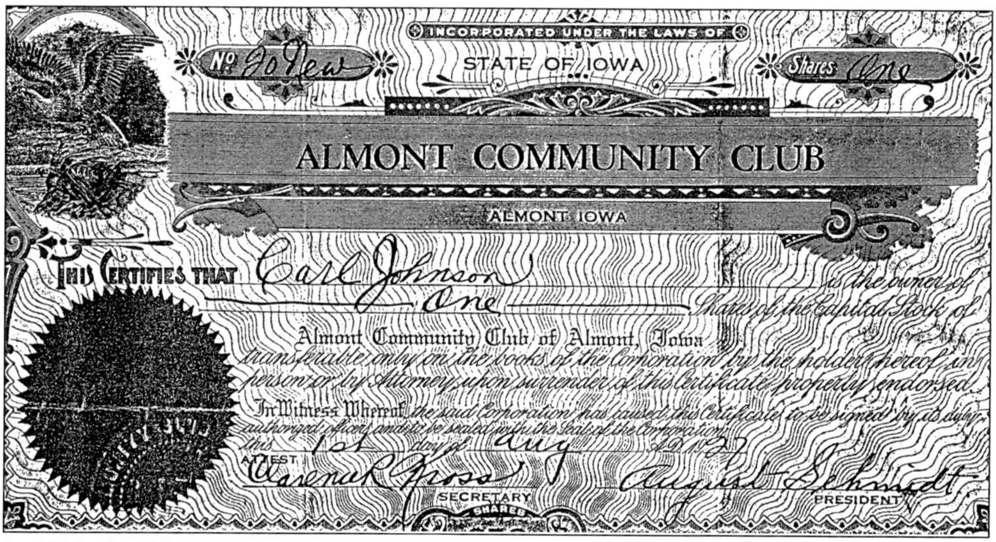

INCORPORATED UNDER THE LAWS OF

No.

STATE OF IOWA

Shares One

ALMONT COMMUNITY CLUB

ALMONT IOWA

This Certifies that Carl Johnson is the owner of One Shares of the Capital Stock of Almont Community Club of Almont, Iowa transferable only on the books of the Corporation by the holder hereof in person or by Attorney upon surrender of this Certificate properly endorsed.

In Witness Whereof the said Corporation has caused this Certificate to be signed by its duly authorized officers and to be sealed with the Seal of the Corporation this 1st day of Aug A.D. 1927

Attest Clarence Kross SECRETARY

August Schmidt PRESIDENT

SHARES

In 1927, the Almont Community Club, in Elk River Township, was selling $50 shares. Carl Johnson was the purchaser of this share and it is signed by Clarence Kross, Secretary, and August Schmidt, President. (Photograph from the Clinton County Historical Society archives.)

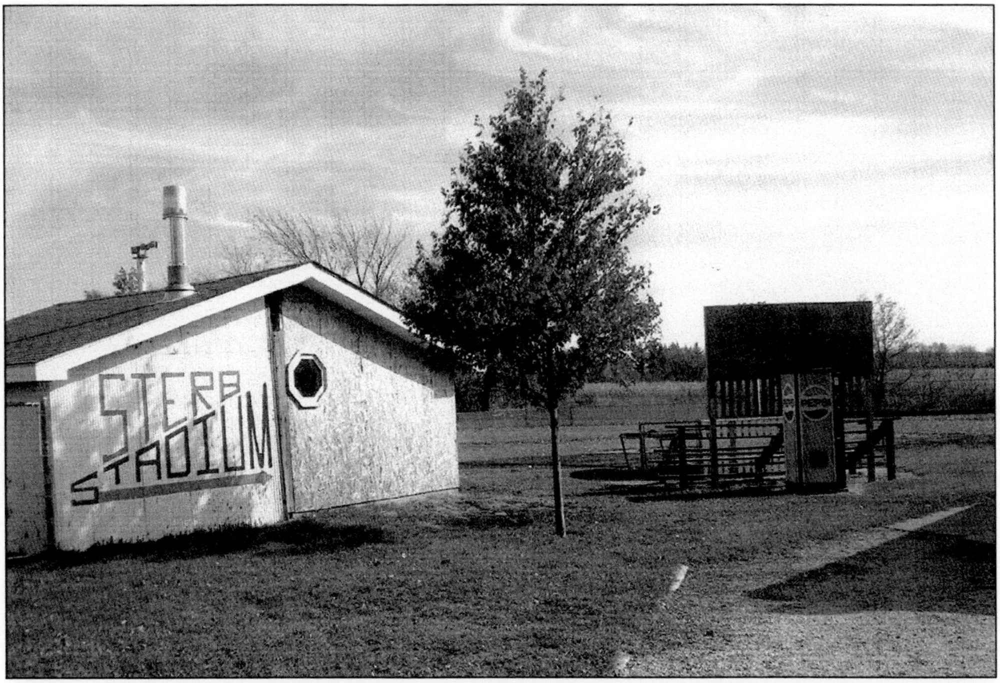

During the 1980s, this wiffle ball park was built next to the C&NW railroad tracks in the Malone area, Eden Township. The park is lighted and the local enthusiasts have their own stadium. (Photograph courtesy of Jule and Jean Luckritz.)

Ramessa, in Eden Township, was once an early station on the Northwestern Railroad line. It was situated on a grade which made it difficult for trains to stop. In the late 1870s, it burned down and it was presumed that the railroad men had set the fire. The station was then located further down the line at Malone. The site of Ramessa is quiet today as shown above. (Photograph courtesy of Jule and Jean Luckritz.)

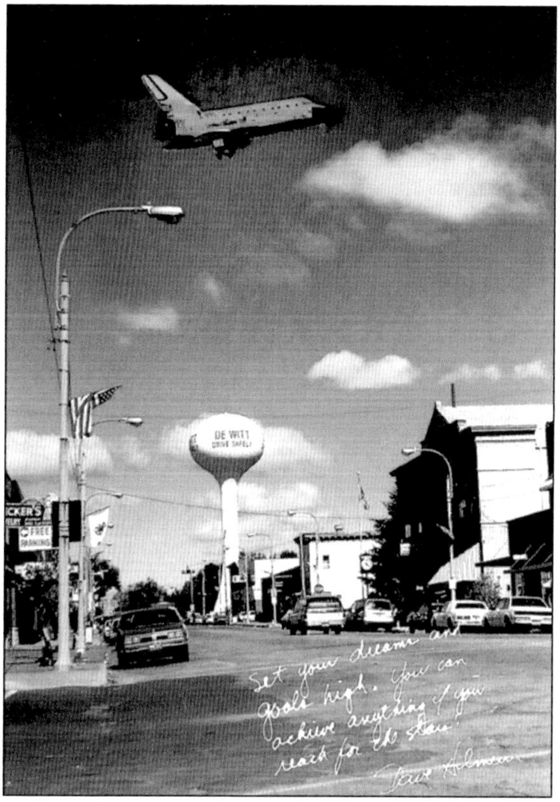

Clinton County proudly stands as the only geographical area in the United States that is home to three astronauts, George "Pinky" Nelson, Dale Gardner, and David Hilmers, in America's unequaled space program. This postcard shows the *Discovery* flight of 1988, which carried two of the astronauts, overlaid over a picture of the city of DeWitt. (Photograph from the Central Community Historical Society archives.)

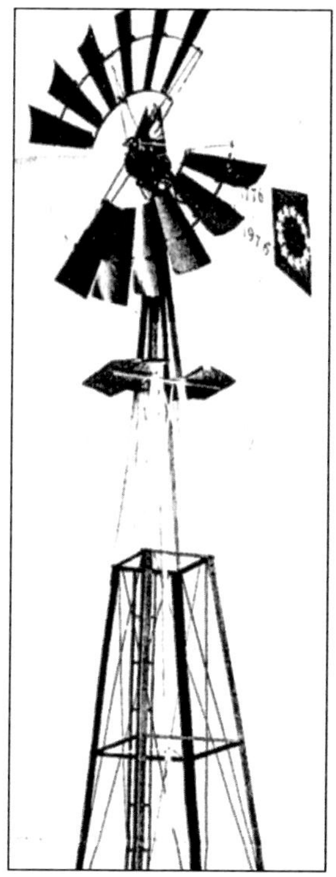

Working windmills are seldom seen on Clinton County farms today, as they were in the first half of the 20th century. During the 1920s and 1930s, when windmills became mass produced and everyone could afford one, August Milder of Jackson County erected over 1,000 windmills in Clinton, Dubuque, and Jackson counties. During that time, a windmill cost around $175 and Mr. Milder could install one in a day once the holes for the posts were dug. The farmer had to dig his own well or have it dug. The windmill could produce 300–360 gallons of water an hour compared to the 700–800 gallons an hour with an electric pump. Windmills are still sold in western states where it just isn't feasible to run electricity to isolated areas. (Photograph from the Clinton County Historical Society archives.)

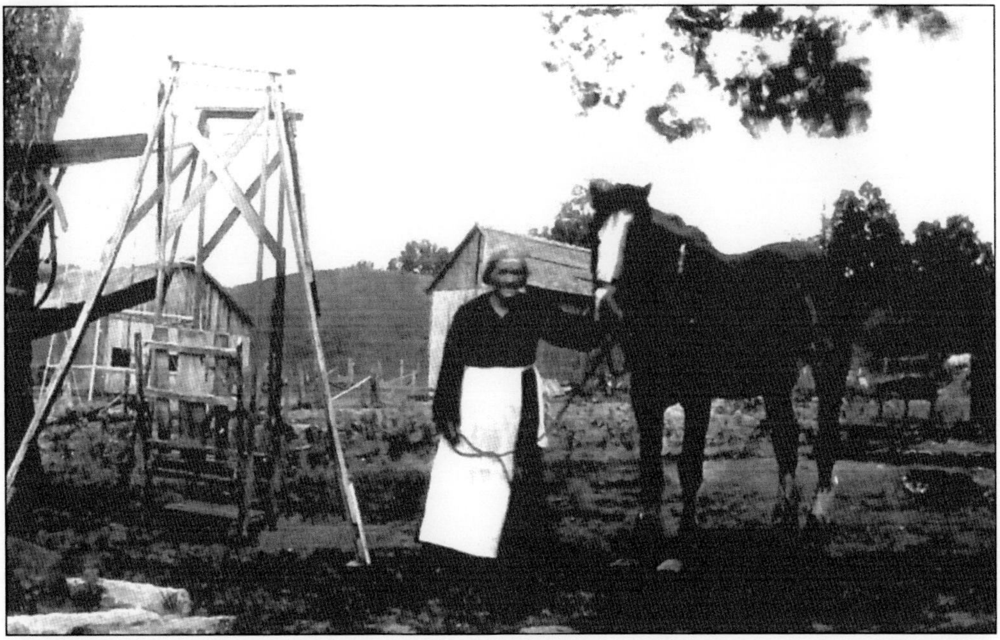

Mary Baird, born in 1830, lived alone on her family's farm in Elk River Township. In the spring of 1915, she lost her life while burning off bottom land on her farm next to the railroad tracks. A trainman spotted her burned body and notified authorities. Mary was the last person to be buried in the Miller/Wilson cemetery. (Photograph courtesy of Carole Gilbert.)

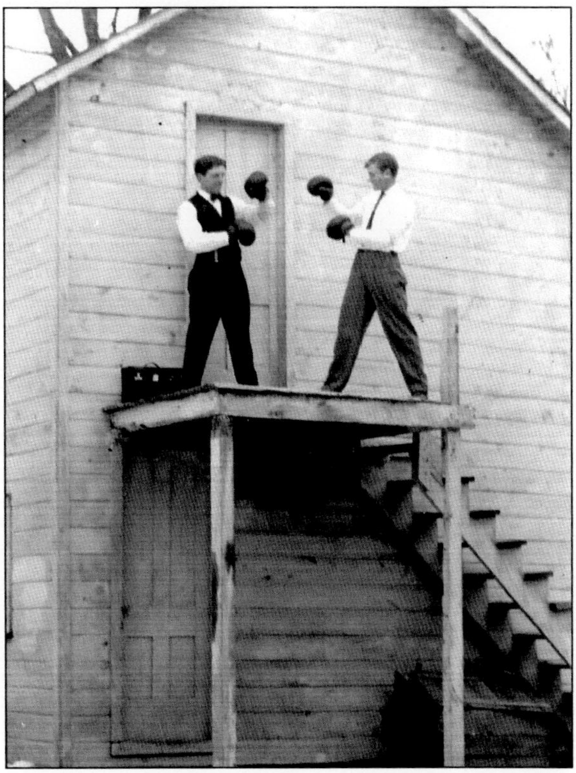

The Boys Club in DeWitt was located in an old barn and frequented by the young men of the city. The photographer captured this picture of two young men posed for boxing in 1908. (Photograph from the Clinton County Historical Society archives.)

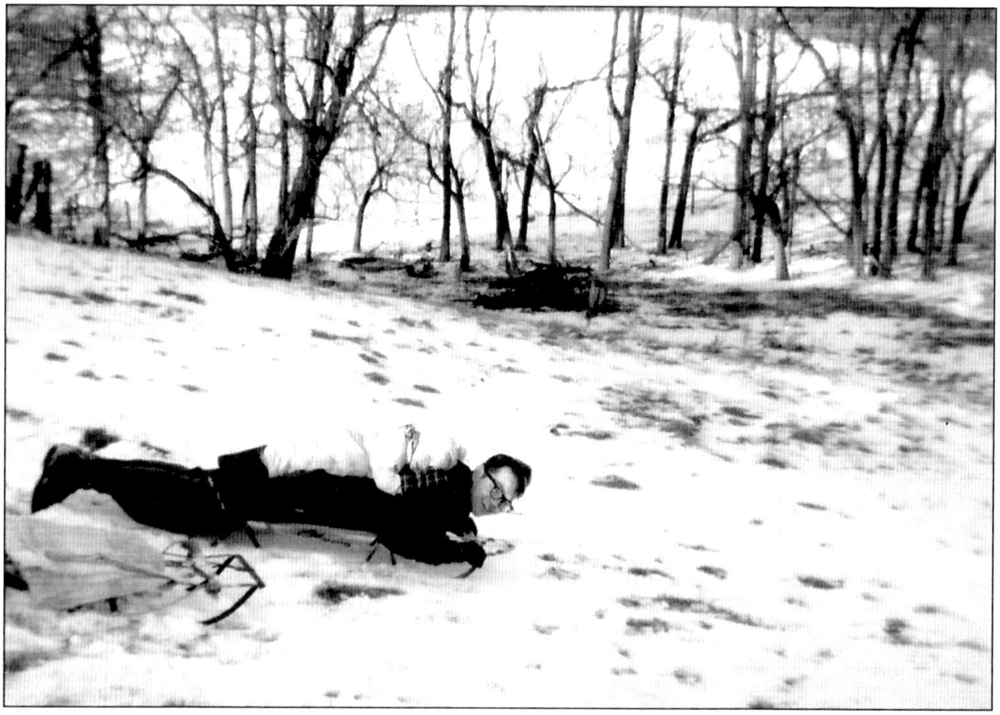

The Clinton County Landfill is located in Lincoln Township on what was once Claude White's farm. Jule Luckritz and his daughter, Dee Ann, are shown sledding down the rolling hills before the landscape was changed forever. (Photograph courtesy of Jule and Jean Luckritz.)

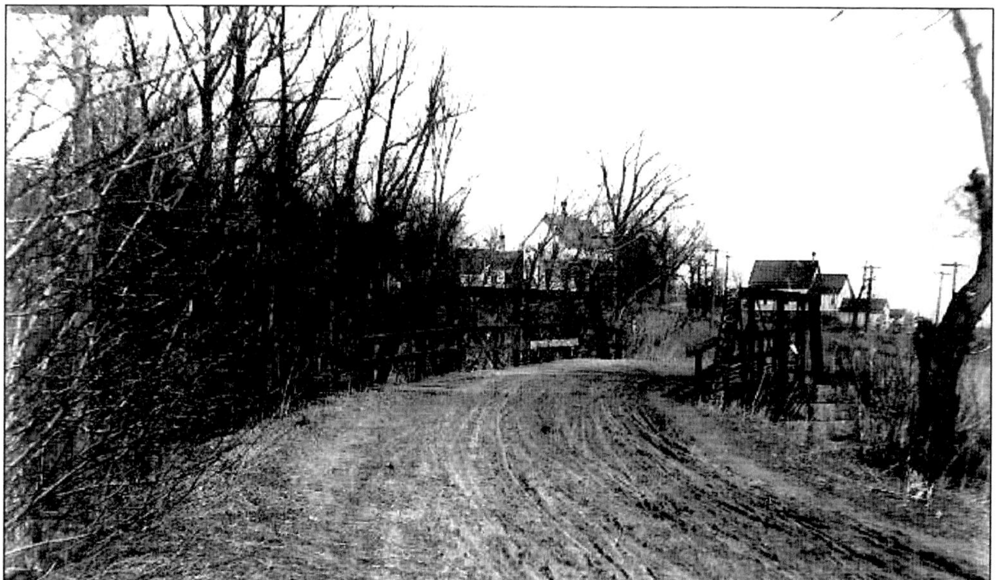

Mill Creek Bridge, Lincoln Township, is shown here as it was in the 1880s. Looking east toward Clinton is the home of Frank Thomas, and northeast of the road is the home of John Lawrence, a local Civil War veteran who is buried in Rose Hill Cemetery in Camanche. (Photograph courtesy of John Hein.)

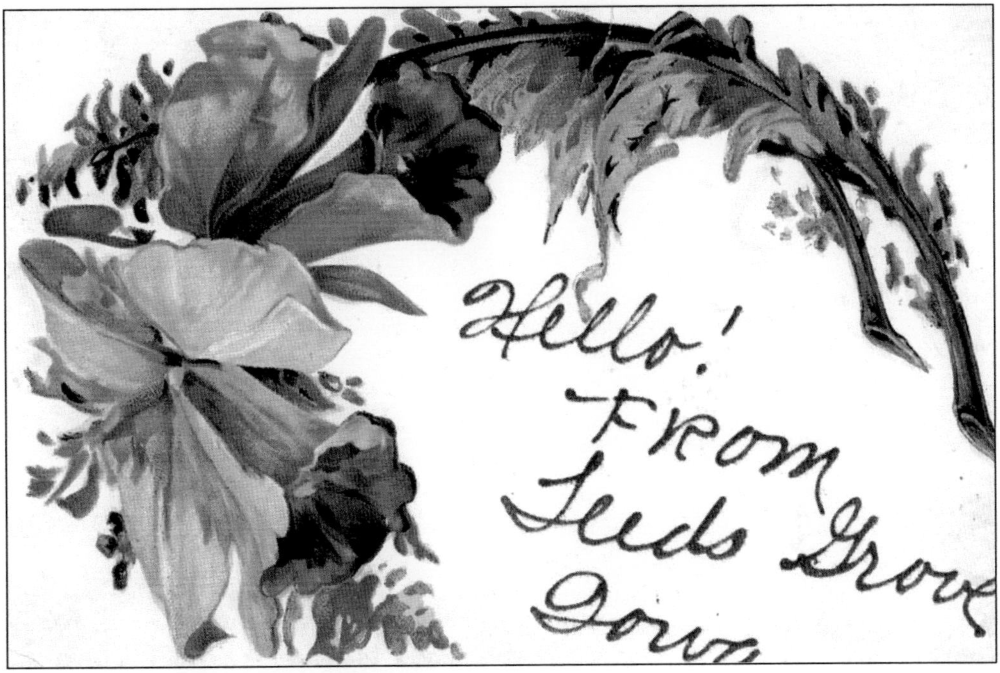

In the final years of the 1800s and the early years of the 1900s, postcards were a popular and stylish way to communicate with friends and relatives. They were as fancy or plain as the author wanted them to be. Without telephones and instant communication, the postal service was the easiest way to keep in touch. (Photographs from the Clinton County Historical Society archives.)

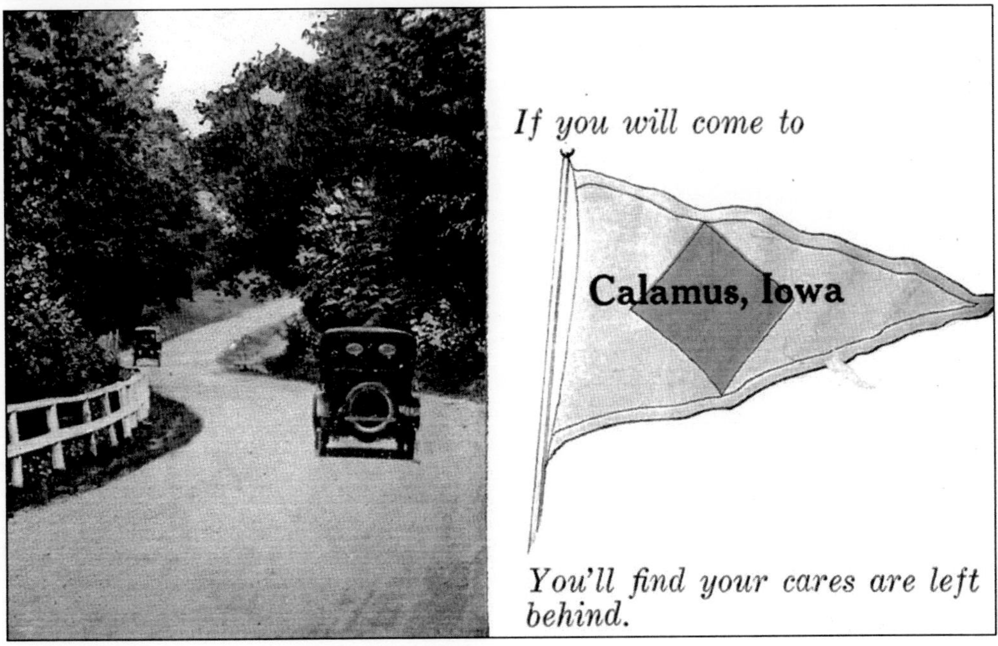

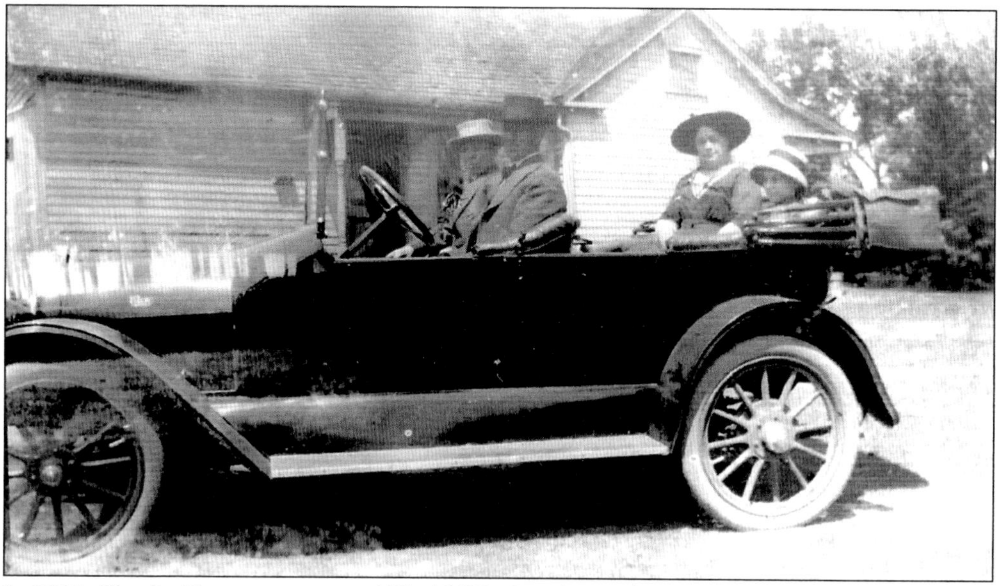

In 1917, Charlie Elsner, a veteran of World War I and son of August and Frances Elsner, shows off his Case car. Charlie had one of the first cars in Sugar Creek, Waterford Township. He willingly took his sister, Minnie Elsner Teshak, her husband, Martin, and their daughter, Irene, for a dusty ride in his horseless carriage. (Photograph courtesy of Arlene Rose Considine.)

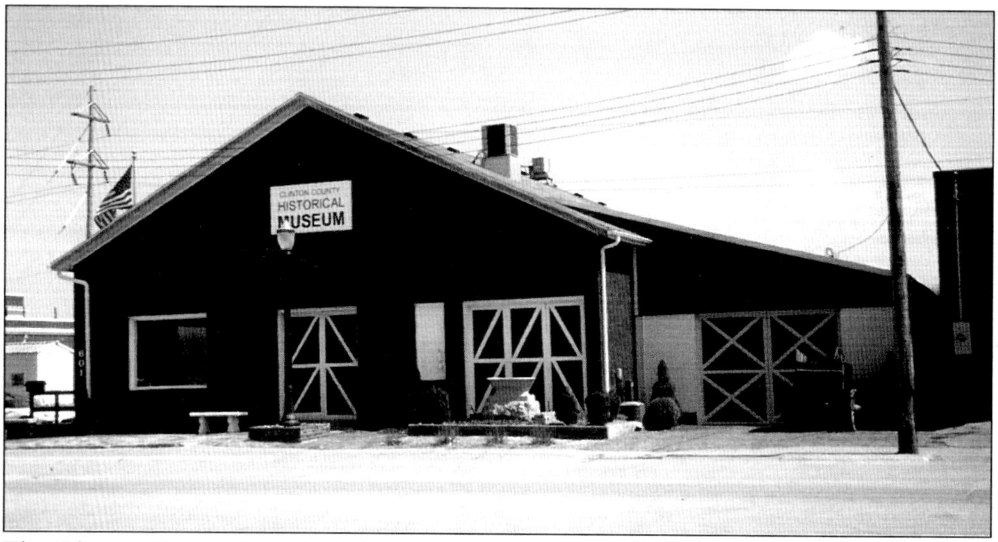

The Clinton County Historical Society museum is located at 601 S. First Street, Clinton, Iowa. The museum building is a riverside landmark which originally was built in 1858 as a commission house for the Mississippi River steamboats. In 1880, it was sold to the Oakes family for their lumber business and was purchased by the society in 1995 for a museum and research library. With the preservation of the history and artifacts of the residents as the society's premise, the museum is an integral part of Clinton County. (Photograph from the Clinton County Historical Society archives.)